THE Shankly LEGACY

THE
Shankly
LEGACY

BERNARD BALE

The Breedon Books
Publishing Company
Derby

First published in Great Britain by
The Breedon Books Publishing Company Limited
Breedon House, 44 Friar Gate, Derby, DE1 1DA.
1996

ISBN 1 85983 045 5

Printed and bound by Butler & Tanner Ltd., Selwood Printing Works,
Caxton Road, Frome, Somerset.

Colour separations by Colour Services, Wigston, Leicester.

Jackets printed by Lawrence-Allen, Weston-Super-Mare, Avon.

Contents

Foreword

by Ian St John

THERE can never be another like Bill Shankly. My life was changed by him, and anyone who ever came into contact with him, even for a few moments, will tell you the same.

Much has been said and written about Shanks, but this book takes the legend and brings it back to life.

There is still a massive Shankly influence on the game and its people. *The Shankly Legacy* is not just an album of memories, it is a very real aspect of this great game of football today.

Shanks would have been proud to see his ideas still in operation and his name still mentioned with the highest esteem. But even his pride would have been nothing as compared to the pride of those of us who knew him.

Ian St John

Birth of a Legend

THERE are comparatively few real legends in the annals of world soccer – Pelé, Puskas and Charlton being three who spring readily to mind, any others requiring a pause for pondering. In British soccer the domestic legends are also in a stark minority – Moore, Clough, Stein, Wright, Matthews, Chapman, Busby and Shankly.

Ah yes, Shankly – on paper not the most successful manager of all time – not even the most successful Liverpool manager of all time. However, there is an Anfield aura even today, more than a decade after his death, that has a distinct Shankly spirit.

The strains of *You'll Never Walk Alone* bring to life the image of Shankly – red scarf draped across his shoulders, hands aloft in salute of his players and of his people on the terraces, mutual adoration creating an atmosphere of camaraderie and understanding born out of pulsating, emotional roots of need – a need for freedom and self-expression and belonging.

Yes, Merseyside has never been the same since that fortuitous day on Tuesday, 1 December 1959, when the board of Liverpool Football Club announced that they had appointed as their new manager, the former Huddersfield, Workington, Grimsby and Carlisle boss – Mr Bill Shankly.

They had blown the whistle to kick off an amazing new era in Liverpool lore. And even when the second whistle had been blown to end his career, the extra time has continued to this day, enriching the whole of British soccer through the work of Shankly's main disciples.

But let us journey back in time to the year of 1913, and the small mining community of Glenbuck a little off the beaten track in the wild, hilly, eastern area of Ayrshire. At the turn of the century Glenbuck was already showing the signs of becoming a ghost town as the rich coal veins, from which most of the local population earned its living, steadily became less and less productive.

Today Glenbuck is easily missed. Its church and its village school have crumbled and voices have become fewer. But back in 1913 – on 2 September to be precise – there was laughter in the air in the village and a wee dram in the glass as John and Barbara Shankly celebrated their latest new arrival, a son and their tenth child.

Villagers called to pay their respects and to greet the newcomer, safely delivered on that warm late summer's day. All was well and Barbara Shankly was delighted with her new son – her fifth. With the delight came relief that there was time to settle her new child ahead of the rigours of his first Scottish winter in the remote settlement amid the harsh haunting hills where lies the body of the legendary John Brown.

With ten children, even if five of them were girls, it could be that the Shanklys were trying to start their own football team. In fact the village had one of the most famous sides in Scotland – as we shall see a little later. But there was another influence in the young life of baby Bill, or Willie as he was often called then, that would surely make some contribution to the career that would later turn him into a legend.

Mrs Barbara Shankly was herself well versed in soccer. Her maiden-name was Blyth and among her brothers were Bob and Bill who were both professional footballers. Bob Blyth played for several different clubs. He was with the mighty Rangers for a while but also came south of the border to play for Middlesbrough and then Preston. Later he returned to Scotland to join Dundee before heading south again to complete his career at Portsmouth where he later became manager and chairman. Bob never made the Scotland side but he was always a better-than-average player and was among the scorers on 21 January 1893, when Middlesbrough beat Newcastle 3-2 in the FA Cup first round. He continued his goal-scoring exploits at all his clubs until creaking joints showed that it was time to hang up his boots and move into the field of management.

Brother Bill's career was very similar. He never played in Scotland professionally but plied his trade in England, first with Preston and then with Carlisle, two clubs which were later to play an important role in the life and times of nephew, young Bill Shankly. Bill Blyth was to play a major part in that as we shall see a little later.

Barbara was not, of course, alone in teaching the kids the rudiments of football. Husband John was also something of a sportsman who enjoyed kicking a ball about. He also had more to offer – superb fitness. John Shankly was quite an athlete and he specialised in what was then known as the 440 yards – a demanding distance run which combined the finesse and speed of the sprinter with the durability of the long-distance runner. It was John who made sure that all his family were physically well-prepared to meet all the challenges that the world would have to offer.

At this stage it might be prudent to take a look at the home environment of the Shankly family. We have already discovered that the one thing they did not lack was fresh air – which perhaps was just as well since the prime employer at that time was the mining industry. A century earlier an ironworks had also been part of the village scene.

The River Ayr flows past the village and into Glenbuck Loch – which was originally formed as a reservoir for the nearby Catrine mills. Today it is chiefly a picturesque mecca for tourists and windsurfers as it nestles neatly amid the naturally sculptured hills.

The Shankly children were fond of the great outdoors. Sisters

Netta, Elizabeth, Isobel, Barbara and Jean used to like to go for long walks in the hills, often taking their little brother with them. In Glenbuck entertainment and recreation was mostly home-grown. There was no theatre, no television, no radio – not even electricity. The nearest emporium of entertainment was a small picture house some four miles away which John Shankly would sometimes visit, walking both ways. He was good at walking – he spent years as a postman. John was also good with his hands and after finishing as the local mailman he turned his hand to tailoring – a skill which he had quite naturally developed, perhaps from all those evenings spent in repairing and adapting clothes for his large family.

The Shanklys were not an affluent family, far from it. Life was a constant battle and much later, when Bill Shankly grew up and came to fully appreciate the hardships that his parents, and especially his mother, had endured he often paid tribute to the 'miracle' that he felt they had performed in seeing all of their children into adulthood.

Barbara Shankly was an excellent cook who could take the most meagre of ingredients and turn them into nutritious meals which kept her children healthy throughout the extremities of the seasons and their own pangs of growth. Husband John meanwhile was a handyman who would, by necessity, turn his attention, not just to his family's clothes, but also to their other needs – warm beds and toys.

It was a gritty experience in which the Shankly children learned the lessons of survival, thrift and rugged determination in the face of daily adversity. Although he was the youngest, Bill Shankly was never spoilt and learned the tough side of life just the same as his brothers and sisters.

While the girls were wandering in the hills, Bill's brothers followed the usual pursuits of young boys living in the countryside. Mischief was a part of their everyday life – but that mischief was always good-natured. Their father was himself an extremely polite, well-mannered and mildly spoken man and he expected the same of his children.

The boys would sometimes accompany the girls on their

expeditions and sometimes the girls would join the boys in their favourite pastime – playing football.

Although Bill was ultimately by far the most famous, each of his four brothers became professional footballers. Alec, being the oldest, was the first to sign a contract. He joined relatively-near Ayr and later played for Clyde. This encouraged the others and James went further afield, taking up the offer to play for Portsmouth who were then one of the leading sides in the newly-formed Third Division South. James went on to play for Halifax followed by Coventry, Carlisle, Sheffield United, Southend United and Barrow. He was by far the most travelled of the Shanklys and, like his uncle Bill Blyth, he never played in his native Scotland.

John Shankly followed his brother James to Portsmouth and later joined Luton then Blackpool, before returning across the border to play for Alloa and Morton. Bob's career went full circle. He started in Scotland with Alloa and then joined Tunbridge Wells Rangers before ending his career back in Scotland with Falkirk.

The adventures of his older brothers were as fascinating as fairy-stories to the wide-eyed Bill who would eagerly await their letters and home visits and pump them for information on every minute of every match. Uncles Bob and Bill Blyth had whetted the appetite, but tales from the lips of his own brothers were even more exciting. Young Bill would sit, face in hands – elbows on knees, soaking up every enthralling second and then demand to be shown the moves that led to glorious goals, sensational saves and terrifying tackles.

Of course, football was not just a part of the Shankly family's life... it was very much the major ingredient in the daily menu of almost every inhabitant of Glenbuck. In the streets and in the back gardens there were boys – and girls – and grown men – kicking footballs, real or improvised. Small wonder then that The Cherrypickers became such a treasured part of Scottish football legend.

The Cherrypickers were a junior football team – but what a team! They started life as Glenbuck Athletic in the 1870s and basically provided an opportunity for young miners to take on their counterparts from other pits. John Shankly Snr. was one of the committee members during the club's history and a look at the life and times of the side a century ago provides us with quite an insight into the very roots of this great game, now seemingly so far removed from its origins.

Glenbuck Athletic's players paid for the privilege of getting a game. They paid for their own white shirts and black shorts and most of their games were arranged by advertising blank dates in the local newspaper. They often played in Cup competitions and challenge matches but did not take part in any League.

The simplicity of soccer then is quite astounding. The first pitch used by the club just disappeared one day when a pit shaft collapsed leaving a crater where once had been Glenbuck's own 'Theatre of Dreams'. The second pitch was sloping. No, it wasn't just sloping, it was actually on a hillside – exhausting if you were wearing big heavy boots, kicking a big heavy leather football, uphill, on a big heavy pitch in the second half. Later Glenbuck moved upmarket a little and used another strip of land alongside the main road. It was known as Burnside Park – yes, it actually had a name – and it was LEVEL! Probably the only level piece of land anywhere in Glenbuck.

As might be expected even 'friendly' matches were never exactly that. The on-field violence, however, paled when compared to the activities of the spectators. In Glenbuck the favoured pastime of the crowd was to pelt stones at the opposition. And as for the referee – that poor referee – he would be subjected to having just about anything and everything thrown at him... And if it was a 'bad game' in the eyes of the crowd it would not be unusual for him to be taken for an early bath in the nearest pond or river. Yet, somehow, there never seemed a lack of opponents or referees willing to risk their necks for a good game of football. It was all part and parcel of Scottish soccer as played in villages like Glenbuck.

Why The Cherrypickers? During the Boer War the 11th Hussars became known as The Cherrypickers because of a story that they once devoured the entire contents of a cherry orchard in Spain. It is believed that there were lads from Glenbuck in the 11th Hussars and so the villagers proudly adopted the name for their local soccer team – a name which eventually became the official title for the club. There is another tale that some soccer-loving lads once ate a massive basket of cherries – with dire consequences – while engrossed in conversation about football, but this yarn seems to be more fantasy than fact.

What is a fact though is that many a great name in Scottish soccer began their career with The Cherrypickers.

Internationals included Alec Brown who played for Preston and then Tottenham, picking up two Scotland caps along the way. Alec was best known in the village for being in the Spurs side that won the FA Cup in 1901. He didn't just play but scored both Tottenham goals in the drawn Final against Sheffield United and then found the net again in the replay which Spurs won 3-1. The whole of Glenbuck celebrated their part in Tottenham's triumph and were rewarded when Alec Brown paid a visit home. As well as his medal, Alec actually took the FA Cup itself along with him, and it was displayed in the window of the village shop throughout his stay.

Willie Muir, George Halley and John Crosbie were among some of the other Cherrypickers who rose to international fame. In fact more than 50 players from the club made the grade in senior soccer, half of them playing in England.

The Cherrypickers were the focal point of the village – a chance for hard-working miners to let off a little steam.

The team also went into the history books for its trophy successes. Among their triumphs were three successive victories in the Ayrshire Junior Challenge Cup from 1889 to 1891, three cups in one season in 1906 and six wins in the Cumnock Cup, to name just a few. Even in their final year – 1931 – The Cherrypickers won the Ayrshire Junior Cup as a kind of Auld Lang Syne victory.

As the village began to wane with the decline of mining in the area, so did its football team until that fateful year of 1931 when the whistle was blown for the very last time and The Cherrypickers were no more. The team had ended but the legend lived on and there was yet more talent to come out of Glenbuck. Tommy Brown was one such talent. He was still a boy when the team folded but his father, John, had been a stalwart member of the side. Young Tommy went on to play for Scotland and for Hearts, Millwall, Leyton Orient and Charlton. John Wallace was another Glenbuck lad who passed into big time soccer. He played for Ayr and Partick Thistle in the Scottish League bringing yet more fame to the village.

And of course, there was another Glenbuck lad who used to cheer on The Cherrypickers every Saturday afternoon – and sometimes kick a ball about on their pitch, dreaming of achieving great things in the game that he loved. Bill Shankly did not become a Cherrypicker. Not that he wasn't good enough he simply wasn't old enough. He had a trial which he passed with flying colours, but at 16 he was considered a little too young for the rigours of the game played Cherrypicker style. A year later The Cherrypickers folded and it was too late.

Shankly would dearly have loved to have joined with so many of his relatives in becoming a member of the famous Cherry-pickers, but it was just not to be. However he always nurtured fond memories of his illustrious village team.

"Aye, the Cherrypickers were a bit special," said Shankly years later. "They were our village team, a good side with a fine record. They provided the miners and their families with an escape from all that work down the pit. The whole village would turn out for some matches and if they won a trophy there would be great celebrations. As a boy I used to watch them and my family were very involved. They played a great part in my early football education."

That was The Cherrypickers – the pride of Glenbuck.

But, of course, life was not just a bowl of Cherrypickers for the mining village and, like everyone else, the Shankly family had to earn a living. For young Bill, schooldays were idyllic. He was keen to learn, happy in his toil and not at all phased by the 'three Rs'. He rarely missed a day at the, now sadly crumbled, village school, and he also joined in with family worship at the village church, now little more than an empty shell, a fossil of a former centre of village life where births, deaths and marriages tolled the inevitable passage of years and generations.

In all too short a time Bill became a teenager and soon he would be out to work. The obvious choice was the mine where everyone else chipped away a living from the not-so-rich underworld of darkness. He was 14 when he joined the small army of rugged, helmeted coal workers and the end of his first day brought him trophies in the shape of blisters – a reward for honest endeavour that he later came to expect from his players.

Bill Shankly was growing up fast and before long it would be his turn to fly the nest, but in the meantime he became a contributor to the family's income with a large portion of his meagre wages.

Years later, when talking about one of his Liverpool stars, Shankly said: "He comes from a tough background. He knows what it's like to come from a poor family. I understand that because I'm from the same sort of background. It was hard going and we were a poor family but we were an honest and a very happy one.

"Times were not good but we didn't let it get us down. As kids one of our most exciting occupations was to be able to collect some jam jars and go and swap them for a pastry to eat."

If his early years in Glenbuck taught him anything, they educated him in the simple joys of family life, dedication and commitment. His childhood also taught him that you don't get more out than you put in, something he regularly reminded his players of many years later during motivation meetings.

His career took Bill Shankly to many far distant parts of the globe that the villagers of his childhood would only dream about. But he never forgot his roots and his roots never left him. Today the Cumnock and Doon Valley District Council is justifiably proud of its most famous son and will eagerly point pilgrims in the direction of Glenbuck although it is a very different place now. No longer do the church bell or the school bell call for attention. There is no morning trek to the mine and no anxious miner's wife waits for the safe return of her family. No crowds line the Cherrypickers touch-line these days. Glenbuck is a ghost village in which the only changing pattern of life is provided by the weather and the seasons. But with a little imagination the Pilgrim can bring it all back to life. The Brigadoon of Scottish soccer and a dearly beloved part of the life of Bill Shankly.

"Like many remote mining villages, Glenbuck has changed quite dramatically since the early part of this century," said Bill. "I was a native of Glenbuck with many happy memories of a beloved family life and the history of the village will not be forgotten. It will always remain in the memories of those of us who spent part of our life there."

Like Shankly himself Glenbuck is far from forgotten but away from the village there was a big wide world awaiting his talents. His family had played a major part in his early years, carving the character who was to become a legend. By 1927 as the world struggled through its decade of depression, Bill Shankly was developing into a hard-working 14-year-old with dreams... dreams of playing football for a living just like his brothers and uncles. And, indeed, the influence of his family was by no means at an end. With that in mind let us look a little closer at the amazing vein of rich football talent that ran through this mining family from Glenbuck.

Running in the Family

WE have sketched the early days, those first formative years that laid the foundation of the character that was to come. But let's just look a little closer at the family influence on the man who, himself, was to become one of the greatest influences on soccer in the twentieth – and probably on into the 21st century.

As we have already ascertained, Bill Shankly's father, John, was a very fit man. His simple philosophy seemed to be – don't ride if you have time to walk, and don't walk if you are able to run. In one sense it was in complete contrast to his son's basic soccer strategy of keeping running to a minimum and making the ball do the work.

John Shankly was celebrated throughout Ayrshire and much of Lowland Scotland for his running ability. It certainly impressed his wife Barbara, who was as sports-mad as the rest of her family. She never made a name for herself in track or field but she had inherited the same 'Blyth Spirit' for which her sporting brothers became famous. She was the perfect partner for John Shankly, a dedicated wife and mother who knew all about health, fitness and the need for personal expression.

There was one smell you would never find in the Shankly household in Glenbuck – cigarette smoke! Neither would you be able to sniff the unmistakable aroma of alcohol. Apart from one bottle of whisky, hidden away to be used for only the most dire medical reasons, John and Barbara did not believe in drinking. Some have attributed this to their religious leanings, but the prime factor was that they both knew that either habit was not conducive to healthy minds and bodies. They firmly believed that a breath of fresh air was better than a puff of nicotine, and that there were better ways of getting a headache than buying it in a bottle.

Barbara's brother Bob was the first to hit the trail to soccer stardom. He was also quite an athlete and, as a sprinter, there were few in the area to touch him. Oddly he earned the nickname 'Reindeer', and this stuck with him throughout his life.

Bob Blyth began his road to success with the Glenbuck Cherrypickers. Like everyone else he had to earn his living down in the mines, but Bob didn't breathe coal dust – he breathed football! When the Cherrypickers won the Ayrshire Junior Cup during those years in the late 1880s and early 1890s, Bob was one of the stars of the side.

Today he would have been snapped up while he was still at school and his career would have been an extension of the classroom, but in those days at the end of the last century there were no such things as schools of soccer excellence. A boy became a man at work and, if he was destined for great things on the football pitch, he would be spotted while he was playing the man's game.

Bob Blyth was spotted by a pair of Rangers' eyes. The Ibrox club was keenly followed in Glenbuck and word reached Glasgow that the Cherrypickers were producing some rare talent. The upshot was that Bob was invited along to play for the mighty Rangers – and Glenbuck had another celebrity in its midst. Of course, life was very different for Rangers players in those far-off days. Rangers had moved to the Ibrox district of Glasgow in 1887 but, even though the club had affluent beginnings, there was neither a sauna to be seen, nor was there a car park full of Mercs, Saabs, BMWs or Porsches.

The Scottish League did not start until late 1890 and, by the end of that inaugural season, honours had been shared by

Rangers and Dumbarton who drew in a championship play-off. Ever the adventurer Bob Blyth decided it was time to move on to pastures new.

Middlesbrough were a much-respected professional club even if they were nick named the 'Scabs' when Bob Blyth joined them. Some strange things happened at that time though and, after a failed merger with another club called Ironopolis, 'Boro reverted to amateur status which really was not worth the trouble to Bob Blyth.

He moved on to Preston which, in those days, had a strong Scottish influence and was a force to be reckoned with – especially after winning the Football League and FA Cup double in 1888-89, the first club ever to do so. That double was particularly memorable because it was the very first season of the Football League. Bob enjoyed his spell at Preston but eventually decided to return to Scotland and play for Dundee.

His nomadic life did not end there. In the twilight of his playing career he made the long move down to Portsmouth where he played out his days and finally became manager from 1901 to 1904. Portsmouth were a leading non-League side then and his spell as manager, followed by chairmanship of the club, laid the foundation for Portsmouth to become – not only a Football League team – but also future champions and FA Cup winners.

Billy Blyth had a similar career but he plied his trade exclusively in England. Another product of that famous Glenbuck soccer nursery, the network of Scottish contacts led to him joining Preston where his brother had previously flown the family flag.

Later Billy joined Carlisle after they had advertised for players in a local Ayrshire newspaper back in 1905. It was a move that was to prove to play a major role in the story of the career of his nephew. Billy stayed with Carlisle for the next nine years. He became a part of the local community and even bought a pub – the Bowling Green Inn – which he kept well into old age.

Although he never entered the field of soccer team management, Billy Blyth did involve himself in administration and later became a director. He was probably the deciding factor when Bill

Shankly and his brother Alec joined Carlisle. It was the start of a long career for young Bill Shankly and his mother, Barbara, must have been comforted to know that her brother was on hand to see that 'Little Willie' was kept safe and well. Bill Shankly was a teenager by this time of course, but still, as the youngest son, fiercely protected by his mum.

In those early years Bill Shankly had seen, read and heard much about the soccer exploits of his two uncles, and had also been given great guidance by his mum and dad, as he explained in an interview.

"I used to be enthralled by the tales of my uncles. I used to listen to every word that they told me, and when they were away I would eagerly await news bulletins – which usually came through my mother. I wanted to hear every little detail. But it was more than just listening to the stories of their adventures – I was picking up tips all the time. I was ambitious you see... I wanted to be like my heroes... I wanted to be a professional footballer!"

There was yet more influence still to come through his family as all his brothers drifted into soccer. His oldest brother Alec was particularly helpful in Bill's education.

"Alec used to teach me a lot. He had a great understanding of the game and passed on many tips to me. He was a thinker and would weigh things up. He used his experience wisely and was certainly a big help to me," said Bill.

"When I was a little boy, Alec told me never to argue with the referee. Don't dissent – you can't win. Fancy getting sent off for talking, he said to me. You won't upset the ref – he's heard it all before. He doesn't score goals or save them – so what's the point of picking on him. That's the sort of advice I was given by Alec. And I listened – I took notice – I remembered – and he was right."

Alec was one of the major family influences on Bill Shankly but, of course, he had his own life to lead as well. His playing career began as a graduate of the Cherrypickers. He was plucked from this soccer orchard by Ayr United. He had been nicknamed Sandy because of his hair which was the lightest of the whole family. To brother Bill, however, Alec was Alec – someone to look up to because he was the first of the family to join a big club.

In the pre-World War One period, when Alec Shankly was at Ayr, the club won the Scottish Second Division championship twice – in 1912 and 1913 – winning promotion to the top division after their second title. Alec also played for Clyde for a while but then the onset of the 1914-18 conflict interrupted his career. After his military service he returned to mining, playing football simply for fun.

It was not the end of Alec's association with soccer however. When Bill embarked upon his career, Alec went with him – almost acting as manager and confidante. Alec was influencing his younger brother's outlook on the game without even kicking a ball.

The next young Shankly to kick a ball as a professional was James – Jimmy to family and friends. Jimmy was inspirational to Bill Shankly for very different reasons. It was not his soccer skills – undoubted though they were. No, Jimmy was a lad who loved his family and always kept in touch, sending money home to help with the family welfare. He would often leave himself short of cash just to be able to do the right thing for the family back in Glenbuck.

In close season breaks Jimmy would be on his way back to Scotland as quickly as he could after the final whistle of the final game. His holidays were all spent in doing odd jobs around the home – and talking football to brother Bill who was always eager to listen.

"Jimmy was outstanding for his human qualities," said Bill, when discussing his family during an interview. "He was a very genuine, honest, caring man – a great example of how people should be to their fellow man… And he was a great footballer as well!"

Jimmy was a defender who was also extremely capable as a robust centre-forward, or striker as they are now known. He also had a spell with Carlisle, but prior to that he had kept up the family connection with Portsmouth – his first club – following that with Halifax before linking up with Uncle Bill Blyth at

Carlisle. He later added Sheffield United, Southend and Barrow to his list of clubs before ending his career in 1933.

Jimmy left behind two goalscoring records that have yet to be bettered. At Southend he hit a record 31 League goals in the 1928-29 season – a feat that was equalled by Sammy McCrory 29 years later, but still never surpassed. Similarly, at Barrow he hit 39 League goals in the 1933-34 season. His may not have been a spectacular career by today's standards – but he certainly left the Shankly mark before retiring and going into business as a coal merchant.

John Shankly was the next brother to leave the Glenbuck nest. There was a very great lesson to be learned from him, and one that has been of great benefit to the many young players who later came under the wing of Bill Shankly.

"My brother John went to a club at an early age and they almost did a heart-muscle in for him as a result of over-training. It was very bad for John and it was a stark lesson for me," said Bill.

John's career kicked off with uncle Bob at Portsmouth. The over-training was, to be fair, at least in part his own fault. He was zealous to say the least and did everything at the double. But there was no restraining influence at the club and his rigorous three-year spell at Fratton Park damaged his health. He went on to Luton after a short spell with Guildford and then returned to Scotland where he played for Alloa.

Despite his obvious frailties he was a true pro and continued to give 100% in all he did. He later joined Blackpool, followed by Greenock Morton, before hanging up his boots. He still refused to shun physical commitment and, after returning home to Glenbuck, he went back to working down the mine. He died while in his fifties, appropriately after the 1960 European Cup Final at Hampden Park in which Real Madrid hammered Eintracht Frankfurt 7-3. John had a heart attack at the match and died later in hospital. Bill Shankly had been at the game with him.

Fourth in line was Bob Shankly, who could almost have performed a double act with Bill. Their outlook was very similar and both grew up to become respected managers. They even looked like twins – although Bob was a little older.

Bob began his playing career with Alloa and then joined Rangers – not THE Rangers but Tunbridge Wells Rangers. They were a major non-League side at the time and had a number of cavalry charges in the FA Cup that had given them a bit of a reputation throughout the country.

Bob Shankly did not stay there for very long. He enjoyed his spell in Kent but hankered after Scotland. Although he spent most of his career with Falkirk, he also had a short time with Alloa. As a player he was excellent but it was as a manager that he really came into his own. He believed in direct, attacking football and always gave his players a firm belief in themselves – even though he personally became very disillusioned once or twice by rough treatment from directors. His pedigree was un-doubted even though his only claim to international fame was selection for the Scottish League against the Irish League in 1937.

His managerial career began with Falkirk in 1950, and he simply transformed them. In the doldrums when he took over, they battled back to First Division status and won the Scottish Cup in 1957. Two years after that triumph he was called to Dundee.

Dundee became managerless in 1959 when Willie Thornton left to take over at Partick. Bob Shankly was his natural successor. He soon demonstrated the Shankly approach and, in the 1961-62 season, Dundee won the Scottish League champ-ionship for the very first time. The following season they reached the semi-final of the European Cup, losing to AC Milan after a two-leg tie that would be worth a book all of its own. Dundee were beaten but they had not lost their dignity. Shankly made sure of that despite unparalleled provocation.

More honour followed until 1965 when Bob Shankly moved on to Hibernian who had been going through turbulent times through the 1960s. Only Jock Stein managed to achieve anything as manager and even he only stayed for one season. In 1971 Bob Shankly became boss of Stirling Albion. They, also, had been going through difficult days and it was not easy for Bob to perform a miracle. But he almost did and his reign as manager, then general manager and finally as director certainly saw the dawning of a new age for Stirling, who are still one of the sides the Premier clubs hate meeting in Cup-ties.

"My brother Bob was only a year or two older than me and therefore I took more in from him. Whatever he did, I knew the same thing would probably happen to me soon, so I listened and learned. We used to exchange views and opinions a lot when we both became managers. When I was at Liverpool and he was at Stirling, my ground was Anfield, while his was called Annfield. When he phoned to tell me he was at Annfield, I said, 'Yes, but I'm at the real one'."

This, then, was the kind of influence that young Willie Shankly had all around him in the family home. Uncles and brothers who had taken their love of football and undoubted abilities and made them do something for them. It was a trait that did, indeed, run in the family. Bill, as the youngest, gained the most from the exploits of all his relatives. It was, if you like, a legacy that had been bequeathed to him. He took it eagerly, invested and enlarged it considerably before passing it on to others as his own legacy to the game that he loved.

But the influence on young Willie was not confined to his family alone. Neither was it exclusive to Glenbuck or the Cherrypickers.

As a boy, Shankly joined the rest of the villagers in cheering on the Cherrypickers – usually playing at home but sometimes at a neighbouring village for an away match. When he started work he began to venture a little further afield. While most of the villagers followed Rangers, Shankly kept his independence. He followed football – the game – not any particular club. As a result of this he would journey to Glasgow most weekends. One week he would be at a Rangers match and the next it would be Celtic. There was no religious divide for him. He believed football to be above that sort of thing. His Saturday pilgrimage by train was to see a match – not a bigoted gathering of some religious clan.

When he was not watching football he was playing it. Reliving some of those moments and skills that had brought forth roars from the crowd at those big games in Glasgow. He was not a hero-worshipper but he had come to admire ability, tactics, tackles, dives and goals.

His early days in the mines developed his sense of humour a stage further. His fellow workers kept up their spirits with gentle repartee, which began upon arrival for the day's toil and barely ceased until after the last 'goodnight' had been called. The lunchtime sandwich break was an interval of story-telling which Billy Shankly found enthralling.

"You have to have a laugh and a joke – it's one of the essentials of life. As a family we had a lot of laughs and then, when I started work, I used to listen to the miners. They were all comedians and they could all tell you a tale.

"As an example, I remember one man telling us how he single-handedly pushed a truck full of coal for a mile down in the pit before he realised that it had come off the tracks. It was funny and it helped everyone to relax, which is why, throughout my career, I've always tried to find something funny to say in the dressing-room before a game. I learned that from my days in the mining industry. People worked hard – very hard – and it was a tough life, but they never failed to see the funny side of things. It was often the only thing that kept them going."

Shankly's days at the pit were short-lived. Basically he came in just as coal was running out. Before long he, and many others, were on the scrap heap – a teenager whose career was over. Unemployment was then common in Glenbuck and the village was slowly disintegrating as its sons and daughters moved out to build new lives elsewhere. Even the Cherrypickers played their last match. A member of the club, Bill never made the first team because he was 'not old enough'. A whole chapter in the annals of the Glenbuck Cherrypickers had been missed.

To keep his head above water, Shankly took on a paper round. Anything would do to help with the family finances. With the depression that was then sweeping the country times were very hard – but there was still football.

About eight miles from his home was the village of Cronberry. It is still there today, on the A70, east of Cumnock. Shankly slung his boots around his neck and set off at every opportunity.

He had had a trial with Cronberry and they liked him – in fact they liked him very much – and he was soon their first choice at right-half. The number-four shirt was entirely his own.

It was the dawning of 1932 when one or two regular spectators began to realise that young Willie Shankly was more than a bit special. He was 19 years old and still a boy among men – though he played like a man among boys. He was already putting into operation that inherent talent fused with the raw edge of his growing-up environment. Like the miners cutting coal at the coal-face he had learned how to hew the ball from every tackle and send the product to the top of the attack for the reward. He could dig deep for a result, honestly toiling without breaking the rules, prepared to shed sweat and blood for this, the favourite part of his life.

"Somebody in the crowd picked me out and from there I went on to play for a professional team," said Shankly, on one of the many occasions that he was asked for a résumé of his career. It was something that he often told youngsters when they asked how they could become professional footballers.

That 'somebody in the crowd' was Peter Carruthers who both reported on the game and scouted for one or two clubs. It was Carruthers who pipped another scout – Bobby Crawford from Preston – to the post and approached Shankly at the end of the 1931-32 season to ask if he would like a trial with Carlisle.

"I couldn't get back home to Glenbuck fast enough to tell my news to the family," recalled Shankly.

Preston were also in the frame but, with uncle Billy Blyth at Carlisle, everything pointed to Brunton Park as being the most sensible place to go for a make-or-break trial game. The official invitation found its way through the letter-box of the Shankly home and, in August 1932, with brother Alec for company, Bill Shankly caught the train to Carlisle.

There was a whole career at stake... a whole life in fact! As it happened, that steam train was not just conveying a young soccer hopeful – it was providing the first leg in a journey that was going to have a major impact on the game. In fact, football was never going to be quite the same again.

A Professional Footballer

BILL Shankly was never an orthodox footballer, even when he was beginning his career. When he and brother Alec stepped down from the train at Carlisle, he was far from convinced that he was doing the right thing. Yes, he was excited. But behind that excitement was that sober streak which made him cautious about this new door that was being opened up to him. It was probably that he had only one trial game in which to prove himself.

Looking at the influence of Shankly today, it is not difficult to piece together the jigsaw pieces of his life that linked together so well to give us a full picture of the man who has left us this wonderful Shankly Legacy. That trial match was just such a jigsaw piece. That very first time that Shankly pulled on a pair of boots at Carlisle, he learned the value of a wise head among young, inexperienced players.

The trial match saw him line up in his customary right-half position alongside Carlisle trainer, Tommy Curry. The Carlisle manager, Billy Hampson, watched the whole thing from the touchline. He was impressed, not only by Shankly's contribution, but also by Curry's. Bill Shankly was also impressed.

"He was a great man, Tommy Curry!" Shankly recalled. "In that trial match he really helped me. He gave me a lot of confidence just at the time when I really needed it. That game was extremely important to me."

The upshot was that young Bill was offered a place at Carlisle as a professional player complete with a contract. His salary? A princely £4 per week. To be honest he did try to send a portion home every week, in emulation of his brother Jimmy, but his mother wouldn't hear of it.

Tommy Curry took Shankly under his wing. He was a tough disciplinarian, but he also had compassion – and an eye for real soccer talent. He was almost a father-figure to young Bill. A role-model from whom Shankly learned much about the care and development of young players. Later, Curry joined Matt Busby at Manchester United and Shankly was distraught when he got the news that Curry was among those who lost their lives in the Munich Air Disaster.

Young Bill quickly became the star of the Carlisle reserves – which was quite an achievement of its own, since he managed to shine even though the side was being defeated week after week. Billy Hampson could not resist giving Shankly his first-team chance and so, after a suitable period of reserve-team soccer, he finally made his senior debut. Carlisle had been having a miserable season with a total of only 14 points from 19 games. Things could hardly have got any worse and so, on New Year's Eve 1932, manager Hampson included Shankly in his line-up for the visit of Rochdale.

The match ended in a 2-2 draw, and Shankly received some praise in the local press. He had done enough to keep his place and by the end of the season he had played in 16 first-team games. Carlisle had not improved their position very much but they had managed to miss having to seek re-election – just. Bill went back to Scotland for the summer break, meeting up with the rest of the family and sharing once again in the emotion of being at home with his loved ones.

Every day he continued training – usually alone. Not for him the long runs favoured by his father – Bill preferred basic fitness routines and a lot of work with the ball. Little boys from the village would act as his retrievers as he practised volleys, free-kicks, goal-kicks and even throw-ins, long and short. He was keen to perfect every skill. He had an eye for detail and it never failed him.

"Your work with the ball is the most important part of the game," said Shankly. "That's what the game is all about... it's called football."

While he was at home in Glenbuck, things had been bubbling at Carlisle. Unknown to Shankly, Preston had not given up on the idea of making him one of their own. Carlisle were having what managers call a 'clear-out' – but Bill Shankly was not one of those being shown the door in the wake of the previous season's disappointments. Players have to be replaced, however, and that can mean money. Times have not changed much in that respect – only the length of the row of noughts on the price tags.

Billy Hampson had decided to leave Carlisle and that came as a blow to Bill Shankly when he heard the news. His spirits rose again, however, when he received a telegram asking him to report back to Brunton Park to discuss a possible move to Preston North End.

Accompanied by Alec once again, Shankly caught the train to Carlisle. The meeting took place at Uncle Billy Blyth's Bowling Green pub. Preston were represented by trainer Bill Scott. In those days the trainer was assistant manager, coach, physiotherapist, kitman, tea-maker and, sometimes, even the cleaner. Today the title doesn't exist. Bill Scott was one of that old school and he reassured Shankly that, although Preston had also been struggling in the division above Carlisle, the club was sound, the future was rosy and there would be first-team football available.

Shankly sat alone with the Preston man – determined that the negotiations and final decision would be entirely his own. Carlisle held their breath – they had real need of the £500 transfer fee. Alec Shankly sat in the next room as his brother and Bill Scott faced each other.

Alec could not believe it when Bill came out and told him he had turned down the move to Preston. It had nothing to do with the £10 personal signing fee – or indeed the extra ten shillings a week in wages – but the fact that Bill was turning down the chance to make progress and show what he could do in a higher division. Alec gave Bill the dressing-down of his life – so much so that he changed his mind there and then. It only remained to catch Bill Scott before he left Carlisle.

Together, they raced to the railway station and arrived just as the train was pulling out. Gasping for breath, they jumped on the moving train, found the startled Bill Scott and, much to his delight, agreed the deal with Preston. All that was left to do was to explain to railway staff why it was that they had made the journey to Preston without stopping to buy tickets.

When he reported for pre-season training with Preston, Shankly was taken along to meet his new landlady – Mrs Hannah Usher. Just as Tommy Curry had been a father-figure at Carlisle, Hannah Usher became a sort of auntie at Preston. Bill stayed under her roof for the next nine years, regularly seeking her advice on a wide range of subjects, from getting his hair cut to getting married. Of course, she never replaced his family in his heart but she proved to be just the sort of 'stand-in' mum that a young lad away from home needed. Once again Shankly was learning.

Preston did not rush their new protégé into action. He began in the reserves and impressed all who saw him. It was not until 9 December 1933, five months after joining the club, that Bill's name finally appeared on the team sheet for the Second Division club. Hull were the visitors, Bill had met them before when his team, Carlisle, had been routed by the Tigers. Now, like himself, Hull had moved up a division – they as Third Division North champions, he as a young man learning his trade. He was obviously learning his trade well as he demonstrated in Preston's 5-0 victory. He stayed in the side for the rest of the season.

Grimsby Town won the Second Division title that 1933-34 season. In 42 League games they scored 103 goals and had the championship wrapped up with a few weeks still to go. But who was going to be promoted with them? There were three clubs in the frame – Bolton, Brentford and Preston. It was all down to the last Saturday of the season. Preston were away to Southampton. They travelled down as Second Division promotion contenders but they made the journey back as First Division newcomers. Their 1-0 win at Southampton had been good enough. As he approached his 21st birthday, Bill Shankly was in the top division.

Once again he returned home to Scotland for the summer and kept himself fit and in practice. His dedication and determination knew no limits – which is more than could be said for the wages he earned. As a First Division player he would now earn £8 per week – the maximum wage allowed to professional footballers at that time.

The following season Preston were a mid-table side – not quite good enough to put in a serious challenge for honours, but too good for the grim prospect of instant relegation. During their promotion season, Preston had reached the quarter-finals of the FA Cup before losing 1-0 at home to Leicester. Could they go even better in the 1934-35 season?… No! Once again they lost 1-0 in the quarter-finals, this time to West Bromwich Albion.

Shankly continued to learn. He trained hard, he played hard and, in the dressing room, he was one of the chief instigators of fun. His upbringing and philosophy of having a 'laugh and a joke', meant that he became the life and soul of the side. Behind that dour mask was a clown trying constantly to escape and reveal itself to the world.

"You can't take life too seriously," he once said. "Football is a serious business but you still need to have a laugh and a joke now and then. If you don't you'll never relax and you'll just go crazy."

He lived up to that philosophy and had a wicked eye for practical jokes and the quick-thinking brain for instant repartee. It never deserted him as we shall see later on in the book. He mostly kept his humour for the dressing room, rarely taking it on to the pitch. His whole concentration for those 90 minutes was on his game and, apart from calling for the ball, the only thing he was known to mutter to himself was how good his team was. He usually did that within earshot of an opposing player, psyching himself up and them out at the same time.

Shankly's whole approach to the game was rugged and determined, but fair. He never flinched a tackle and would slide in where others feared to tread. But he was no fool, no cannon-fodder, a dispensable caveman sent in merely to victimise opponents. Not for Shankly were misplaced elbows, crafty ankle-taps, hair-tugging, kidney punches or spitting. He was a tough guy whose countenance would terrify Rob-Roy but he recognised that his opponents were human-beings in the same profession as himself. Uncompromising during the game, his was the first smile and handshake when the final whistle blew.

One opponent remarked; "He was frightening to look at – a real bruiser – but when he tackled it was the ball that was his objective. If you got in the way it was your own fault. It was a bit like running across the track in front of an express train – if you were hit you knew it."

For all his tenacity Shankly rarely suffered injury. Minor bruising he shrugged aside with the adage that injuries were only a problem if you allowed them into your mind. He hardly ever did and consequently the number of games that he missed could be counted on the fingers rather than a calculator.

The 1936-37 season was an up-and-down affair with Preston still not the finished article. League form was virtually unpredictable with both unexpected victories and defeats. The FA Cup was different however. In the third round Newcastle were beaten 2-0 as Preston steeled themselves for the big occasion. The Magpies were then a top Division Two side and might well have sprung a surprise on Preston – but the lads from Deepdale were the masters of the day. Fellow First Division side Stoke City were next in line. They had already caused Preston problems that season but, with the FA Cup at stake, there was no holding Shankly and Co. They won 5-1 with Frank O'Donnell hitting a hat-trick to add to the one that he scored against Newcastle.

Exeter gave Preston a scare in the fifth round. They were struggling at the bottom of the Third Division South and had nothing to lose. Their visit to Deepdale on 20 March 1937 was a real chance for glory. They hit three goals – but Preston were up to the challenge and scored five of their own, Frank O'Donnell once again throwing a hat-trick into the ring.

The Preston fans were beginning to get excited by now and a couple of trains were needed for the trip to London for the sixth-round game at Tottenham. Spurs were then a Division Two side and confident Preston strode through to the semi-final with a 3-1 win.

It was back to North London for the semi-final against West Bromwich Albion at Highbury. Frank O'Donnell hit another two to take his FA Cup tally to ten – and Preston triumphed 4-1. Bill Shankly had his first-ever date at Wembley to meet Sunderland on 1 May 1937. Back in Scotland, the Shankly family and all their friends and neighbours were thrilled to bits – and Mrs Usher was quite excited too.

The day was to end in tears. Frank O'Donnell scored his customary goal but Sunderland, inspired by Raich Carter, hit three of their own. The champagne – or most of it – remained on ice. Shankly sat emotionless in the dressing room, looking at his loser's medal. It is almost a Cup Final custom that the losing team will console each other by determining that they will be back next year. In this, Preston were no exception.

The influence of Bill Shankly on the Preston side was growing by the week. He rarely had a bad game and was fast developing into a major star of the First Division. The 1937-38 season proved to be the best yet for Shankly, who celebrated his 24th birthday shortly after that memorable campaign.

In the League, Preston had developed into a major force and were pulling in the crowds both at home and away. By the last day of the season they were within one point of the leaders, Arsenal, and a record Preston crowd of 42,684 packed into Deepdale to see them go for gold in their final game – against Arsenal. The history books reveal that the Gunners won 3-1 and clinched the championship, Preston finishing third behind Wolves. But the books do not tell the whole story by any means. Just before half-time, Preston's Jimmy Milne broke a collarbone.

There were no substitutes in those days and the heroics of ten-man Preston thrilled the crowds but, unfortunately, lost the game.

The season was not over though. There was still the FA Cup Final to come. Yes, those words in the loser's dressing room that previous May had come true. Preston were back at Wembley.

Before he journeyed to the FA Cup Final again, there had been another two landmarks in Bill Shankly's career. On 2 February 1938, Preston were playing, of all teams, Liverpool, at Deepdale. The 2-2 result was not particularly memorable – though it was a greater cause for celebration by mid-table Liverpool than by title-hunting Preston. No, the remarkable moment of the match was the ball hitting the back of the net from the boot of Bill Shankly – his first-ever League goal.

And there was another milestone in Shankly's career when he was picked to make his debut for Scotland in the highly-charged international against England at Wembley in April 1938. But more of that later – the FA Cup awaits.

The campaign began on 8 January 1938, with a 3-0 win over West Ham of the Second Division. All the Preston goals came from inside-right George Mutch, who had been bought from Manchester United for £5,000 a few months earlier. First Division Leicester were dispatched 2-0 in the next round, and then a hard-fought 1-0 away win at Arsenal saw Preston into the quarter-finals. Once more they were drawn away in London, this time to Brentford who were also a First Division side.

That hurdle was jumped with a 3-0 result and Preston found themselves facing Aston Villa for the semi-final at Bramall Lane, Sheffield. For the first time in the campaign Preston conceded a goal – but with two of their own they had successfully booked their passage to Wembley for the second successive season. That part of the promise, at least, had been fulfilled. Huddersfield were waiting for them.

Once again the Preston fans were in full voice when the teams appeared from the dressing rooms. In the crowd was a large group from Glenbuck – a party trip had been organised, in the conviction that this was going to be Bill Shankly's finest hour.

The game was tense. Both sides came close but no goals were forthcoming. The Preston defence was like a rock and the Huddersfield team matched them. The BBC radio commentator was Tom Woodroffe. He watched the minutes tick away into extra-time. It was a deadlock. With one minute of extra-time to go the commentator told listeners; "If they score now, I'll eat my hat!"

The ball went out of play and Bill Shankly picked it up for the Preston throw-in. All that practice that he had put in during the summer came to his assistance as he summoned all his strength and sent in a very long throw to the feet of George Mutch. George collected the ball, jinked past Huddersfield's Eddie Best, and steamed into the Yorkshire side's goal area. Defender Alf Young completely mistimed his tackle and Mutch went down like a sack of potatoes. The crowd groaned, the last chance had been lost – or had it?

The referee's whistle had not been to end the game – he was pointing at the spot! It was a penalty! Mutch was nursing his bruises. He looked around to see who was going to take the penalty. All his team-mates walked away. Shankly nodded to him and smiled. Mutch placed the ball on the spot. The silence seemed almost deafening. Then came the thud of boot meeting ball – another thud as the ball hit the inside of the bar – the unmistakable sound of a leather ball sliding down the netting – and the silence was shattered into a million pieces as that packed sea of Preston supporters erupted in a great roar of approval.

There was barely time to restart the game before the whistle blew to conclude the match. Preston had won the FA Cup, the promise now fully realised, and Bill Shankly sat in the dressing room gazing at his winner's medal that had been presented to him by King George V1. Shankly was elated and the memory of that moment stayed with him for the rest of his life. He often recounted it to his players later, when it was time for their greatest moment.

"When the whistle blows at Wembley and you've played in the FA Cup Final, and you've won it – that, boys, is the greatest thrill of your life. The feeling is unbelievable. You've won the FA Cup and everyone knows that you're the best."

The Preston team on that great day reads like a soccer who's who – Holdcroft, Gallimore, Andy Beattie, Shankly, Smith, Batey, Watnough, Mutch, Maxwell, Bob Beattie, Hugh O'Donnell. Six of them were internationals at a time when caps were honours rather than confetti.

The 1938-39 season saw Preston lose their grip on the FA Cup in the sixth round. Runcorn, Aston Villa and Newcastle had all been overcome, but Portsmouth proved to be a bridge too far – and it was a long low-key journey back to Deepdale. Someone said there was always next year... but there wasn't. After that season there would be no more FA Cup Finals for seven long, gloomy years.

In the League, Preston had a reasonable campaign but eventually finished ninth in Division One, 15 points behind champions, Everton. Shankly went back to Scotland to escape for his summer break – but there was no escape from the approaching gloom as the clouds of war gathered across Europe.

By August of 1939 those war clouds had turned even blacker, threatening to turn into a major storm. Football ceased to be the chief topic of conversation in the offices, factories, shops and pubs of Britain. However the new 1939-40 season started on schedule. Shankly was approaching his 26th birthday and still had his usual air of optimism. The first few results were far from encouraging.

On the morning of 2 September 1939, Bill Shankly opened his birthday cards, delivered to Hannah Usher's house. Preston were at Grimsby that afternoon and he had saved his cards for the day even though most had arrived early. He was given a ribbing by his team-mates and a few gifts as well. There were no gifts from Grimsby during that game though – they beat Preston 2-0. After the game the home side presented their defeated visitors with a box of fish. Bill took his share back to his digs.

The next day the nation gathered around its radio sets to have its worst fears realised – Britain was at war with Germany. The government immediately issued a number of safety decrees including a ban on gathered crowds. The football season was instantly over, little more than two weeks after it had begun.

At a time when Bill Shankly's career was about to reach its peak, he, like many others at that grim time, found himself being tackled and brought down by something more foreboding than any soccer opponent. His career was over – or at the very least, on hold until further notice. He had been thrust out of work and was now joining the rest of the world in posing that one unifying question – now what?

Braveheart

BILL Shankly never shirked anything in his life. At school he never shirked his class-work. When he went to work at the mine he never shirked his toil there either. He never shirked his responsibility toward his family. He never shirked a tackle on the soccer pitch... and he never shirked his duty when he received the international call, either in the soccer stadium or in World War Two.

His progress at right-half for Preston attracted many onlookers. Among the fans were scouts from other clubs and among these were representatives of the Scottish Football Association. They already knew a great deal about Bill Shankly. The very fact that he was a Shankly – and a nephew of the Blyths – was enough to make him worth having a look at... but the reports coming out of Deepdale made it all the more essential for them to come and see for themselves. He was reported to be a bit special – and so he was!

The call came, and it wasn't just Bill who was proud – the whole of Glenbuck celebrated. Especially did they celebrate because his international debut was to be made at Wembley on 9 April 1938, against the old enemy – the oppressors from over the border – England!

At one minute to three, on that April afternoon, the two teams faced each other in front of a packed Wembley Stadium. As well as Shankly, Preston had provided three other Scots – Andy Beattie, Tom Smith and George Mutch. Others in the side were Dumming, Anderson, Brown, Milne, Walker, O'Donnell and

Reid. England had their own star line-up – Woodley, Sproston, Hapgood, Willingham, Cullis, Copping, Matthews, Hall, Fenton, Stephenson and Bastin.

You could barely hear the whistle for the roar of the crowd. The game sprung into action and Shankly eagerly awaited his first touch of the ball. It came after eight minutes but as he attempted to play the ball, a wild tackle came in from Wilf Copping and almost ended Shankly's part in the game there and then. Copping was playing in his 14th international for England. He was aware of Shankly and had no qualms about showing him who was boss as quickly as possible.

The tackle was so fierce that blood oozed from a nasty gash, the solid leather stud of Copping's boot having torn through Shankly's thick sock, shinguard and flesh. Today it would have meant a red card and a stretcher – but on that day it brought a sharp look, a quick bandage and on with the game. Shankly wanted his revenge but there was no opportunity as the two men never came into contact again throughout the rest of the game... but there was no handshake between them at the end.

Shankly had the greater satisfaction though – because of the scoreline. Scotland were victorious 1-0. The all-important goal had come from Tommy Walker of Hearts after just six minutes – perhaps that was the final incentive that Copping had needed to launch his attack. Copping later repeated his assault on Shankly in a League match – again resulting in that desire for revenge. But it never came – Copping retired before it ever became possible.

The old enemy was vanquished and Bill Shankly had played his part. He was an obvious choice when the Scottish selectors met again to pick their team for the next international – this time in Belfast against Northern Ireland on 8 October 1938. Because of their FA Cup Final commitments, Bill and his Preston team-mates were unavailable for the international against Holland in Amsterdam in May of that year. Scotland won 3-1 and were good value in Holland – but they were even better in Belfast, securing a 2-0 win.

But for an interruption in his career, Bill Shankly would

probably have gone on to a huge collection of caps. As it was, he played in the next Scottish international against Wales at Tynecastle on 9 November 1938. The Welsh gave the Scots a run for their money but the home side eventually prevailed and finished on the better side of the 3-2 scoreline.

There were two more international calls for Bill Shankly that season. On 7 December 1938, Hungary were the visitors and the game was played at Ibrox. Hungary put up a good fight but the Scots won the day with a convincing 3-1 victory. The Scots were on a roll. Shankly was playing out of his skin and couldn't wait for the next international date on the fixture list – 15 April 1939. The venue was Hampden and, once again, the opponents were England.

There was no Wilf Copping in the England side this time – but there was Joe Mercer, Stan Cullis, Stanley Matthews and Tommy Lawton. England were still smarting from their 0-1 defeat of the previous year at Wembley. Another Scotland victory would give them the Home International championship for the first time in four seasons.

Jimmy Dougal put Scotland ahead and that was how it stayed on the rainy afternoon in Glasgow – until the seventieth minute when the Hampden roar was silenced by an equalising goal from England's Pat Beasley. England had their tails up and Matthews began to terrorise the home defence. Eventually the Scots cracked and, after two defenders were left sprawling by the will-o'-the-wisp Matthews, Lawton found space to knock the ball into the net. Shankly later commented that, hearing the ball bulge into the Scottish net just then, was one of the worst sounds that he had ever experienced. England won 2-0. The Home International championship was shared equally by the English, the Scots and the Welsh.

It was disappointing for Shankly because his heart had been set on beating the English and helping Scotland become champions of Britain. The season came to a close. There was no Cup Final this time and the 1938-39 campaign proved to be unproductive in League matters as well. Preston finished ninth in the First Division – one place above Grimsby – two places above Liverpool – and ten places above Huddersfield, who were also, later, to play a part in Shankly's life.

Still, there was always next season – except that, this time, there wasn't! Oh yes, pre-season training was normal. Bill reported back to Deepdale after his usual summer break back home in Glenbuck. The summer had not been quite the same however – the radio had been turned on more than usual as news bulletins changed hourly to give the latest developments of the gathering clouds of war over Europe.

Back at Preston, training was gentle during the first few days. Shankly renewed acquaintances and looked forward to the challenge of the new campaign. Being good 'also-rans' in 1938-39 was not good enough. There had to be a medal or two for 1939-40. This season saw numbers on players' backs, as a compulsory measure, for the first time. The campaign kicked off on 26 August 1939 – and by the time it finished, Shankly's Preston had failed to win a game. In fact they had failed to even score a goal. They finished in 19th place – below them were Portsmouth and Blackburn, with Middlesbrough at the very bottom. The reason for this apparent demise in Preston's fortunes was that only three games were played before the season was officially abandoned as Britain entered World War Two. Preston had played three, drawn two, lost one and had a 0-2 goals tally.

Although the Football League was abandoned, special wartime competitions were started to provide some relief for the beleaguered British public. Shankly remained with Preston for a while as the club became part of the Northern League. Here he found himself playing alongside young Tommy Finney – who Shankly later described as the greatest player he had ever seen. Shankly had much to say about Finney as we shall see later. The respect was mutual too – Finney admired the no-nonsense approach of Bill Shankly and appreciated the encouragement that he always gave to the younger players at Preston.

In the 1940-41 season the Preston fans had plenty to cheer about. Not only did their side win the Northern Regional League, but they also reached the wartime Cup Final at Wembley. Arsenal were the opposition and a hard-fought game resulted in a 1-1 draw. The replay was at Blackburn and, in their own corner of the country, Preston were determined not to let it slip. They won 2-1.

Don't make the mistake of thinking that professional footballers hid in the dug-outs when war broke out. Like all professionals they had to wait and see. A few enlisted in the forces instantly, but of those who didn't, many found other ways of making their contribution. Bill Shankly spent the first few months working at a local firm as a labourer – and then found another job as a riveter in an aircraft factory. He did not enjoy that because he did not like working indoors surrounded by the metal carcasses of aircraft. He still liked the wide open spaces of the football pitch.

At the end of the 1939-40 season – in June to be precise – he decided to enlist and became a member of the Royal Air Force. He was able to continue playing for Preston because he was stationed at Padgate, near Warrington, not too far by train from Deepdale. For a while he was then sent to RAF Cosford, where the emphasis was – and still is – on physical training. Bill did not stay there too long however, he was posted in December 1940 to Manchester – which meant that once again he was within easy travelling distance of Preston. He continued to turn out for them as often as he was able but he also played for the Balloon Barrage Depot (Bury), who competed in the Manchester and District RAF League.

Not content with that, Shankly also stepped between the ropes of the boxing ring. He had always nursed a passion for boxing – a passion that stayed with him for the rest of his life. In the RAF he boxed at middleweight and was good enough to win a trophy.

It was a topsy-turvy time for the whole world – soccer did not escape it and, of course, neither did Preston or indeed, Bill Shankly. There were wartime internationals of sorts at both Hampden and Wembley in which Shankly was involved no less than seven times. In fact his last international call-up, in 1944, was to end on something of a sour note. He was asked to test the fitness of a suspect knee injury by kicking a goalpost. He refused point-blank, saying that he wouldn't do anything so stupid even with his good leg. The authorities did not appreciate his attitude and Bill certainly didn't appreciate theirs. He was withdrawn from the squad and never saw another Scotland shirt in his size.

Away from the international scene, clubs were able to temporarily recruit any player who happened to be stationed within a reasonable distance of their ground. Bill Shankly would have happily continued to turn out for Preston in between fulfilling his RAF obligations – but the Army put paid to that when they commandeered Deepdale in 1941, putting Preston out of action for the rest of the war. The club received £250 a year for the use of their ground – but that was no compensation at all as far as Shankly was concerned... and there was worse still to come.

Being in the RAF meant that Shankly found himself being posted to various camps all around Britain. As a result he played for number of different clubs – among them were Luton, Cardiff, Norwich, Bolton and Arsenal. It was while he was playing for Arsenal that he sampled both the sweet and sour sides of human nature.

Shankly played a major part in Arsenal reaching the 1943 League South Cup Final at Wembley. He was looking forward to seeing the famous twin towers again and was stunned when some of Arsenal's old players – who had not been with the side since the war started – reappeared and were given preference over him. He had played in every round of that Cup competition but was to be displaced for the Final. By way of compensation, the club offered him a free ticket for the match. Needless to say, he told them in no uncertain terms what to do with it. His passion for the game won out though and compelled him to go and so he bought a ticket and watched from the terraces as Arsenal beat Charlton for the Cup.

There was another bit of bad news for Bill during those war years. He suffered a nasty knee injury which stayed with him for the rest of his life. It was in November 1941 and he was still with Preston, playing away to Halifax. He travelled back to Manchester on a bus with his knee looking like he'd stuffed the ball down his trouser leg. The pain was searing and he finally agreed to go to the hospital and get it checked.

At first they diagnosed a broken knee-cap and told him he

would never play again. Later, an Army Medical Officer said that it was simply cartilage trouble. Normally that would mean an instant operation to rectify the condition. Unfortunately Bill's op was not so instant. He waited – and continued to play – for another two years before his knee was finally put right. While it never stopped him playing, that knee injury nagged at him periodically throughout his years.

But it wasn't all bad news for Bill Shankly. True, the news that his father was unwell did not make him very happy – but his compassionate posting opened up new avenues to him – one of those avenues being a complete departure from everything he had previously known.

The RAF posted him to Glasgow. A train ride from the camp could get him back to Glenbuck whenever it might be necessary – but it also meant that he was in one of the hottest soccer cities in the world.

Although he had never truly taken sides when he had journeyed regularly to Glasgow in those earlier years to watch both Celtic and Rangers on alternate weekends, he would really have liked to have played for Rangers. Perhaps this posting would bring that ambition to reality! If not, perhaps it might be Celtic's shirt that he would be wearing. Wrong again! It was Partick Thistle who were the nearest, and it was their dressing-room that would become home to him.

On his Partick debut on 2 October 1943, he injured his knee again, and this time there was no avoiding surgery. Partick made all the arrangements and the operation was carried out with the minimum of fuss and with great success.

As part of his rehabilitation training, Shankly would run a couple of miles most days around the Bishopbriggs Camp, where he was stationed. Unknown to him, there was a deal of careful attention being paid to him by someone else on the camp – a teleprinter operator. She was not a football fan and didn't recognise Bill – or even his training companion, ABA heavy-weight champion Jock Porter, who used to join in with those daily running sessions.

At last Bill noticed her and, being a true romantic at heart, he took her presents of cheese on toast and similar delicacies. He discovered that this young lady was in similar circumstances to himself in that she had also been posted to Bishopbriggs Camp because her mother was not well. Shankly became more and more fascinated. For the first time in his life he began to realise that there was room in his heart for more than just football and his own natural family. He also found himself wanting when it came to the emotional courage department. Eventually, however, he summoned up all his bravado – and asked her out. Not for him the joys of a cinema, the theatre or even the fish and chip shop. No, only the very best for this young lady – he took her to watch him play for Partick against Celtic.

It was the start of a beautiful friendship that grew and grew until finally it led all the way to the altar in a church in Glasgow on 29 June 1944. William Shankly took Agnes Fisher to be his wife – and from there on, Bill and Ness were an item. Notice that they were married during the cricket season when Bill had no playing commitments!

Shankly continued to play for Partick and it was something of a wedding anniversary present when, a year after their marriage, he played in the Summer Cup Final in June 1945 and helped his side beat Hibs 2-0. Now he had wartime Cup medals from both sides of the border.

At long last the doves of peace took to the skies over Britain, replacing the ugly black clouds that had hung over the nation for far too long. The Shanklys were to leave Glasgow as Bill was still officially a Preston player. A huge party was thrown in their honour by the supporters of Partick and both Bill and Ness had tears in their eyes as they said their last farewells and departed, laden with gifts and showered with genuine affection.

Before leaving Glasgow, there was another new experience for Bill when he became father to a daughter. Barbara Shankly was born in the summer of 1945, a Glaswegian girl and the pride of her mum and dad.

In January 1946 Bill Shankly was demobbed. Britain's 'finest hour' had come and gone in those preceding years. Bill Shankly's was still to come.

Lessons

POST-WAR Britain began a party that lasted almost as long as the war itself. Dance halls were crowded – at speedway tracks, the roar of the crowd drowned out the din of the straining motorbikes – and at football grounds attendances were huge. First Division turnstiles clicked to a standstill as gates of 30, 40 and even 50 thousand became the norm.

For Shankly the boom continued at Preston. He was out of the RAF and out of the war – but into serious soccer action. After a break of seven years, League Football returned on Saturday, 31 August 1946, and in the next four seasons nearly 157 million spectators watched League matches. At Preston they had their share as North End kept among the leaders for much of that first post-war season. In the event they finished in seventh place, ten points behind champions Liverpool.

When the whistle blew to start that season Shankly was nearly 33 years of age. He was captain of Preston and showed it. He knew that he did not have too many playing years ahead and so he was determined to play each game as if it was his last. Come to think of it, he hadn't changed very much.

There were some memorable moments in these final boom years. Many of them were created by Tom Finney whom Shankly believed was the best footballer he had ever seen. More of Finney later. On the downside was Charlton Athletic, who were fast becoming a bogey side for Shankly and his Preston gang. Charlton had dumped Preston out of the FA Cup during the 1945-46 season with a win of 6-1 over two legs in the fifth round.

The following season they did it again, this time winning 3-2 in the sixth round. Despite all his efforts Shankly was never again to play in an FA Cup Final. Nevertheless, he left his mark on the competition by appearing in a record 43 consecutive FA Cup-ties for Preston.

Amazingly, that record would never have been created if some directors of Preston had had their way. When Shankly returned to the club as a full-time professional following his demob – some members of the board were opposed to taking him back. It was his age – his best years were gone, – said some. He would not be the same now that he was married and had a daughter, said others.

How wrong they were! Shankly was as committed as ever and there was certainly no problem with his age. His rugged approach, his tenacity in the tackle, his clan chieftain style in the soccer onslaught were all as keen as ever. If Preston did not want him, there were many other clubs who would put down the red carpet for him. But – Preston did want him – the majority of the board decided that they did not just want him… they needed him!

Shankly responded in his own inimitable style – vindicating those who had supported him, politely ignoring those who had not.

Of course, Shankly was not going to stay a first-team player for ever. He was well aware that one day he was going to have to stand down – but he was also well aware that he wanted to stay in the game and be a soccer boss. To this end he had taken a correspondence course in physiotherapy, and when Preston chairman, James Taylor, suggested that it was now time for Shankly to consider himself as a second-team player, with the special assignment of bringing on young players, he was not too dispirited.

His first-team days were not completely finished though. There was much haggling between himself and Preston. The club wanted to keep him on as a reserve player-coach, and offered him a testimonial benefit. Shankly was annoyed by that. He felt that if he was due any sort of bonus it should be in appreciation of what he had already done in his 16 years at Preston – not as an enticement to convince him to stay longer.

While the talking was going on, Carlisle were patiently waiting in the wings. They had approached Shankly to offer him the post of manager. He was still something of a hero at Brunton Park and his reputation, both nationally and internationally, had made him just the kind of big-name that they wanted to attract as their new boss.

Shankly was not keen to leave Preston – but he was a man of principle and he was not prepared to lower his personal standards of ethical conduct. Carlisle offered to match his £14 per week salary and, with his uncle Bill Blyth still being involved, they put up a good case for his signature. The rift between himself and Preston continued to grow and finally he made up his mind that Carlisle was the place for him.

His annoyance at the club was tempered by the fact that a few months after his departure Preston were relegated, and also that the Preston Supporters Club made a special presentation to him – which underlined the point that the lack of appreciation for Shankly was just confined to the boardroom.

On 19 March 1949, Shankly made his exit as a player. Preston held on to his playing contract in a bid to prevent him playing elsewhere or seeking a high fee – so he simply announced his retirement as a registered player. For that last game, which Preston lost 3-1 to Sunderland, Shankly was 35 years old.

On 22 March 1949, he was formally appointed manager of Carlisle – replacing Ivor Broadis who, ironically, had played for Sunderland in Shankly's last game.

Between that last game for Preston, and his new challenge as manager of Carlisle, there was time for Bill to reflect on the lessons he had thus learned from his early days of innocence in Glenbuck to the heady heights of Hampden and those final days of anger and depression at Preston.

So what were those lessons that had carved Shankly's career thus far? What had he learned up to now that was to carve that career in the future – and indeed, that would have an effect on British soccer that has lasted right up to today?

Bill Shankly was a deep-thinking man and also a great orator. He rarely refused an interview – not because he liked the sound of his own voice – but because he was passionately interested in his subject. He often reflected on his early days and earnestly believed that they were the major influence on his life.

"When I went into management for the first time, I had a lot to draw upon. You have to learn from life – from your experiences. Remember them, think about them, and then use them to improve yourself." He said in interview.

"I learned a lot about the game from my brothers and uncles. With my brother Alec I learned about discipline where referees are concerned. He always said that you should never have a go at referees because it was a waste of time – and he was right. I never had a go at referees. When I was playing I used to sometimes even congratulate a referee when he gave a decision against us. People used to think that I was crazy but that didn't bother me – I just used to do things my way from what I had learned from my brother Alec.

"As an example, a referee might give an offside against us when we had put the ball in the net. I would say, 'good decision referee. You were right there'. I'd chat to them. Next time there was a 50-50 decision – he'd most likely give it our way because I'd been all right with him. It's all good psychology – and psychology is very important in football.

"Denis Law was the same, and perhaps he got some of that from me. He used to chat to the referees and linesmen and they would get to like him, he was a nice little boy. They would be more inclined to give him the benefit of the doubt in a situation.

"That was all because of what my brother Alec taught me. I also learned from another brother, John, who had a good career spoiled by wrong training – asking too much too soon of a young body. That taught me a lot, not just for myself, but also for the care of players in general and youngsters in particular. Never over-train! You can ruin a player by applying all the wrong training. That was a big lesson for me and I'm sure that it helped in the success of Liverpool years later.

"One of the most important things was having a sense of humour. It does wonders for everyone. That is something I learned from the mines. The men there worked incredibly hard and sometimes it was only their sense of humour that kept them going. The exaggerated stories that they told still make me laugh.

"I remember one old man saying that he pushed a coal truck with a ton of coal in it for over a mile in the mine before he realised that it had come off the rails. Now that sort of story would get a good laugh and make the men happier at their work. As a player I used to do the same sort of thing. I would keep a bit of banter going in the dressing room before a game – and even on the pitch sometimes. I remember being asked what was my best season and I said that it was the year I hit 15 hat-tricks.

"Having a laugh before the game relieves the tension and makes for a good team spirit. If people can laugh together they will also work together. Laughter is a very unifying factor. You can sit in a theatre with 1,000 people that you don't know. But when the show is over and you've all had some good laughs, those same people are talking to each other on the way out as if they had known each other for years. Now that kind of spirit is extremely important in football. I saw it in action in the mines – I used it as a player – and then I used it as a manager.

I had also learned such things as dedication, practice, being professional and having the will to win. I had seen all these things in the players I had played alongside and I had seen the benefits of them all. There are many important factors in professional football and these are just a few of them. It's a bit like a list of the ingredients with which to make a wonderful cake. Every ingredient, however small, is very important. A good cook must have a real eye for detail, and I knew that a football manager must have a similar one... even the smallest thing must be absolutely right.

"A good manager needs to know everything about his players, but he also needs to know what they go through both mentally and physically. The more experience you have as a player, the more you're able to understand your players when you become a manager. You won't get the best out of them unless you can put yourself in their position.

"Being a manager does not just mean coaching players. You have to coach your coaches – or trainers as we used to call them. It's no good them training your players a certain way if you want them to perform along different lines during a match.

"And then there are the directors. I had met many directors and officials when I was a player and I learned that they too are all different individuals with different ideas and ambitions. A club may have a board of directors in which each one is totally different. Some of them are just happy to have a good seat, meet everyone, and that's it. Others want to pick the team, talk to the press and almost act as dictators.

"Being a player, I had met all kinds – and that gave me a good grounding. I knew what to expect. It was not always my ambition to be a manager, but I'd always taken an interest in what made clubs and people tick. I think I would urge all players to get the most from their playing days – not necessarily in earnings, but in experience, knowledge, wisdom. It is a wonderful thing to be able to learn a trade, and even if a player has no intention of becoming a manager one day, he can still learn the trade. Take everything in – think about it. Managers are not born – they evolve! Every player is an apprentice manager and, if he wants to, he can go on to get his scholarship. If there is no interest in management, the player has still had a worthwhile education and career during his playing days."

Shankly had certainly had his education. He believed that he peaked as a player in the post-war years – and there are many who feel that the war years cheated him of an illustrious playing career. But even allowing for that terrible interruption, Bill Shankly had still placed himself in the category of great and memorable players.

It is a well-known story that he handed over his Preston number-four shirt to Tommy Docherty, who joined the club from Celtic for £4,000 as a replacement for Shankly. He wrote a note to Docherty congratulating him on taking over as the greatest right-half in the world. He also added these immortal words – "Just put the shirt on and let it run around – it knows where to go!"

But letter-writing was not the prerogative of Bill Shankly. When the news broke of his retirement as a player and his launch into a new career as a manager, he received shoals of letters from well-wishers both in the game and regulars on the terraces. Not one was pleased to see him go – and many expressed anger at what they saw as shabby treatment of Bill by the Preston board. There were many tributes – among them some sincere and emotional words from one of the greatest names of soccer history – Joe Mercer.

Mercer wrote a letter congratulating Shankly on his appointment as Carlisle manager, but lamenting what he saw as 'the passing of a great player'. Although there had been no quarter asked, or given, whenever the two met on the pitch, they shared an empathetic distinction – they were both great professional footballers. As Mercer said: "The game will be much poorer without you Bill!" He meant as a player of course – but even Mercer did not realise that the greatest Shankly impact on football was in the future and still to be seen.

Already the Shankly Legacy was in operation. After he had departed from Preston, young players who had gained from his inspiration and encouragement were forming the nucleus of the next generation of the club. Shankly left in March 1949 and, as we have already said, the club was relegated at the end of the 1948-49 season – but there were better days ahead for Preston.

Tom Finney and Co had a good 1949-50 season in the Second Division, but came of age in 1950-51 when they finished as the division's clear champions – five points ahead of runners-up Manchester City. The Shankly approach to coaching had already had some effect. His coaching work with the reserves and young players at Preston was bearing fruit after his departure.

Shankly put into practice the things he preached and Preston became the first club to benefit from what we all now know to be – The Shankly Legacy.

The Gaffer

IT was 4 April 1949 when Bill Shankly moved in as manager of Carlisle United. The set-up was one that can only really be described as 'prehistoric'. The ground was shabby and rather run-down. The players were less than enthusiastic. With patched-up surroundings theirs was a 'patched-up' approach to the game. They went through the same monotonous training routines day after day and it was almost as if they were undergoing a life-sentence at HM Prison Carlisle, rather than Carlisle FC, members of the Football League since 1928.

Shankly's recollection of Carlisle in those days was one expressed with his usual honesty.

"When I came back to Carlisle as manager, conditions were just as bad as they had been when I was a player. I knew that much had to be changed. I was still learning but I was enthusiastic and that much at least I knew I could put into the players and the supporters."

Within a matter of days Shankly had won his first trophy. Carlisle beat Workington 2-1 at home, in the Final of the Cumberland Cup. It might not sound a lot but to a man with the passion and drive of Bill Shankly, winning even an egg-cup would be a matter of personal pride and achievement.

An eye-witness of those early days was Geoff Twentyman, then a 19-year-old with high hopes but little first-team experience. Later he became a player and then a scout for Liverpool – his educated eye for soccer talent owing much to the time he served with Bill Shankly. He remembers well the winds of change at Brunton Park.

"I was a part-time player when Bill Shankly arrived. I was just 17 when I got into the first team at the end of the 1946-47 season. When Bill Shankly arrived he changed everything. He took a lot of interest in training methods and we found that our regular routine became totally altered.

"He was like a breath of fresh air for Carlisle. The supporters liked him and the players responded to him immediately. He didn't just make changes – he took a personal interest in everyone. He knew all about our private lives and would give anyone who was misbehaving in any way a real talking to. He never betrayed a confidence and it was useless trying to keep anything from him.

"Very often he would call you in for a bit of physiotherapist treatment, which he was very good at by the way. But as he worked on you he would talk to you about yourself. It might be about your game, it might be about your family... anything. When he got you on that couch it was a combination of physiotherapy and psychiatry."

The effect of Shankly's new regime was immediate – but it did not show in the results of the games played. There was one solitary win out of the seven remaining games of that season. But Shankly had learned another lesson – that of patience. His time for rebuilding was the summer.

His first task was to make his presence felt and he certainly achieved that. He demanded new kit for the players – his first move in giving the team the psychological lift it needed. He ordered a spring-cleaning of the ground from the terracing to the dressing-rooms. Wherever there was work going on Shankly would be seen – with a brush sweeping the dressing-rooms – with a hammer repairing seating – even with a pen-knife, scraping mud from the first-team's boots. Shankly was demonstrating the same industrious characteristics as his father. He would never ask anyone to do something that he was not prepared to do himself – and that applied as equally to the junior players as it did to the chairman.

Another of Shankly's masterstrokes was his relationship with the press. He soon let it be known that he would talk freely to the media and all who came into contact with him were totally impressed by his style and commitment.

By the end of the season Carlisle appeared to have been hit by a hurricane. The townsfolk responded with their feet and attendances at Brunton Park rose rapidly. Within a few weeks Shankly had introduced that elusive 'feel-good factor', that politicians have strived to convince us of for many generations. In Carlisle it was real! Shankly had already become the proverbial 'white knight', who had ridden in on his charger to rescue Carlisle from the gloomy depths of soccerdom's lower reaches.

Much later on, in reflection, Bill Shankly said that he was simply putting into practice all the things that he had been learning as a player. He even said that he had been planning to go into management ever since he started as a player, and that he had been studying for just that purpose. Be that as it may, there is no getting away from the fact that two of Shankly's greatest attributes had come into play – his boundless enthusiasm together with his positive attitude.

To Bill Shankly, a ground was never half empty – it was always half full. His players were never injured – they just had a temporary strain. His team hardly ever lost – even if the other team won. It never bothered him that, with Carlisle being such an outpost, his team had to travel so extensively – away games were business trips, to be enjoyed and bring back results. Home matches meant that the opposition had to face his mighty players after an horrendous journey to Brunton Park. That was what he told his players.

His management style was set in concrete right from the start at Carlisle. Think positive, be positive, play positive. This book is about the Shankly Legacy – the style that is still prevalent today through the activities of his many disciples. They don't come any more positive than Newcastle, where Kevin Keegan's Geordie Revolution owes much to the Shankly Legacy – which itself is indebted to those early days at Carlisle – as Bill Shankly himself was quick to admit.

"I had a lot of success as a football manager, and it was really at Carlisle that I learned the job. Of course, I had many ideas before I ever went to Brunton Park, but at last I had the opportunity to try those ideas out. That's why I say that it all started at Carlisle and that is where I learned so much."

One of Shankly's signings during the early part of his managerial career was Paddy Waters, a former team-mate at Preston and a quick-thinking half-back from Dublin. After seeing Brunton Park, Waters was looking at the rail timetable to see how quickly he could return to Preston. It was the persuasive powers of Bill Shankly that made him decide to give Carlisle a go.

"We can do a job here Paddy," said Shankly. "It might not look very pretty – but we can make this the greatest club in the world."

Yes, even in those days, the Shankly ploy of including everyone in the 'we', and exaggerating the potential to gargantuan proportions, was very clearly in operation. Shankly had taken management by the scruff of the neck and turned it into something entirely different. If you think that a statement like that is, in itself, an exaggeration – How about this:-

"When I was at Carlisle, I used to talk over the loudspeaker to the crowd – explaining my team selection to them, and saying why I had selected one player in preference to another. I used to talk about how we had played in our last match and this sort of thing. The crowd really appreciated me taking them into my confidence and I much preferred the personal touch rather than writing something in the match programme."

That was nearly 50 years ago. Today we have Clubcall and similar club phone lines. In terms of soccer public relations, Shankly was way ahead of his time. Some today still haven't learned the lesson of good rapport with the fans and the press, while others did take on board the Shankly approach to public relations. Denis Law, Ian St John and Kevin Keegan are great examples of former Shankly players who can not only handle the spotlight, but also take advantage of it.

Another signing was Billy Hogan, a brilliantly clever player who Shankly captured from Manchester City. It was a mystery to everyone why City should allow such a tremendous player to leave the club – but later it was discovered that there was a question mark over Hogan's health. The Manchester club were undecided about it, but Shankly had no qualms at all. Hogan appreciated Shankly's confidence in him and repaid it with some outstanding performances in the forward line. Shankly's assessment was a good one as Hogan remained at Carlisle until his retirement in 1955.

Shankly was building a new side and, in fact, a new era for Carlisle. He sought public confidence and got it.

"I am very much a crowd's manager and I think it is as important to instil confidence into the crowd before a match as it is the players," he once said.

He would talk to anyone at anytime about football. Supporters would drop by at Brunton Park for a chat – and perhaps to drop off a few gifts of dairy produce, which Shankly always ensured would be divided equally among his players. He would not let anything disrupt the unity of his team.

Enthusiasm ran high in Carlisle but he would not allow anyone to consider that trophies were just a matter of time. Before the new season he told the local football reporter; "Producing a good team might take a couple of seasons. If we don't get immediate results we will get them eventually – but we'll only get them through playing real, well-organised football."

The crowds responded and attendances were very good for a Third Division North side at, what was then, an outpost of the game.

There were no motorways then and the railways were pre-Beeching – which meant that the steam trains stopped everywhere and took an age to reach a place like Carlisle.

At the end of Shankly's first full season in charge, Carlisle had definitely improved – finishing ninth in the table instead of 15th as they had in the previous season. They finished on 47 points – only eight behind division champions, Doncaster. In the FA Cup, Carlisle ventured beyond round one for the first time in three years. They dispatched Lincoln and Swindon before facing Leeds in the third round. The Yorkshire club proved to be a bridge too far and Carlisle crashed 5-2.

The year passed quickly. Soon it was time to report back for training for the 1950-51 season. Shankly was still building his new team but at the same time he was learning his new trade. His training ideas were being put into practice and his players were becoming accustomed to what were almost revolutionary systems. For years players had been sent out to do road-work – running the bone-jarring streets of the town – hardly ever seeing a football except at the end of a practice session which had already sapped their energy and enthusiasm. Shankly changed all that.

"You play on grass so you'll train on grass," he said. And instead of the marathon running, the Carlisle players found themselves with a ball at their feet as soon as they had warmed up. It was Shankly's belief that the ball was something that his players had to be totally comfortable with and, just like breaking in new shoes, there was only one fail-proof method. He would organise his players into groups for passing, tackling, head-tennis and five-a-side matches in which possession and ball-playing was non-stop.

Did it work?... Didn't it just!

The Shankly system saw Carlisle improve still further in the 1950-51 season – but it was a campaign of high drama. Even before the season started the team on the terraces was playing its part. Season ticket sales were at an all-time high and the talk in Carlisle was non-stop soccer. Everyone had been infected by Shankly disease.

The season started with a flourish. Cheered on by the supporters Carlisle staked their claim for a place among the leaders. Still Shankly relentlessly sought improvement. Others in the game were beginning to realise that Shankly was bringing something different to football – among them the directors of Grimsby Town.

Bill Shankly was approached in the autumn of 1950 as Grimsby were struggling in Division Two. Shankly was tempted. The chance to challenge clubs like Manchester City, Birmingham, Leeds and Blackburn – not to mention Preston – was very hard to decline. There was more money on offer as well. Bill, ever honest, talked to the Carlisle directors. They fully understood what they were asking him to turn down – and to make the pill a little easier to swallow, they offered him a bonus if Carlisle finished in the top three. Shankly agreed and in November an announcement was made that he would be staying at Brunton Park. Everyone got back into their seats.

In December 1950, Shankly's powers of persuasion meant that Paddy Waters agreed to join Carlisle.

"When I came up here, Carlisle were struggling financially – but the support was amazing," said Waters. "There we were in the Third Division North and pulling in an average home gate of about 16,000. My first home match was against Southport. We won 2-0 in front of 17,000 people.

"There was a great team spirit at Carlisle and always a competition to keep your place. Shankly always made sure he had a strong reserve team and that makes for a very determined side. It was just the same at Carlisle in the early 1950s. The place was really buzzing while Shanks was in charge. He lived for football. He was totally football-mad."

Perhaps that was part of Shankly's heritage. His family, and all the friends of his childhood environment, were bitten by the football bug. It was not something that he kept to himself either. Shankly's soccer disease was highly contagious. He passed it on to whomever he came into contact with. The disease still flourishes in Merseyside to this day.

There was further drama in January 1951. Carlisle had sailed through the first two rounds of the FA Cup with wins over Barrow and Southport. Then the draw for the third round was made and Carlisle were drawn away to the mighty Arsenal.

Bill Shankly grinned, wrung his hands with delight and then uttered the immortal words – "Arsenal? – I've never heard of them!"

The Gunners hit Carlisle with every bit of artillery in the first 20 minutes – but they could not score. Shankly's men hit back but the game remained in stalemate at 0-0. When Arsenal arrived at Carlisle for the replay, Shankly stared at them as they came into the ground... then he rushed in to see his own players.

"Boys, boys," he said, clapping his hands. "I've just seen Arsenal get off their bus. They should all be in hospital, they're in a terrible state. The centre-forward can hardly walk!"

"He was a great confidence booster and a great man to work with," said Paddy Waters.

On this occasion, however, the psychology didn't work. Arsenal won 4-1, and the defeat also affected Carlisle's promotion hunt.

"We seemed to fall a bit flat after that Arsenal defeat," Waters commented. "We had a run of draws which might have been victories if it hadn't been for that Arsenal Cup match."

Carlisle finished the season in third place, enough to warrant Shankly receiving the promised bonus – but not enough to win promotion for the club. For Shankly those final tables revealed two other stories – both from Division Two. Preston finished as Second Division champions, while Grimsby finished at the very bottom.

When the referee blew his whistle to finish the 1950-51 season, Shankly took stock of his position. Carlisle had given him a great springboard into management. He now knew without any doubt that his ideas would work... They had worked. But as he soul-searched he knew that if he was going to make progress it would have to be elsewhere. He knew that Carlisle were never going to reach the heights of the big-city clubs. He was frustrated by the club's inability to increase its financial profile and by the end of his meditations he knew that he had to resign.

Of course there were those who tried to talk him out of it – but Shankly was always a very single-minded man. Once he had plotted his course he would doggedly stick to it, regardless. His departure from Carlisle was fairly civil, almost amicable in fact. His next stop would depend upon the response to the letter he had sent to Grimsby Town, applying for the manager's job at Blundell Park which had become vacant at the end of the season.

Grimsby's board of directors could not believe their luck. Their original offer to him had been as coach with a view to becoming manager at a later date – and now, here he was actually asking for the job. It was the best news they had received for more than a year.

Shankly officially became manager of Grimsby Town in July 1951. Little known was the fact that they were not the only club in the running. Some months earlier, when he was considering his future at Carlisle in the light of Grimsby's original offer, Shankly had applied to Liverpool for the vacant manager's job. To his surprise he had even been invited for an interview and had been seriously considered for the post. Lack of management experience was his only drawback – otherwise the course of soccer history might well have been accelerated by eight years.

Of course, behind the scenes there was Bill's family, now with another daughter, Jeanette. Whatever move he made, Shankly felt that he was doing it as much for Nessie, Barbara and Jeanette as for himself.

"He was a good father, hopeless at helping in the home – but the girls thought the world of him. He was not very good with things like washing machines, but he was first class with the cooker. It wasn't that he could cook, but if his team lost he used to take it out on the cooker by giving it a thorough clean. That's why I used to quite like it when they lost now and then," smiled Nessie.

The prospect of moving to Grimsby was not a fun idea to Nessie Shankly. Living just a stone's throw from Brunton Park in Carlisle, meant that she was not too far from her family in Scotland and there were frequent visits to and fro – which compensated a little for the amount of time she sacrificed her husband to football. But Grimsby was almost a southern club in Mrs Shankly's eyes and she braced herself for life in North Lincolnshire.

Grimsby Town was a different proposition for Bill Shankly. Once again he had joined a club which had potential but lacked the financial clout to make it a big outfit. The club had history – that was beyond doubt. Only three seasons earlier Grimsby had been in the First Division among the game's elite. In the 1930s the Mariners had twice reached the FA Cup semi-finals. But there was a serious danger that the club would always be among the also-rans – the nearly-men, whose supporters lived in a fantasy world of rosy optimism.

Add to that the fact that Shankly had taken over a side that had just been relegated to the Third Division North – a division that they had last seen in 1926 – and it was clear that the new boss would have to call on all the past experience that he had thus far gained... and then some!

On the Fish Docks

THE Shankly Revolution Road Show rolled into Blundell Park with a mission rather different from the Brunton Park campaign. Grimsby had been a somebody in the First Division and had more of a latent would-be-giant about it than the innocent never-been-there attitude of Carlisle.

Having just been relegated to the Third Division North, there was a mood of depression in the Grimsby camp. Shankly had his work cut out – the players and staff were fed-up, the board was divided between cynicism and nostalgia for past glories and the supporters had a dose of all three commodities – in short the place was psychologically in a shambles.

But the sheer energy of Bill Shankly soon skittled the cynics. He breezed into Blundell Park like a breath of fresh air, armed to the teeth with the guile that had already stood the test of Carlisle. Within a week he had won over the depressed and silenced the club's critics. He busied himself with talking to the local press and whipping up enthusiasm. To get as many locals as possible involved, he invited local amateurs to contact him for a trial. He also spent hours talking to local football organisations, making sure that he was preaching the Grimsby gospel every inch of the way. The team woke up!

The *Grimsby Evening Telegraph* was thrilled to find someone in their midst who would, and could, give an interview at a moment's notice. He used the media to his own full advantage, and well before the the season started the supporters were captivated by this unusual Scotsman who had practically convinced them that their team could walk on water.

One change, however, immediately upset one member of staff. The chief groundsman was upset because Shankly insisted that all training took place on the pitch. The directors also became upset when Shankly barred them from the dressing-rooms immediately before a game – and told them so in no uncertain terms.

But for everyone who got annoyed, albeit temporarily, there were many more who were delighted by this new broom that was sweeping all the cobwebs from the corners,and dust from beneath the mats of Blundell Park. The existing players were fired up by Shankly's work in which he revelled as trainer as well as manager. He loved to play and would give practical demonstrations on how he wanted his players to perform.

Four new faces were brought in – Jimmy Hernon from Bolton, Walker Galbraith from New Brighton, Bill Brown from Queen of the South and Alec McCue, his former player from Carlisle. It is a tribute to Shankly's player assessment that he signed Jimmy Hernon, who was an outstanding player when he joined Grimsby shortly before his 26th birthday. Many wondered how Shankly had managed to sign a player who was, in truth, more worthy of a place in Manchester or London. The truth was that Shankly had done his homework. He knew that Hernon was suffering from TB and that, just like Billy Hogan at Carlisle, there was a question mark hanging over his future fitness. Shankly was also aware, however, that Hernon would feel a whole lot better if he lived near the seaside and – since Grimsby's ground is actually in the seaside resort of Cleethorpes – Shankly had just the bait to capture him. Ironically Hernon has outlived Shankly.

The new 1951-52 season began, and the full force of Shankly's pre-match routine was soon felt by his players. He would coax them, encourage them, stir their self-pride and convince them of their invincibility. Then he would leave them to think about it

– returning a few minutes later to excitedly tell them about the poor condition of the opposition.

"So-and-so is limping – he won't last the game... They look scared stiff lads!... Their goalkeeper's got his hand well-bandaged under his glove... One of their reporters has just told me that they've been dreading playing us all week..." The Shankly directory of ways of rubbishing the opposition was inexhaustible of course. Many a Grimsby player said later that they all felt six inches taller by the time that they went out on to the pitch.

The fans were not left out either. Once again Shankly picked up a microphone before the game to tell the supporters of his choice of team. It misfired at Grimsby though! The good folk of North Lincolnshire were rather less tuned in to Shankly's broad accent than those in the border lands of Carlisle. It wasn't that they didn't appreciate his talking to them – it was simply that they couldn't understand him. The practice was ditched!

The start of the new season was littered with disasters. The first game was at Chesterfield and it was an immediate defeat for Grimsby. The second game was at home to Lincoln. The game ended with only nine Grimsby players on the pitch. Goalkeeper Stan Hayhurst broke a finger and Alec McCue broke his leg. To add insult to the injuries, county rivals Lincoln won the match.

Assistant manager George Tweedy was brought out of retirement as first-team goalkeeper and made 32 appearances at the age of 39 to give his playing career an unexpected final lap. After such a devastatingly bad start, things could only improve and Shankly steered his men on to greater achievements. As the season unfolded, Grimsby gradually took on the look of serious promotion challengers. Attendances soared and suddenly it was as if the clock had been turned back in Grimsby – the good times were rolling again, courtesy of Bill Shankly.

The grins turned to a grimace at the end of the season though as Grimsby finished second in the table behind Lincoln City. They had won 29 of their 46 League matches and lost just nine. It was an excellent achievement for his first season in charge and had certainly restored faith in Grimsby's future. Unfortunately, having finished three points behind Lincoln, they failed to gain

promotion as only one club from each section of the Third
Division was elevated to the Second Division.

Lincoln proved to be something of a bogey side that season as
they also denied Grimsby a place in the third round of the FA
Cup, beating them 3-1 in round two, the Mariners having beaten
Darlington 4-0 in the first round.

The following season confidence was high at Blundell Park.
Apart from a £6,000 signing for Fred Smith from Manchester
City, Shankly kept his squad together. Smith, incidentally, is
still remembered by long-term Mariner fans for once scoring four
goals in seven minutes in a 7-0 hammering of Hartlepool.

Grimsby began the 1952-53 season with a flourish. They were
undefeated in their first nine games. The tenth was against Carlisle. True to the way these things always seem to go, Shankly's
current side lost its proud record against his former club. However the Grimsby promotion bid continued and all seemed to be
going well until a collapse around Easter time. From then
Grimsby could not put a foot right and ended the season in sixth
place – seven points behind champions Oldham. The FA Cup run
did get as far as round three, but Bury proved to be too strong to
the tune of 3-1.

At the end of the season Shankly realised that his squad had
done their best but it just wasn't enough. It was time for
investment, time for the board to dip into their pockets and put
their money where their apparent ambitions were.

It came as a bit of a shock to Bill when the Grimsby board
shuffled its feet and changed the subject when money came into
the conversation. It was probably at that end of season debate
that he realised that he had gone as far as he was likely to go
with the club. It saddened him because he liked the place and he
liked the people. He wanted to restore to them the major club of
the past, but it was now becoming obvious that he would have
to work more than a miracle if he was going to achieve that.

This feeling of depression soon gave way to irritation. Grimsby
was one of the best supported clubs in the lower divisions –
rarely experiencing attendances of less than 15,000, and sometimes as much as 20,000 plus – especially since Shankly had

been in charge and raised the spirits of the club and its pilgrims. He felt let down by the board and his annoyance was felt at home where wife Nessie was missing that easy access to her Scottish roots. In the past they had been able to help each other's varying moods with words of encouragement – but now, they were both at a low ebb together. There was no problem between them – there hardly ever was – but they were both casting their eyes in the direction of a move.

The Coronation of 1953 came and went and Shankly tried to lift his own spirits for the start of the 1953-54 season. It was hard work. Come the big kick-off and Grimsby lost five of their opening eight games – gaining seven points from a possible 16. Then came some light at the end of Shankly's personal dark tunnel – he was approached about taking over as manager at Workington. That might not sound the most exciting prospect in soccer – but it meant a fresh challenge with another club that was struggling at the foot of the Third Division North. It also meant a return to the North-West, not a great distance from Ayrshire and the Scottish haven of both his and Nessie's families.

He met the directors of Workington in mid-December and said he would give a decision immediately after Christmas. He and Nessie discussed the possibilities over and over until finally the die was cast. As a good Scot he allowed New Year's Day to pass but then, the very next day, he told the Grimsby directors that he was leaving. Much was said to change his mind, but it was too little and it was too late. Once Shankly had decided on something he could not be altered from his course.

On 6 January 1954, Bill Shankly moved into his new office at Borough Park, Workington. He was only the second manager in their Football League history. Mind you, they had only been in the Football League since the 1951-52 season. Their record was frightening. They had finished bottom of the Third Division North in their first season, second from bottom in their second and, only a few weeks before the board approached Shankly, they had suffered their record League defeat, hammered 0-8 by Wrexham.

Well, if Grimsby the fish town was the frying pan, then Workington soon proved to be the fire. Shankly was already aware that the ground was a little Jurassic – but he had not realised that it was still lit by gaslight. Neither did he realise that there was a ground-share arrangement with the Workington Rugby League side – which meant that the pitch was almost always like a ploughed field. As a player, Shankly was renowned for his precision passes along the ground. He liked his teams to play the same way. At Workington that was rendered impossible. The groundsman, Billy Watson, who was also general maintenance man, did his best to provide Shankly with a decent surface, but he was fighting a losing battle.

However, the two were united in adversity and became good companions, often to be seen huddled around Billy's boiler with massive mugs of tea, talking football for hours on end. If Grimsby had been a culture shock, Workington proved to be something closer to a cardiac arrest. As manager, Shankly had countless tasks to perform which had very little to do with improving playing results – even to the point of making up the players' wages – Workington never having considered that this was a job for the administration department in the shape of the club secretary.

No electricity, facilities that resembled an ageing cow-shed, a pitch that seemed to demonstrate agriculture more than it did soccer culture, a job that included all manner of strange diversions – and no car! That was the world of the Workington manager – and yet Shankly was not as disgruntled as might have been supposed.

"Deep down I enjoyed it," he once said. "It was an experience, the like of which, few people would ever come across. When I sat in the luxury surroundings of Liverpool years later, it made me appreciate them all the more when I thought back to places like Workington. Even while I was at Workington I had a kind of a thrill from being in such conditions – a bit like being in the trenches. I thought, 'if you can survive this and come out of it with honour – you won't have done too badly.' It was a tremendous challenge."

Shankly turned on the inspiration tap and things began to happen at the club. At first it was results on the pitch. His very first game in charge was a 2-2 home draw with Carlisle – yes, his old club and almost local rivals. The Workington fans were delighted, it was a good result for them. In the following matches, the side took 11 points from a possible 18 – great success, compared with the 12 from 42 that they had captured before Shankly became the boss.

From a dangerous re-election place at the bottom of the table, Workington clambered to twentieth out of 24 clubs – their best-ever finish since joining the League. Attendances were on the incline and a new mood of optimism was coursing through Workington's veins. One of Shankly's favourite moments was an unexpected 2-1 victory over Grimsby – unexpected, that is, as far as people outside Workington were concerned.

Having tasted, what was to them, success – Workington's directors were 'over the moon'. They gave the go-ahead for changes in the squad and Shankly took them at their word, releasing six players and putting eight more on the transfer list. By the beginning of the next season, six new players were brought in – Ernie Whittle had joined during the latter part of the previous season and there were summer signings in the form of Stewart McCallum, Ken Rose, Wilf Billington, Des Jones and Jimmy Fleming.

It had been a busy summer. At home Shankly had been turning-to with hammer and nails, paint and wallpaper in order to make their new house as comfortable as possible for his family. In the street he had become something of a local overnight celebrity, constantly being stopped by well-wishers and inundated with invitations ranging from judging local talent and beauty contests to giving talks for the local WI.

Perhaps the best news was from the Workington board, who agreed on few matters, but finally did decide that it was time to separate from the Rugby League club. At last there was the chance to improve the playing surface and the possibility of improved football.

The 1954-55 campaign got off to a slow start. There were some fine victories but some hiccups too – although it must be said that the team's performance was improving all the time. Steadily, Workington found themselves higher in the table than they had ever previously experienced.

It was around this time that one of the most chronicled incidents in Shankly's early management career took place. For those who haven't heard it, Workington were on a train to London for a second round FA Cup game with Leyton Orient. By sheer coincidence, on the same train was the legendary Hungarian team, also travelling to London, after beating Scotland 4-2 at Hampden with another of their majestic performances that had made them such a part of football folklore.

Once Shankly heard that the Hungarians were on board the train he took his players to meet them, and spent the rest of the journey with Ferenc Puskas and Co as if they were all one squad. Shankly later swore that Workington's 1-0 win at Leyton Orient had been helped by his team rubbing shoulders with these Hungarian greats.

The sequel to the story is that a postcard arrived addressed to Bill at Workington several days later congratulating him and the team on their victory at Leyton Orient. It had been sent by the Hungarian Football Association. It's an old story, but for the purposes of the Shankly Legacy it goes to show the quick-thinking opportunism of a man who knew the workings of a player's mind better than any other manager before or probably since. Shankly laid down the path with incidents like this. Many others have followed as we shall investigate later on in this tribute book.

As 1954 drew to a close, there was talk in the air at Workington that had never been dared to mention before... promotion! Shankly had moulded a side that were serious contenders and, even more than that, he was creating a strong future for the club by attracting teenagers to form up-and-coming reserve and youth squads that were designed, not only to maintain a steady flow of talent that would continue the trend already achieved, but could also save the cash-strapped club a comparative fortune in transfer fees in the future.

Workington did not win promotion – but they did finish in eighth place – in itself almost worthy of an open-top bus ride around the town. The mood was good in the town and Shankly was happy enough with everything that had been achieved so far. His three-year plan was on schedule.

But then there was that board of directors. Shankly hated attending board meetings at the best of times. He was never a directors' man. He did not fit easily into the stiff collar and tie brigade. Before he joined Workington it was the board who had picked the team each week. Shankly had diplomatically put an end to that practice but he still had to regularly sit in on board meetings, which he found both infuriating and hilarious at one and the same time. He likened the board members to both stage comedians and Chicago gangsters – depending on his disposition at the time.

Just when Shankly felt that he needed some further investment to improve Workington's finishing position, he was reminded that the club was still being run on a shoe-string and that, far from there being any more money available, players would have to consider a proposed pay-cut in order for Workington to remain in existence.

The new 1955-56 season began in earnest. The players and the supporters were itching to continue where they had left off just a few months earlier. Within a matter of weeks Workington were in the top four of the division and looked like a side seriously challenging for the championship. All who saw them were convinced that they had a very good chance of success. Attendances were good but still the board were fretting over finances and agreed to raise extra cash by charging more at the turnstiles.

The prospect of the supporters being asked to hand over more of their hard-to-come-by cash sat no better with Shankly than the previous idea of cutting the players' salaries. He was powerless to stop the board taking such drastic measures but he was not at all happy about it. Once again he was finding himself in the situation in which he had halted the decline of a club, increased their income at the turnstiles, and now needed a little more cash to put the icing on the cake with promotion. Once again he was faced with a board of directors who did not share his enthusiasm for 'speculate to accumulate'. Once again he was becoming frustrated.

The most amazing situation then arose as Shankly made a playing come-back. He was never out of kit and boots during training – but a phone call from Huddersfield manager, Andy Beattie, gave him the chance to perform before thousands once again. It was not for a competitive game of course. Andy Beattie, a pal from his Preston playing days, wanted Bill to turn out in a testimonial match under floodlights on 14 November 1955.

The problem was not in persuading Bill to play – it was in containing his excitement. The day arrived – a Monday – and, after putting his Workington players through their paces, Shankly went to a League meeting at Manchester and then on to Huddersfield for the match, which was both entertaining and successful.

Beattie and Shankly locked heads after the match and chatted about their experiences and their lots in life. It was then that Andy Beattie dropped the bombshell that was to open a major new chapter in the Shankly story and set off a chain reaction that still has its ripples in today's soccer.

"Bill, I don't know if this is of any interest to you – especially since you are now used to being the boss at these clubs – but I need an assistant here at Huddersfield. I need someone to bring on the young players as you've been doing at these other places and as you started to do at Preston. So how about joining a First Division club Bill?... What do you say?"

The Final Stepping Stone

SHANKLY was not expecting such a suggestion from Andy Beattie. The trip to Huddersfield had merely been a night out – a chance for him to pull on his boots again for a match in public. Although it had been a testimonial – a 'friendly' – Shankly showed that he had lost none of his competitiveness. To him, the words 'friendly' and 'match' could never be room-mates. His after-match chat with Beattie was nothing more than a finishing-off to a great day, which is why Beattie's question came as such a bolt from the blue and white.

Bill Shankly did not take long to deliberate. His situation at Workington had been troubling him for some time. It wasn't the club, or even the job – in his way he was quite enjoying himself. It was the lack of potential! He had found it very difficult to get players from outside the immediate Workington area and he knew that there was not going to be enough talent from such a small area to seriously develop. The financial state of the club meant that as soon as players showed promise there would be a demand to sell them on. In fact the entire outlook at Workington was obviously one of very limited horizons.

It was that lack of future thinking and progress that troubled Bill Shankly more than anything else. He liked the club – it had that old-fashioned appeal that he found both irritating and yet still refreshing. Also, of course, he didn't want to earn a reputation as the manager who never saw a job through.

All this flashed through his shrewd, Scottish mind and within seconds he was able to give a reply to Andy Beattie, telling him that he would indeed be interested in joining Huddersfield. Within just a few days Huddersfield had confirmed the job for him and he had stated his case to the disappointed but understanding Workington board. There were handshakes all round and Bill Shankly was off to West Yorkshire to start work with former giants Huddersfield Town.

In the 1920s, Huddersfield won the League championship three times in succession and were among the leading clubs throughout that decade. Those were the days of Herbert Chapman, the hugely-successful innovator, who went from Huddersfield to Arsenal and continued his times of triumph. Anyone following Chapman had a hard act to follow. Cecil Potter, Jack Chaplin, Clem Stephenson, David Steele and George Stephenson had all tried with varying degrees of success.

Andy Beattie had taken the hot-seat in April 1952 and it had proved to be more difficult than he had previously imagined. By the end of the 1951-52 season the club had been relegated to Division Two. The following season Huddersfield had finished second and were promoted back to the First Division. Things looked as if they were getting better again but it was still a struggle and by the time Beattie approached Shankly he had already attempted to resign. He was finally talked out of it by the directors, who suggested that he might get more involved with the be-suited side of management – and a little less with the track-suit side.

When the Shanklys arrived in Huddersfield at the end of November 1955, they were warmly welcomed by both the press and the supporters. Bill had been specifically engaged to look after the reserves – and that is exactly what he did. Andy Beattie realised that he had made a big mistake. He recalled to mind the times that they had been team-mates at Preston, remembering Shankly's dogged determination to stick to his job. They had often exchanged heated words in those days – something that Beattie had long ago forgotten.

Almost from the first day at Huddersfield that same uneasy relationship continued, and it was not unusual for raised voices to be heard coming from the direction of the manager's office.

Shankly stuck to his guns and his job, bringing along young players through the reserves. He would have nothing to do with the first team. Perhaps it was that sort of determination and single-mindedness that rubbed off on at least two of the Huddersfield reserves – reserves who would later become house-hold names... Denis Law and Ray Wilson.

The first team struggled, while the reserves went from strength to strength and were unbeaten for months. The rivalry between the two men grew even deeper as Shankly's wicked sense of humour got the better of him. If Beattie dropped a player, Shankly would tell him that he had been promoted.

"You've got to be playing well to get into my side son," was the sort of comment that Shankly would bestow on a demoted player – getting under Beattie's skin at the same time.

Shankly was on good terms with Matt Busby at Manchester United and admired Busby's style. He would often refer to United's young players in glowing terms – something that was extremely rare for Shankly to do. He studied Busby's methods and was not too proud to admit, later, that he had adopted some of them for his own successful sides.

Shankly's passion for the game overtook everyone once again. He was the complete opposite to Andy Beattie. The manager was 'Mr Beattie' to everyone, Shankly was simply 'Bill', the bloke who would stop for a game of football – even with the kids in the street. Shankly loved playing in training games, whether they were five-a-side or whatever – and he always organised it so that he was in the best team. It wasn't just that he loved football – it was also that he loathed defeat.

Shankly even used to play with a group of fathers and sons from the houses where he and Nessie lived. Almost every Sunday afternoon he would take a ball and go round the houses to see who would come out to play. If he could have survived without sleep, Shankly would surely have spent every night kicking a ball around a street-lamp.

Relegation to Division Two at the end of the 1955-56 season put even more pressure on Andy Beattie. The board continued to back him, at least in public, but Huddersfield's Caesar was struggling to retain his laurels, while Bill 'Mark Anthony' Shankly was leading the reserve legions to conquest after conquest. Everyone was thinking the same thing – but nobody was actually saying anything.

As the 1956-57 season got under way, Huddersfield's situation worsened and Beattie's personal gloom finally got the better of him. He had already bought a small business for his retirement and, after a 4-1 home defeat by Sheffield United, Beattie once again tendered his resignation. This time he was determined not to be talked out of it. To his credit he recommended that Bill Shankly was the man to replace him. Although the two men had had their moments, they still had a mutual respect for each other and an understanding that they were basically different. After Huddersfield their friendship continued much as it had before.

Shankly was contacted that same evening while he and Nessie were out with friends. He accepted the job immediately and the next day spoke to the local press.

"I will work hard for the club but I won't make any predictions. I expect to get a hundred per cent effort from the players. I gave that when I was playing and that is all I ask of them – a hundred per cent effort. I want them all to fight for Huddersfield Town."

The effect was immediate. The atmosphere at the club changed. Shankly's style of management was very different from that of Beattie. He was always available and approachable. The players, the press and the supporters all found that Shankly's door was ever-open to those whose interest was football.

Shankly's first League game in charge was against Yorkshire rivals Barnsley. It was an away match and was a dream start – Huddersfield came away with a 5-0 win. The players responded to their new boss and demonstrated their willingness to perform. Regrettably, the new-found energy did not last long. They did, indeed, give of their best – but it was not enough and the season ran out of steam with Huddersfield finishing in 12th place.

The crowds filtered back though – especially for the FA Cup run, which saw Huddersfield getting as far as the fifth round before losing 1-2 to Burnley, at that time one of the Football League's major clubs. Some 164,000 fans had witnessed the Cup battles and had been really encouraged by the spirit that they had seen.

Some of the players were getting a little long in the laces and Shankly knew that changes were inevitable. As the older heads departed, the likes of Denis Law, Kevin McHale and Ray Wilson were given greater responsibilities despite their tender years. Shankly was following that faith in youth that had been the hallmark of his friend Matt Busby. The maxim was that if you were good enough – then you were old enough.

The 1957-58 season was little better. There were good days and bad days – and at least one day of absolute disbelief when Huddersfield lost 6-7 at Charlton, after leading 5-1. To make matters worse, Charlton had been reduced to ten men early in the game. Shankly blew his top, but not until the team coach stopped halfway home. It had taken him that long to get over the shock.

Another shock that season was the Munich Air Disaster, in which so many Manchester United players and officials died – including Tom Curry who had been one of Shankly's trainers at Carlisle. Curry had become one of the chief right-hand men to Busby at Old Trafford and Shankly had nothing but admiration for what he and Busby had achieved. Shankly took the news of the plane crash very badly. It might come as a bit of a culture shock to Liverpool fans to discover that their hero was, in fact, something of a Manchester United fan. It was their set-up that earned his admiration, however, and of course Matt Busby himself – whom Bill Shankly once described as a 'truly wonderful man'.

The 1958-59 season was a slow starter, to put it politely. Huddersfield suffered a number of early defeats and all Shankly's work seemed to be going nowhere. There was one very welcome oasis in this desert of results, when Huddersfield – down to ten men – gave Liverpool a 5-0 hammering, a match which Shankly often chuckled about, even years later, when he was the boss at Anfield.

Unfortunately the season ended with Huddersfield in mid-table once again. The FA Cup produced a good third-round result against West Ham. Having been held 1-1 at home, Huddersfield travelled down to Upton Park and stormed all over the Hammers – beating them 5-1. A 0-1 result at home to Luton saw the club's exit from the competition in the next round.

On paper Huddersfield had scarcely improved in the Shankly regime – but in fact, Bill had put together a very promising outfit. It seems a mystery why they were not more successful more quickly. Their style of play had developed into a much more entertaining strategy and the supporters were enjoying what they were seeing.

Behind the scenes Shankly was learning all the time. He still saw himself as a player-coach who was not actually playing. He did his utmost to avoid the paperwork and kept as busy as he possibly could with the players. He endeared himself to all the players because he was one of them. It is a rare person who can be 'one of the boys' and still remain the boss – but that was something that Shankly mastered well. He always kept a close eye on the interests of his players and dealt with them in the same way as he himself would want to be dealt with. In response, the players were always prepared to do their best for him.

Shankly was still learning the art of management – as he readily admitted.

"I learned from my playing days and I also learned something almost every day of my management and coaching career. Sometimes it was using things that you had learned earlier – but you learned even more by putting them into practice in different situations."

The Shankly wordology was already almost legendary. The

time to worry was when he stopped talking! He mostly talked about football of course, reliving past experiences, past matches, anecdotes – giving advice from his own adventures. But Shankly could also suddenly start talking about television programmes or his beloved gangster or western films.

Most of all, he liked to laugh. He was a great leg-puller and joker. He had been the same as a player and had developed it into an art form. His pre-match team talks were quite unique, as much about rubbishing the opposition as giving out orders and tactics to his own men. Those sort of pep talks had worked equally well at Carlisle, Grimsby and Workington and now Shankly was using them to great effect, yet again, at Huddersfield. Team spirit was high – even though the club's League position was a little lower than everyone would have liked.

There are some amazing stories from those Huddersfield days as have been recorded elsewhere. But in his quest for a striker, Shankly came close to signing a 'young man' who was exciting everyone at Middlesbrough. Huddersfield could not fund the deal, otherwise Shankly could well have captured no less a person than Brian Clough. Another name that Shankly considered was Ian St John, but once again Huddersfield were unable to stump up the cash. The same thing happened when he asked about Ron Yeats.

Huddersfield had been spending what extra cash became available on long overdue ground improvements. They had still not installed floodlighting at this stage, and as far as the board were concerned the first priority was to avoid getting into debt – and the second priority was the ground. Team improvement was relegated to a lagging third.

The club directors pointed out that it was the home-grown young talent that was the club's future – either by becoming long-term first-team players or by being sold on to give Huddersfield a more flexible bank balance.

Shankly was frustrated. He did understand the dilemma – but he was also aware that no club would ever climb to the heights of the game without investment in the purchasing of new players who had already proved themselves elsewhere.

Still, Huddersfield progressed. The 1959-60 season saw them get off to their best start for years. They were among the division leaders and the club was beginning to think that perhaps, after all, this was going to be their year. The inevitable happened however. A couple of injuries left the side unbalanced and the results began to go wrong again. Shankly was desperate to add depth to his first-team squad, but there was still no money forthcoming from the board. He began to consider his position.

One of Shankly's problems was that he and his family were genuinely happy at Huddersfield. They liked the place and had made many friends. That in itself was worth a lot to Bill who had seen Nessie so very unhappy in the days at Grimsby. He did not know what to do for the best. As it happened the matter was taken right out of his hands.

Much happens after football matches, and it was after Huddersfield had lost 0-1 at home to Cardiff, on 17 October 1959, that one of the most momentous events in the history of modern football took place. Two men approached Bill Shankly and bluntly asked him; "How would you like to become manager of the best club in the country?"

It was typical of Shankly that the question did not phase him.

"Why, is Matt Busby packing it in?" he joked.

The two men shared in the joke and then introduced themselves as Tom Williams, chairman of Liverpool, and Harry Latham, a member of the board. They explained that their then manager, Phil Taylor, had a health problem and was therefore having to retire. They wanted a quick replacement, and they felt that Bill Shankly was the man for the job.

Shankly could have reminded them that he had previously applied for the job back in 1951, and that they had, then, not believed that he was up to it. However these were different directors – and Shankly was not the man to bear a grudge. He said that he would give the matter some thought and then get back to them.

Bill could hardly wait to get back home and tell Nessie. To put it politely, she was less than delighted and a few harsh words were exchanged – but Shankly knew what he wanted, and his wife was well aware that soon she would be packing again. During the next couple of weeks negotiations continued. Phil Taylor resigned on 14 November 1959 and the press got wind of Shankly's impending move to Anfield. At that stage Bill had told no one except his family and it was a little ironic that on 28 November, Huddersfield were at home to Liverpool. The Yorkshire side won 1-0 and the papers speculated. For several days nothing more happened and then, on 1 December 1959 at a board meeting, Shankly formally resigned. The board were angry but kept their cool and forced a month's notice out of him. However, with the following week proving that the working relationship had completely broken down, it was obviously pointless for him to stay.

Bill Shankly was sad to leave Huddersfield – very sad! The town was sad to lose him too. Years later when Huddersfield moved into their current 'superstadium', various items from the Leeds Road ground were auctioned off. One fan paid several hundred pounds for an old loo seat – simply because it was the one that Bill Shankly had used.

In December 1959, Shankly left Yorkshire for a new throne and a new kingdom. He was on his way to become the King of the Kop.

The Great Adventure

FOR most of us, the career that Bill Shankly had enjoyed up to 1959 would have been enough to set us up in anecdotes for the rest of our lives. He had played at the highest level in club football, been capped by his country, and gone on to coach and manage four different football teams. It was in 1959, however, that Bill Shankly's greatest adventure was about to unfold.

Shankly had long been an admirer of Liverpool. They were one of the biggest clubs in Britain, but he was under no illusion as to its position, the club was in very poor shape. This giant among soccer clubs, for all its size and support, was an ailing giant. The ground was in a state of neglect and the team were going through a bad spell. Support, although large, was more motivated by tradition than anything that smacked of excitement at that time.

Shankly immediately began to woo the press – giving the locals the things that they wanted to hear.

"I am very pleased and very proud to have been chosen as manager of Liverpool Football Club – a club with so much great potential. It is my opinion that Liverpool have a crowd of followers which ranks among the greatest in the game. They deserve success – and I hope to be able to do something toward helping them to achieve it. I make no promises except that I shall put everything I have into the job I have so willingly undertaken."

That was Shankly's official statement. The press loved it, the Anfield faithful loved it – and Shankly meant every word of it. He also knew that there was quite a task ahead of him – as he revealed later. In the years leading up to his appointment Liverpool had hit a serious decline. Since joining the Football League in 1893, the club had had a proud record. Yes of course, they knew the meaning of defeat just as they knew the meaning of relegation – but they had also won the championship five times and, since 1905, they had remained a strong First Division side. The very suggestion that Liverpool might crumble was close to blasphemy – yet crumble they did, and the 1953-54 season became a total disaster with no less than 23 defeats and only nine victories out of their 42 League matches. They were relegated.

From 1954 until the arrival of Bill Shankly, Liverpool had been marking time in the Second Division. In 1955 they finished in 11th place, the following season they improved to third – and in 1957 finished in exactly the same spot. The next two seasons saw them at fourth and it was becoming obvious that the club was going nowhere. To make matters even worse, Everton had remained in the First Division and Manchester United had twice won the League championship in those same few seasons.

It was no wonder that Shankly looked upon the club as such a sleeping giant.

"Candidly, the place was a shambles when I came. I knew that Liverpool had the best supporters in the world. I knew that their potential was tremendous – those are the only reasons that I came. The people reminded me of the Glasgow people, the Scottish people, and I had seen them in action.

"When I was with Huddersfield, in one game we beat them 5-0 and we only had ten men. It kind of saddened me to see such a great club in such trouble. When I joined Liverpool I had battles – not just battles on the field, but political battles, battles in the boardroom. I had to get them to see things the same way as me.

"The team was run-down, the ground was run-down – mind you the war had a lot to do with that. It was just not good enough for a club like Liverpool – and I had to convince the directors that I knew what was best for the club.

"I had been to Anfield many times as a player, and I knew that the supporters were just fantastic. I was only interested in the good of the club and to bring success to those loyal fans. I was only in the game for the love of football – and I wanted to bring back happiness for the people of Liverpool."

Shankly had already experienced the hardships of being in charge at clubs without money – clubs which, when the niceties of initial lip-service were over, appeared to have no ambition to move forward. He was no fool. He had learned to read directors and he could always read situations. Even though his own enthusiasm for Liverpool was bubbling over, he was fully aware that his own personal excitement alone would not be enough to bring the success that was needed.

After he had been at Liverpool for a while he even took Nessie for a walk around the training ground and asked her if she still felt that he was right for having taken the job. Nessie just smiled and said that if his ambition was to be manager of a First Division football club, then this was the best chance yet for him to realise it. Her comment was enough to heap extra coal on his fire and from then his enthusiasm and determination burned ever brighter.

He continued with his battles and there was a little improvement during that season, followed by even more during the next. However, Shankly knew that there was a need to invest and, fortunately, just around the corner was the man who would come to his rescue. The man who would help him to make Liverpool one of the greatest teams 'the world has ever seen' – Eric Sawyer!

"They had no money to start with. After about 18 months of being there, a man came on to the board called Mr Sawyer. He was on the accountancy side at Littlewoods Mail Order. He was a bit sick too at seeing Liverpool not making any progress.

"Well, I read in the *Sunday Post* that Ian St John was up for sale, and I knew that if we were going to get anywhere then he was the sort of player we needed. So I went to a board meeting and told them. Someone said, 'We can't afford to sign him' – Mr Sawyer said, 'We can't afford not to sign him!' So we went up to

Motherwell the following week and we saw him play – not that that mattered... we didn't need to see him play. The next day we signed him and brought him to Liverpool.

"Now that man, Mr Sawyer, was the beginning of Liverpool. He was someone who was willing to spend money. He said to me, 'If you can find the players, I'll find the money!'

"St John played in a Liverpool Cup match at Everton and, although they won 4-3, he scored our three goals and set the place on fire. That was in the May, July came and we wanted Yeats – a tower of a man, a fantastic player. We had wanted him for a while. In the end Dundee United finally said we could have him for £30,000. I arranged for us all to meet in Edinburgh the very next day, and we signed him.

"So Mr Sawyer was the man who found the money, and St John and Yeats were the foundation stones, the greatest signings for Liverpool. They were the beginning of the new lease of life for Liverpool Football Club.

"Yeats was tremendous at the back and St John was marvellous up front. He played his own game magnificently but he also brought on Roger Hunt, who proved to be another great player.

"It was important to me that we get things right down the centre. Yeats was in the centre of defence and looked after that department. St John was in the centre of the attack and led the hunt for goals. Everything else was built on these two and that's why I believe that they were the most important signings that Liverpool ever made."

When Shankly joined Liverpool there was, of course, already a recognisable side. He did not make changes purely for the sake of it or to try to assert himself by an outward demonstration of tackling the club's problems. Shankly's motivation came from within. He did not simply put a coat of gloss on rotting wood. Shankly earnestly believed in cutting out all the dead wood, filling the gaps with something better and only then applying the gloss.

That is how he set about his task at Anfield. But he had help that he both liked and respected – Bob Paisley. The two men knew each other well. They had played against each other a number of times and shared very similar views of football and the way it should be played. Their sense of humour was similar too – something that was vital in the day-to-day running of a football club. Both of them loved boxing and both of them loved a good yarn. Paisley became first-team coach with Liverpool just a few months before Bill Shankly was appointed manager. It was a soccer-marriage made for success.

"We hit it off from the moment that he arrived and it was an absolute pleasure to work with him throughout our time together," said Paisley

"He was a team man, totally dedicated to football – and in particular Liverpool Football Club," reflected Shankly. "He had a sharp wit as well. I remember when we were playing Leeds in the 1965 Cup Final at Wembley. Leeds had Albert Johansen in their side. He was a very good black player from South Africa, very good indeed. During the game Peter Thompson took the ball to the corner and was stuck there with Johansen and another Leeds player pinning him into that situation. Someone said: 'He's snookered!' Quick as a flash Bob replies; 'Aye – behind the black.' That was typical of Bob Paisley, very quick, wonderful sense of humour – and he knew the game."

Another member of the coaching squad was Joe Fagan, who had been in charge of the reserves for a year when Shankly arrived. They knew each other too – Shankly had tried to sign Fagan for Grimsby several years earlier. Fagan welcomed Shankly's appointment and Shankly had no qualms about keeping him on as reserves coach – a job that was to grow tremendously in importance during the Shankly regime.

Reuben Bennett had also been at Liverpool for about a year before Shankly arrived. At one time it had been thought that he might have been appointed manager instead of Shankly – but Bennett was more than happy to play lead violin to Shankly's conductor. Bennett was a Scot who demonstrated many of the typical Scottish traits that Shankly himself championed. He loved to tell exaggerated stories, give appalling reasons for every defeat, cheer on Scotland to beat England every year, have a good laugh and generally be a positive influence behind the scenes. Most of all he knew his football.

Albert Shelley was also around. He had officially retired but was totally unable to stay away. He was an odd job man with little or nothing to do with coaching. However he had been at Anfield for so long that he was almost part of the furniture. He was unpaid at Anfield but busied himself doing odd jobs – repairing, painting, sweeping, whatever seemed to be needed at the time. He was not a coach but he contributed greatly to Anfield's feel-good factor and he was considered by Shankly and his men to be a part of the team.

"We used to have a little room by the manager's office," Shankly explained. "It was only small, but we had a table-top football pitch permanently set up to help with our discussions. Everyone tried to pile in there to discuss the game that was coming up, or else look back on the previous one. Everyone had the chance to speak their piece and we had some really useful meetings in that little room." That little room became famous as 'The Boot Room' – often said to be the nerve centre of Liverpool – the place where matches were often won or lost.

Shankly called them all together at the start of his new job and explained that they were all going to keep their responsibilities, and that there would be changes made which, he felt, would benefit both the club and them as individuals. Above all he sought mutual co-operation – a striving for the common good of Liverpool Football Club – and, most importantly, he sought their loyalty as he pledged his own to them.

He gave the same message to the club captain – Ronnie Moran – who openly admitted that he felt that his education started with Shankly's first day in office.

There was so much to put right at Anfield that a lesser mortal than Shankly might have changed their mind and left. But Bill Shankly was not like that. He ordered a complete overhaul of the club's training ground at Melwood. He instigated a thorough programme of ground and facilities improvement at Anfield – and he stepped up the training schedule to something that he considered as more worthy of professional sportsmen.

"Everything hinges on training and preparation, and I wanted things doing in a certain way, with much more emphasis on having the ball at your feet rather than endless running and exercises," said Shankly. His new approach was welcomed by players and coaches alike.

Success did not come overnight. Indeed, his first two games were bad defeats with not one goal scored and seven conceded. However there was a gradual improvement. A very patient man, Shankly knew that there would be no great success without investment – which is why he was so delighted to find such an ally in Eric Sawyer, and also by the speed at which words changed into action and he was able to capture both Yeats and St John. He felt that Liverpool had turned a corner and, as was so often the case, he was right.

St John and Yeats were not the first signings that Shankly made however, and they certainly were not going to be the last. Prior to their arrival, Sammy Reid had been bought from Motherwell, Kevin Lewis was captured from Sheffield United, and with the purchase of Gordon Milne, for £16,000, from Preston, Shankly had broken his personal Liverpool signing record. Gordon's dad, Jimmy, had been a team-mate of Shankly's at Preston and Bill was hoping that the Milne ability was going to run in the family. As it turned out he was not disappointed.

But it was the signings of Yeats and St John which proved to be the most significant. They were the master strokes that finally brought the painting to life. Roger Hunt was already at the club, a young man finding his feet in the first team. In May 1961 St John was added. In July 1961 Yeats was signed. Now Shankly felt that he had a real chance of winning promotion from the Second Division. He had an impressive squad with goalkeepers Bert Slater and Jim Furnell – an outfield of Alan A'Court, Gerry Byrne, Ian Callaghan, Roger Hunt, Tommy Leishman, Kevin Lewis, Jimmy Melia, Ronnie Moran, Ian St John, Dick White and Ron Yeats.

The fans were delirious as the Liverpool machine thrust into top gear and hit 99 goals in that remarkable season. Roger Hunt broke the club's scoring record tally with a personal best of 41 League goals. Even FA Cup defeat at the hands of Shankly's old club, Preston, did nothing to dampen the ardour as Liverpool raced to 62 points out of a possible 84. The Second Division championship was wrapped up two weeks before the end of the season and even more than that – the club had had a heart transplant. The fans, always noisy, had organised themselves into an all-singing, all-chanting choir – the like of which the world of football had never before experienced. Their songs and their chants had depth and meaning. An incredible new phenomenon in soccer history had been created and the Liverpool team had been increased to more than 50,000.

Shankly continued to make changes – some alternative training here – a new angle of psychology there – and, of course, new players where they were required. The first season back in the First Division was satisfactory with Liverpool finishing in eighth place. The only blot on the Mersey landscape was that rivals Everton finished as champions. A bonus was that Liverpool had travelled as far as the semi-finals in the FA Cup before going down by a single goal to classy Leicester. There were other bonuses too. Young Scots goalkeeper, Tommy Lawrence, had been promoted from the reserves and proved himself to be first choice for the next 400 games.

Shankly knew that he still needed another option for the side. He had just signed Willie Stevenson from Rangers and, just as the 1963-64 season dawned, he took another look at a 21-year-old who was said to be performing wonders at Preston. Peter Thompson was that player – the fee was £35,000 – and Shankly had the final piece to his jigsaw.

The fans were having a party at every game. It wasn't just that Liverpool were winning but that they were playing great football and scoring goals – lots of them. Their FA Cup run ended in the quarter-finals but the League championship was still in their sights – and the possibility of wresting it from the the grip of Everton was just too great an opportunity to let slip through their fingers. A victory over Arsenal secured the title and what a victory it was. Arsenal, who have rarely had a leaky defence, were completely over-run by 11 Liverpool footballers, 50,000 Liverpool fans, and a Liverpool manager who made every single tackle, headed every high ball, took every throw-in and hit every shot. It was no wonder that Liverpool won 5-0!

Shankly and his men deserved their acclaim. Not just the homage that was paid by all those adoring Scousers – but from all over Britain where soccer fans had watched their television screens with awe as Liverpool had marched relentlessly on – storming to that wonderful championship.

As he held the League championship trophy for the first time in his life, Bill Shankly could have been forgiven for borrowing those immortal words: – "I came, I saw, I conquered!"

But the great adventure was not over – in many ways it had only just begun. This championship win was Shankly's first – and it was the first for Liverpool in 17 years. But there were more challenges to face. One trophy that had always eluded the club was the FA Cup, and there was also the prospect of tackling the cream of Europe – a completely new departure for the club and its fans. Yes, the great adventure was still very much alive.

The 1964-65 season saw Liverpool finish seventh in the table. Perhaps it was the European challenge that affected their League campaign. It was still a good League season and many observers felt that, if there had not been the distraction of the European Cup, Liverpool would almost certainly have retained the League championship.

Teenage defender, Tommy Smith, had been drafted into the side after fully serving his apprenticeship. Geoff Strong was signed from Arsenal in November 1964 for £40,000 and, as Merseyside had now become the hottest spot on the world map of pop music, the Kop Choir adopted *You'll Never Walk Alone* as its own personal anthem.

Liverpool's debut in the European Cup was quite decisive. In their opening match they travelled to Iceland and trounced Reykjavik 5-0. Back at Anfield they won the second leg 6-1. They were not destined for European Cup glory that season – but it was certainly the start of something big. Liverpool's first assault in Europe ended in the semi-final, when they were beaten 4-3 on aggregate by Inter-Milan. The games could not have been more dramatic if they had been created by Hollywood film-script writers. Liverpool won the first leg 3-1 with the Anfield Faithful playing their part and putting the fear of Merseyside into the Italians. The return leg was won by Inter, 3-0, and even the most independent of spectators were forced to admit that the refereeing was suspect, to say the least, and possibly rather more sinister than that.

Yet there was something to treasure from that season – a unique moment in soccer history. The moment when a Liverpool captain held aloft the treasured FA Cup for the first time in the club's history. Leeds had been stiff opposition. It was a mighty clash between Shankly's fluid form of football and Revie's robotic spoilers. Don Revie had turned Leeds into a super side – very effective, very successful... but not very pretty. Shankly knew that trying to get something out of Leeds would be like trying to loosen the grip of a corpse.

As we saw earlier, Gerry Byrne broke his collarbone early on in the game, but bravely battled on right to the end. Leeds never knew just how badly he had been injured. Even his team-mates didn't know until the end of the game. Shankly did not want anything to spoil their concentration. Just imagine how Byrne must have felt when he heard that final 90 minute whistle, and realised that his agony was going to be prolonged for another half-hour.

The blank score-sheet did not remain that way for long. Roger Hunt took just three minutes of extra-time to find the net. The Liverpool fans were in the ascendancy for a while, until their celebrations were brought to an abrupt halt when Billy Bremner hit a Leeds equaliser as the first half of extra-time approached its close. The tension mounted at Wembley as the fans of both teams did their noisy best to lift their favourites for the last quarter of an hour. With only five minutes remaining, a piercing cross from Ian Callaghan was met by a headlong dive from Ian St John and there was that glorious 'swish' as the ball hit the back of the net.

Wembley was witness to an amazing feast of festivity as the Liverpool fans savoured that glorious moment when their club broke its 72-year-old 'duck'. The names of all the players resounded around the stadium, but then there was an incredible increase in volume as the chant changed to 'Shank-lee... Shank-lee.'

Shankly raised a Liverpool scarf as his personal tribute to the team on the terraces.

"They were magnificent," said Bill Shankly later. "They played their part in the win. I don't think Wembley had ever seen anything like it before. We had the usual after-match get together, but the next day we went back to Liverpool by train and I don't think anyone was prepared for the reception we were given when we travelled from Lime Street Station to the Town Hall. The city was packed with people – wherever we looked there was just a mass of people, crowds and crowds of them, an absolute sea of red and white. It was one of those sights that you could never forget."

But there was still more to come... much more!

Conquering Europe

FOR a decade or more, Liverpool had lived in the shadow of Everton who had been League champions in 1962-63, and who had retained their First Division status throughout with style – dominating the Mersey soccer scene. Not too far away, Manchester United had recovered from the shock of Munich and the now world-renowned Busby Babes had taken the championship and the FA Cup. Liverpool fans had looked on with their faces pressed up against the window of success for years. Now, at last, they had something to crow about – and Shankly was determined that this would be no fleeting moment. He was building for the future.

"We were still not a rich club and money had to be spent wisely. I wanted to see youngsters brought along better, and I wanted to make sure that we were getting value for money when we bought players. We were not in a position to spend a lot of money on a player and just keep him in the reserves. That's why I was more interested in players from the lower divisions. It was easier to get them to come to a club like Liverpool. First team or reserves, it didn't matter so much to them because they were happy to be a part of one of the biggest clubs in the land. I was looking for bargains and I got them. We got Ray Clemence for just £18,000, Kevin Keegan for £35,000 – now these were bargains – we could afford them. Our scouts were very important to us – a part of the team."

The 1965-66 season dawned with the fresh challenge of the European Cup-winners' Cup. But Shankly also wanted to win the championship again, and the club had another task which was new to them – defending the FA Cup. Shankly was undaunted – he was a winner and he wanted to win everything – over and over again. He gathered his team of winners from the previous season – the likes of Ray Clemence and Kevin Keegan were, as yet, still to come.

The League matches were ticked off one by one. There were more wins than draws – and more draws than defeats. Liverpool had suddenly become the team to beat. Their successes in recent seasons had attracted thousands of new fans, many of whom had never even been near Merseyside. The euphoria of Anfield's faithful supporters was highly contagious. English soccer was on a high and Liverpool soccer was 'over the moon'. Shankly's side was competing with Manchester United for the title of England's greatest soccer attraction. Anfield was packed for every home game and, wherever Liverpool played away, their hosts experienced their best crowds of the season.

By December 1965, Liverpool were at the top of the table having dispatched a number of top clubs with high scoring that came as a result of their efficient, determined approach and their ruthlessly confident style. They were not just winning – to quote Bill Shankly they were, 'playing real football. They were frightening.'

However, Liverpool were not invincible. Shankly's old Preston pal, Tommy Docherty, put one over on them when he took his young Chelsea side to Anfield for the third round of the FA Cup. Chelsea's 2-1 victory in front of the Kop was the shock result of the day.

But if the FA Cup had gone, the European Cup-winners' Cup was still very much alive. Juventus were the first hurdle. By soccer standards they were not so much a 'hurdle' as a 'Beechers Brook'. The first leg was in Turin and the Italians won 1-0.

However the victory was not a comfortable one and although the Juve fans cheered – they were not convinced. They had every reason to be concerned because Liverpool completely controlled the second leg and cantered home to a 2-0 success.

Belgium's Standard Liege met a similar fate in the next round and Honved of Hungary were next in line. Any result over a Hungarian side was good news for English football and when Liverpool dispatched Honved to earn their place in the semi-finals, the whole of the Football League applauded. There was a sharp intake of breath when the semi-final draw was made – Liverpool were to confront Celtic.

There were 70,000 fans crammed into Parkhead and Liverpool were on the rack from the start. Celtic scored, but however hard they tried – and they did – they could not get another. Back at Anfield, on a night of high drama, Liverpool left it late but then, first Tommy Smith and then Geoff Strong, playing through a severe pain barrier, put Liverpool into the Final against Borussia Dortmund on the neutral ground of Scotland's Hampden Park.

The Final was another game of high drama. At the end of a rain-soaked 90 minutes, the score stood at one each. Extra-time was all cut and thrust – but it was the Germans who finally drew blood and were the ultimate winners, 2-1. Yes of course, Liverpool were disappointed – but their European education had certainly been furthered.

There was consolation in that Liverpool had already won the League championship again – another title, another trophy, another party and another crack at Europe. They thought it was all over...

There was still another party to come on Merseyside. For Liverpool fans it was a bit extra special – but even Everton fans were dancing in the street. Anfield hero, 'Sir Roger Hunt', as the Kop had dubbed him, was on the score-sheet as England triumphed in the 1966 World Cup.

It seemed that the city of Liverpool had the Midas touch in the mid-1960s. Everton had won the FA Cup and had also had two players in the all-conquering England World Cup side. Pop music of that era seemed to be the monopoly of Merseyside, and even

Bill Shankly in the colours of Preston North End in 1938, the year he won an FA Cup winners' medal with the Lancashire club.

Left: Shankly in the blazer and tie of Huddersfield Town, the club he managed from 1956 to 1959.

Top: April 1964 and Shankly shares the adulation from Anfield's adoring fans as skipper Ron Yeats lifts the Football League championship trophy after the Reds' 5-0 hammering of Arsenal.

Bottom: The Liverpool team which Shankly selected for the 1965 FA Cup Final. Back row (left to right): Milne, Byrne, Lawrence, Yeats, Lawler, Stevenson. Front row: Callaghan, Hunt, St John, Smith, Thompson. Like his father before him, Gordon Milne missed the chance of a Wembley Final through injury. He was replaced by Strong (not pictured).

Top, left: *The summer of 1966 and Bill Shankly arranges the silverware including the Football League championship trophy, won for the second time in three years, and the FA Charity Shield.*

Top, right: *Shankly raises a glass in celebration after the FA Cup semi-final victory over Everton at Old Trafford in March 1971. The Reds were beaten by double-winners Arsenal in the Final.*

Bottom: *Liverpool in 1968-69. Back row (left to right): Strong, Clemence, Lawrence, Byrne. Middle row: Graham, Hateley, Wall, Ross, Arrowsmith, Thompson. Front row: Callaghan, Hughes, Hunt, Yeats, St John, Smith, Lawler.*

Yet another night of European glory at Anfield. Chris Lawler is foiled by the AEK goalkeeper during the UEFA Cup second-round first-leg game in October 1972. Liverpool went on to win the trophy.

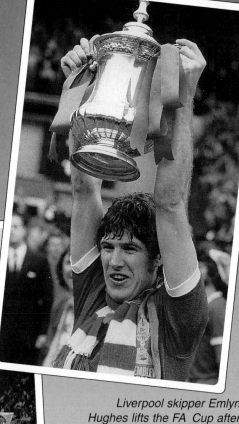

Liverpool skipper Emlyn Hughes lifts the FA Cup after the Reds' crushing victory over Newcastle in the 1974 Final. It was to be Shankly's last trophy for the Reds, for he announced his retirement, to the shock and dismay of the club's supporters.

Manager of the Year, Bill Shankly, with the aid of a young helper, lifts the trophy he won in 1973 after guiding Liverpool to yet another League championship triumph coupled with victory in a European Final.

Brian Clough, then Leeds United manager for a brief but controversial spell, casts an admiring glance at Bill Shankly before the start of the 1974 FA Charity Shield game at Wembley.

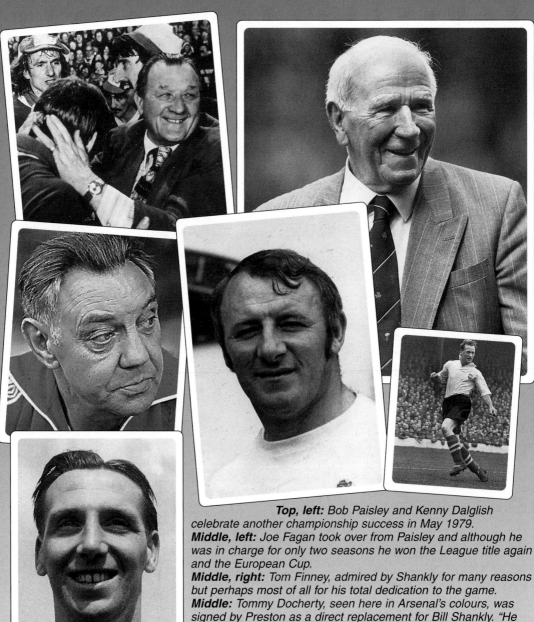

Top, left: Bob Paisley and Kenny Dalglish celebrate another championship success in May 1979.

Middle, left: Joe Fagan took over from Paisley and although he was in charge for only two seasons he won the League title again and the European Cup.

Middle, right: Tom Finney, admired by Shankly for many reasons but perhaps most of all for his total dedication to the game.

Middle: Tommy Docherty, seen here in Arsenal's colours, was signed by Preston as a direct replacement for Bill Shankly. "He was the same sort of player as me," said Shankly. "I would have loved to have had him in my team."

Bottom: Centre-forward Tommy Lawton. "You had to stop the ball getting to him," said Shankly. In 1939, Lawton had scored in a memorable England win at Hampden when Shankly was in the Scotland team.

Top, right: Sir Matt Busby. There was no argument about it as far as Bill Shankly was concerned. "Matt Busby is the greatest manager who ever lived," he once said.

Top, left: Denis Law has no doubt that he owes a great deal to Bill Shankly, who once said of him, "He was very polite and willing, very dedicated and worked hard. That's important."

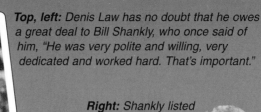

Right: Shankly listed George Best among his all-time favourites with these words: "He was a very special player, a truly great one … Best was a gem."

Middle, left: Ferenc Puskas lines up before Hungary shocked English football at Wembley in 1953. He later signed for Real Madrid, who dominated the early years of the European Cup. "Real has some fantastic players, " said Shankly, "But the pick of them all was Ferenc Puskas."

Bottom, left: "Pelé was marvellous, but Eusebio had the edge for me," said Shankly. "I think he could do all that Pelé could do, but he was just that little bit faster – and that made him the better of the two."

Top, left: Diego Maradona in a pose familiar to English football fans. Shankly's early assessment: "At 19, he has all the natural skills, but he does everything at breakneck speed. He should learn to slow down. If he can learn not to try to do everything, he can be the best in the game."

Top, right: Shankly once wanted to sign Ian St John for Huddersfield, but the directors would not provide the cash. Eventually he took him to Anfield and proclaimed later, "St John was my first great signing for Liverpool."

Bottom, left: "Ron Yeats could have played in the Second Division with no other defenders and won," said Shankly. "Strong as an ox. There were very few in the game in the same class."

Bottom, right: "Larry Lloyd was the ideal replacement for Yeats," said Bill Shankly. "He came into the reserves to learn how we do things. Then, when his time came, he was ready."

the Prime Minister's constituency of Huyton was only a good free-kick away from Goodison or Anfield.

The first-team squad remained much the same for the 1966-67 season, at least for most of it. However the season proved to be not one of the best for Shankly and his men. The League season was creditable but a little disappointing compared with all their recent successes. Liverpool finished fifth in the table, made a fifth-round FA Cup exit at the hands of rivals Everton, and a first-round triumph over Petrohil Ploetsi of Romania seemed hardly worth the trouble when Ajax taught them a lesson or three in the next round.

In his heart of hearts Shankly knew that he was going to have to replace some of the players who had been so loyal to him and given their all in laying the foundation of the great Liverpool revolution. It was not easy for him. Shankly had always firmly believed that loyalty was a two-way affair. But he also knew that, for the good of Liverpool Football Club, there had to be new faces.

"We went down to Watford for the third round of the FA Cup and we came away with a 0-0 draw. They were a Third Division club and, although they played very well, we should have beaten them. We didn't. We gave a bad performance and we had some changes to make.

One of those changes joined the club before the end of the 1966-67 season. He had been playing for Blackpool. Shankly had been urged to go and see him as soon as possible because several other clubs were also interested.

"I went along to see Blackpool and Blackburn. Matt Busby and Jimmy Murphy were there, probably watching the same player. It was a nothing sort of game with little at stake – but the boy I was watching turned it into a Cup-tie. The great Bryan Douglas was playing, but he was completely overshadowed by the Blackpool lad. Some players you think might be a bit risky to buy – but I knew that this boy would definitely not be a risk. I tried to buy him then and there, but they made me wait."

Shankly's patience was rewarded. Not many days passed before 19-year-old Emlyn Hughes became Liverpool's latest signing and was about to prove, once again, that Bill Shankly was one of the shrewdest managers ever to take part in the soccer transfer market.

As Shankly restructured his masterpiece, Gordon Milne and Willie Stevenson moved on. Ray Clemence was signed from Scunthorpe and Shankly gambled a club-record of £96,000 on a centre-forward whose son was later to become even more famous and successful than himself. Tony Hateley was Shankly's new hope. Years later, Mark, the son of that great hope, became one of soccer's top strikers.

The 1967-68 season once again saw Liverpool in pursuit of the major domestic competitions. In Europe also, the club had qualified for what was then known as the Inter-Cities Fairs Cup – a rather over-stated name for what is now simply called the UEFA Cup. The tale resulted in anticlimax, however, as Liverpool bowed out of each competition – albeit with honour. In the League, Liverpool finished third behind champions Manchester City and runners-up Manchester United. The tremendous haul of League, FA Cup, League Cup and Inter-Cities Fairs Cup fixtures had proved too much for them.

The Liverpool fans were still happy, Anfield was still packed for match after match, and everyone was having a good time. But it wasn't good enough for Bill Shankly. He was still rebuilding. He wanted more trophies and, most of all, he wanted to bring home some silverware from Europe. His friend, Jock Stein, had won the European Cup with Celtic in 1967, and in 1968 another friend, Matt Busby, had done the same with Manchester United. Shankly needed his moment of European glory.

The 1968-69 season soon came around. Liverpool's pre-season preparation went smoothly. The club had lost the amazing Gerry Byrne whose injuries had finally ushered him into retirement, but gained a new one in Alun Evans, at £100,000 from Wolves, the most expensive teenager that Britain had ever seen. Once again however, the optimism at Anfield, the driving ambition that coursed from Bill Shankly through his staff and players, all came to nothing. The Fairs Cup campaign was lost on the toss of a coin, which was the decider chosen by the wise men of UEFA in those days. The FA Cup run had hardly broken into a trot before Leicester fatally wounded Liverpool's aspirations in the fifth round.

Everyone was taking the League Cup seriously by now and Liverpool enjoyed their best run to date, beating Sheffield United and then Swansea. Highbury was their not-so-happy hunting ground though and Liverpool were simply fodder for the Gunners. Perhaps the League would yield some treasure? No! Liverpool were runners-up again, Leeds taking their turn at supremacy.

And so the show rolled into the 1969-70 season, one that was to prove to be a time of difficult decision. Even without filling the trophy cupboard, Liverpool had achieved much. They were still the team to beat for most clubs, their support was as strong as ever and they were still playing good football – but they were not actually picking up the medals.

Everton were champions that season, Liverpool finishing in fifth place. Their League Cup run was halted by Manchester City after the Reds had beaten Watford. That Watford win was significant because later Liverpool were again drawn against them, this time in the FA Cup. Watford gained a shock win and Shankly knew that the team he had built, improved after another poor result at Watford and now, defeated again by Watford, was at the end of the road. The Fairs Cup campaign ended in the second round – and so it was back to the drawing board.

"That defeat at Watford told me that we were going to have to disband the team and build a new one. We had created a great Liverpool team. We had won things and put pride back into Liverpool. Now it was time to create another great Liverpool team, one that would be even better. My best spell as a player was between the ages of 28 and 33. You can still play as well as ever and you have gained in experience. After that age you start to decline, some quicker than others. We had several players who were at the end of their best time and we had to replace them."

It meant the end of the Liverpool days for goalkeeper Tommy

Lawrence, Roger Hunt, Ian St John and Ron Yeats. Larry Lloyd and Alec Lindsay joined the club, Ray Clemence was promoted from the reserves, and greater responsibilities were given to Emlyn Hughes. Ian Callaghan and Peter Thompson were still performing brilliantly and were well worth their first team places.

With Liverpool going through such a period of transition, it was not such a surprise that the 1970-71 season looked set to be another without a trophy. But the much younger side began to get its act together at the halfway stage of the season and the fans witnessed a soccer Super Nova – the birth of a whole new star team.

The Fairs Cup was put out of reach by Leeds of all teams. They were in the competition too and a 1-0 aggregate win was enough to extinguish Liverpool. The League ended with them in fifth place again – but there was still the possibility of the FA Cup. Merseyside held its breath when Everton and Liverpool were drawn together in the semi-final to be played at Old Trafford. Ultimately, Liverpool won and were on their way to Wembley to meet newly-crowned League champions, Arsenal.

History now reminds us of the cold facts that Arsenal won the double that season. It does not record the tremendous fight they had to gain that 2-1 victory through extra-time. The new-look Liverpool team of Ray Clemence, Chris Lawler, Tommy Smith, Larry Lloyd, Alec Lindsay, Ian Callaghan, Brian Hall, Emlyn Hughes, Alun Evans, Peter Thompson, John Toshack and Steve Heighway, had played well. Shankly was always disappointed to lose but he knew that he could be satisfied with his new team's performance.

An interested observer at the game was a young lad who had only just signed for Liverpool. He was only 19 and he had the whole world at his feet. His name was Kevin Keegan.

Once again there was optimism in the Anfield camp when the 1971-72 season approached – and with good reason. Liverpool had a new secret weapon in Keegan, who was set to make his debut in the first match of the campaign, at home to Nottingham Forest. The Kop choir were in great voice as the Reds won 3-1, and of course, Keegan scored on his debut.

The secret weapon had quite an impact and played a leading role in a 15-match unbeaten run in the second half of the season. It was still not enough. Derby won the championship, leaving Liverpool to fill third spot behind Leeds. The domestic Cup campaigns also fizzled out, as did the European Cup-winners' Cup, in which Liverpool had been given a place since Arsenal had done the double in the previous season.

"You can learn much more from defeat than you ever can from winning," said Shankly – and during those few seasons Liverpool had certainly had an education. It wasn't that they had done much wrong – but they had not yet achieved the perfection that Shankly was seeking. By the standards of most they were doing very well, but they were not doing great, and that was Shankly's goal – greatness!

Peter Cormack was added to the squad before the 1972-73 season. He was a £110,000 investment bought from Nottingham Forest and at last Shankly had the squad that was going to bring home the bacon. The League Cup was looking good when Liverpool reached the fifth round for the first time, beating Leeds, among others, to the obvious delight of the Kop. Tottenham put paid to any further ambition in that competition. Manchester City ended Liverpool's FA Cup hopes in the fourth round.

The League was a different proposition. Liverpool were storming when they went into their Easter programme. Leeds were the visitors and a capacity 55,000 fans packed into Anfield to cheer on the Reds. Cormack and Keegan was the double-act that stole the show with a goal apiece – two points and the championship. That win was enough to confirm that Liverpool could not be bettered.

The streets of Liverpool were lined again as the championship party got into full swing – but the season was not yet over. Shankly allowed only moderate celebrations. The reason was that his men had not only fared well in this country – they had also reached the semi-finals of the UEFA Cup. In yet another twist of fate, they had been drawn against the holders – Tottenham Hotspur. As it was, a 2-2 draw was enough to earn

Liverpool a place in the Final because of having scored an away goal in the second leg.

Borussia Dortmund were Liverpool's opponents in the Final, which was also a two-leg affair. That season the German side was probably the best in Europe and Shankly knew that he would have to summon every ounce of experience, confidence, effort and psychology if his team were to add a European crown to their League title.

The first leg was at Anfield, and the worst possible scenario for a manager opened on the day of the match. A rainstorm swept across Anfield and, after a goal-less half-hour of play, the match was abandoned. Shankly had a knack for turning bad news to his advantage and so he used what he had seen of the opposition to change his tactics and psychologically charge his players for the replay which was to take place the next evening. The tall, imposing John Toshack was brought back into the side and the order was to pump high balls to him and to the onrushing Kevin Keegan.

Shankly had spotted weaknesses in the Dortmund defence and meant to exploit them. The Toshack-Keegan pairing worked perfectly. A high ball to Toshack, nod-on to Keegan and the Germans were caught back-peddling. Keegan scored twice and another came from Larry Lloyd. The Germans were stunned – Anfield was ecstatic. The return leg was still to come and that had a drama that was all its own. More torrential rain threatened the match, but it continued with the two teams battling it out on a surface that was as slippery as an ice-rink.

Borussia Dortmund, roared on by their home crowd, threw everything at Liverpool and scored twice. Liverpool tightened their defence still more and remained under siege. The Germans were desperate but gradually they ran out of steam and when the final whistle blew, Liverpool had captured their very first European trophy.

It was a marvellous moment for Bill Shankly. He had become the first manager to take his team to the League championship and a European victory in the same season. He had achieved it by steering 16 players through a gruelling 64 games. Once again Merseyside rang to the chant of 'Shank-lee... Shank-lee'.

Few teams manage to retain trophies, so a repeat performance in the 1973-74 season was asking a lot – even for Shankly's amazing Liverpool. They did not try to defend the UEFA Cup, of course, since they had qualified for the European Cup. They gave it a good shot too, but narrowly lost to Red Star Belgrade in the second round.

The League Cup was still a no-go area for Liverpool and their fifth-round exit was at the hands of Wolves. The League championship campaign was probably disrupted by the pressures of other competitions, perhaps a little too much being asked for a second successive season of stamina-sapping soccer. Liverpool finished up as runners-up to Leeds.

The FA Cup held the key to Shankly's next moment of potential glory. The third round almost caused their faces to become as red as their shirts. Kevin Keegan's old club, Doncaster, were visitors to Anfield and it was only a late equaliser from Keegan himself that saved the day. Liverpool won the replay and then went on to beat Carlisle, Ipswich, Bristol City and finally Leicester City, to book their place in the FA Cup Final. Their opponents were Newcastle United.

The teams that faced each other at Wembley that year read like a soccer who's who. For Liverpool the line-up was Ray Clemence, Tommy Smith, Peter Thompson, Emlyn Hughes, Alec Lindsay, Brian Hall, Ian Callaghan, Peter Cormack, Kevin Keegan, John Toshack and Steve Heighway. Newcastle's team was Billy McFaul, Frank Clark, Pat Howard, Bobby Moncur, Alan Kennedy, Jimmy Smith, Terry McDermott, Tommy Cassidy, Malcolm McDonald, John Tudor, Terry Hibbitt and Tommy Gibb – the only substitute used in the game.

Liverpool probably gave their best-ever display. They scored three goals without reply. Kevin Keegan opened the scoring, Steve Heighway added a second and then Keegan made it 3-0. The fans partied and once again Shankly's name rang around Wembley.

Shankly enjoyed himself. He waved to, and applauded, the supporters, he joked with his players and even the directors. He was still enjoying the atmosphere of it all at the after-match banquet – and again the following day, when the streets of Liverpool were lined to welcome back the Anfield heroes and the FA Cup.

In front of Liverpool Town Hall, tens of thousands of fans erupted when the players came out to show them the trophy. But you could have heard a pin drop when Bill Shankly spoke to them – a brief speech that was, in its way, to become historic.

"Since I've come here to Liverpool, to Anfield, I've drummed it into my players time and time again, that they are privileged to play for you. And if they didn't believe me then, they do now. I've drummed into them that they must be loyal, that they must never cheat you, the public. The Kop is exclusive. It is an institution – and if you're a member of the Kop you're the member of a society. You've got thousands of friends around you, all united and loyal."

The crowd roared their approval.

Two months later there was disbelief as the news spread like wildfire through a dry forest – Bill Shankly had decided to retire.

Aftermath

WHEN the press gathered at Anfield on 12 July, they assumed that it was simply to welcome Ray Kennedy, whom Shankly had bought from Arsenal for £200,000. Few signings come as a complete shock and, while Shankly had played this particular card close to his chest, there had been hints from various quarters thereby giving the 'gentlemen' of the press an inkling as to why they had been summoned to Anfield.

They had not one inkling, however, of what was to follow the introduction of Ray Kennedy. All the usual questions were asked – and all the usual answers were given. Then, Liverpool chairman John Smith revealed that he had a further announcement to make.

"It is with great regret that, as chairman of the board, I have to inform you that Mr Shankly has intimated to us that he wishes to retire from League football."

There was total silence for a moment as the bombshell hit its target. Everyone waited expectantly for the next part of the statement – something like; 'Liverpool Football Club has asked Mr Shankly if he would remain for one more season.' But that half-expected, half-hoped for statement did not come. As the chairman resumed his seat, the room turned into an uproar as the various media reporters realised that this was not a false alarm, it was not a joke or some sort of publicity gimmick. Bill Shankly really had decided to call it a day. It was the end of an era – No! It was the end of an epoch.

Bill Shankly explained himself to the press.

"It was not a decision that I've taken quickly or lightly. My wife and I have been thinking about it for 12 months and we feel that it is time to recharge our batteries and take a rest from the game."

John Smith added that the club had accepted Shankly's decision with reluctance and wanted to place on record their deep appreciation for all that he had done. Deep appreciation! The sincerity was there, but 'deep appreciation' was not exactly an apt epitaph. Shankly had completely transformed the club. He had taken Liverpool from being Second Division also-rans to their first FA Cup success, to League championships and to one of the top prizes in Europe.

In 1959, Liverpool had been a giant in slumber – or decay. In his 15-year reign Shankly had turned it into an international institution.

When Shankly resigned he was beginning to look his full 61 years. The strain of perpetual optimism in the face of soccer management was beginning to tell. Shankly later gave further explanation of his decision and its timing.

"When I had come to Liverpool the place was a shambles. The team was not doing as well as it should, the ground was in need of a coat of paint and the training ground was a mess. But the potential was tremendous. The crowd was fantastic and it reminded me of Glasgow and the Scottish people.

"I had fought the battles on and off the pitch. I had fought the battles in the boardroom as well as everywhere else. Most importantly, I had made the people happy. They needed success – it mattered a great deal to them and their lives. If their team was doing well then they could handle everything else that life threw at them.

"All the arguments had been when I had conquered my Everest. Very few people achieve that – but I had, and I left when I had. I was still the manager when I decided to retire. I did not have to go – I chose to go."

And go he did – there and then! His replacement was Bob Paisley, Shankly's right-hand man. It was Shankly who recommended Paisley for the job and it guaranteed the continuation of Shankly's unique style of management.

Of course, that was not the last that Liverpool saw of Bill Shankly. He was regularly seen at matches, although he did try to keep a low profile and after a while declined boardroom tickets for ordinary seats. He also kept his promise of going on to the Kop to watch a game.

"It was not bravado," said Bill. "I was their man and they were my pals. The Kop was a unique place. I promised a Kopite that I would stand with them on the Kop when I retired – and I kept that promise."

It could be said that the Shankly Legacy was bequeathed on that 12th day of July 1974. Bob Paisley took over but little changed on a day to day basis, other than that Shankly's familiar footsteps and voice were now missing.

But Shanks was still around. He deliberately avoided getting involved in training or anything else behind the scenes, even though he was urged to call in at any time. At first he would turn up for training and have his own personal work-out – just to keep the joints in good order – but he avoided getting near the team's training sessions.

After a while he was seen less and less at Melwood and there are conflicting stories about his relationship with the club that he had served so well. He was offered an 'upstairs' post – that of General Manager. It was a sop more than a constructive move for the betterment of Liverpool Football Club, and that was exactly how Shankly read it – hence his instant refusal. He was a fiercely independent man who still had little time for members of boardrooms.

It is said that he had an uneasy relationship, especially with John Smith, because the chairman wanted to be more 'hands-on' in the buying and management of players.

Shankly made no categoric statement, neither did he point the finger – but he dropped hints and planted suggestions that took little growth to reveal their true meaning. He loved Liverpool Football Club, its players and its supporters, but he felt a little cheated. Shankly had given much of himself to the club and he had taken much from his family to sacrifice to the club too. He felt that the club could have been more generous in its rewarding of him.

Perhaps Shankly's true feelings are also reflected in his early morning cups of tea with Howard Kendall at the Bellewood Training Ground, after Kendall was made manager of Everton in 1981.

"We used to see him quite often," said Kendall. "I was thrilled because all of us at Everton had had tremendous respect for him. You could ask his advice and opinions and he would give willingly. He just loved to talk football but he would never talk down to you, or patronise you. He didn't say: 'Well, when I was in charge at Liverpool we used to do such and such…' He wasn't like that. It would be difficult to get him to talk about Liverpool. At times it was as if he had shut the club right out of his mind.

"He much preferred to talk football in general, without talking specifically about Liverpool, although he would dip into personal experience to tell you a funny story or two.

"Probably the most profound advice he ever gave me was to get into a tracksuit as soon as I turn up for work. He said that it showed the players that there was work to be done and acted as a deterrent to people in suits who wanted to bog you down with administrative work. I took that advice on board and it is rare that you find me at work without a tracksuit on – unless it is at a match."

Before the days of taking tea with Kendall, Shankly had much to occupy his time. As the 1974-75 season began, Liverpool were involved in the FA Charity Shield at Wembley against Leeds. Shankly agreed to lead out the team. He did the same two weeks later in Glasgow, when Liverpool were the visitors to Parkhead for a testimonial game for Billy McNeill, and took on Jock Stein in a psychological war of words before the game. Shankly had physically retired – but mentally and emotionally he was as highly charged as ever.

The boy from Glenbuck had another big date in his 1974 diary when he went with Nessie to Buckingham Palace to collect his OBE. He was quite emotional on the day although he maintained a confident countenance for the Royal Family and the press.

Shankly was still the biggest name on Merseyside and it was just as difficult for him, even in retirement, to walk along the street without being asked for a handshake or an autograph as it had been when he was still the Anfield boss. He had bequeathed a part of his legacy to these people while he was still manager of Liverpool Football Club. He had given all Merseysiders self-esteem, happiness and hope. They could not let him go that easily.

He turned up at rivals Everton for their first home game of the season and, when the word passed that he was there, he received a standing ovation from the 40,000 crowd.

Shankly felt alienated from the man who had replaced him, Bob Paisley, after Paisley asked him not to keep turning up for morning training sessions. It was a very awkward moment. Kindly, Bob Paisley tried to explain in the best way he could – but he did not have Shankly's way with words. Probably he didn't realise either how difficult it was for Bill Shankly to suddenly stop doing what he had been habitually doing for the last 40 years or more. There was no real animosity between them but the bond that they had shared for the last 15 years had been severed and things could never be the same again. Shankly knew that he had left a very handsome legacy and he now felt that its – or his – full value had not been appreciated.

Tranmere Rovers played on Friday nights and Ron Yeats had become their manager. Bill began to watch them regularly and then, in November, he was appointed as consultant to the club. John King was assistant to Ron Yeats and well remembers the reaction to Shankly's presence.

"There used to be a buzz go around the ground when he came to see a game. If the Queen had turned up there would not have been greater excitement. You have to remember just what Bill Shankly meant to the man in the street on Merseyside. He was one of them, but not just a face in the crowd – he was their leader. This worship was not restricted to Liverpool fans, or even football fans. Everyone on Merseyside thought the world of Bill Shankly.

"There was great delight at the club when he agreed to become consultant and I remember that the crowd for our first home game was huge. I think a lot of Kopites had turned up to wish him well. We were playing Preston, whose manager was Bobby Charlton, and we won 3-1. You would have thought that we had just won the League, the Cup and just about everything else. The atmosphere was fantastic.

"I wish we had been able to take better advantage of having him around but he had other commitments and couldn't always be there. We had some good results but a lot of bad ones too, and in the end we were relegated. Poor Ron paid for it with his job and I became manager for the first time. Bill was still around and helped a great deal. I learned a tremendous amount from him."

Derby County attempted to get Shankly on board but, after much deliberation, he turned them down. Nevertheless, his phone rarely stopped ringing and often the calls were from club managers seeking his advice.

Shankly also kept in touch with Matt Busby and would often pop over to Old Trafford, even going into the dressing-room before a match to help Manchester United players with their preparations.

His ability as an orator meant that he was in great demand as a public speaker, his colourful wit and story-telling capabilities often creating more laughter and applause than professional comics booked at the same functions.

Shankly's easy style and superstar manager status also had him in great demand from the media. He hosted his own show on Liverpool's commercial station, Radio City, and he was also a popular choice as co-commentator for television match coverage – especially when Liverpool games were being televised.

He also still found time to play football and he would enthusiastically take part in matches with Everton's schoolboy set. Shankly would play among the under-14s and still feel the same elation whenever his side scored and the same stab-wound whenever there was a goal for the opposition.

Mike Lyons was involved with the Everton youth training at the time and remembers Shankly's boyish enthusiasm.

"I've never seen anything like it. There was Shanks, well into his 60s, mixing it with the kids, playing his heart out and motivating his side to do the same, moaning if there was a free kick against him and shaking hands and patting lads on the back whenever his side got a goal. He was just like one of the kids himself.

"He used to come to me and give me a match report afterward. He once said; 'Great game today Mick. We won 19-17!' It was almost as if he were back in the school playground. Most importantly he enjoyed himself and I always got a kick when I saw that."

Shankly also caught up on the reading in which he had intended to immerse himself for some time. For a Scot, what else could that reading be but Burns. He would read it, consider it, read it again and then think about it long and hard for some time before moving on to the next item. Nothing touched him like Burns and he would often quote from it as much for his own pleasure as his audience's.

Bill also tried his hand at gardening but that was much more in order to please Nessie and spend some time with her than it was for his own horticultural interest. He was the first to admit that his gardening exploits were generally failures – a rare admission indeed. He would chuckle as he revealed that he had often pulled up Nessie's prize blooms thinking that they were weeds.

Apart from these few asides, football still dominated Shankly's life. He could not keep away from it and did not particularly want to. Those who knew him best believed that he was secretly annoyed at himself for retiring just when he did. He had become increasingly distressed at, what he considered to have been, shabby treatment by Liverpool. Yes, he had been offered a further position at the club, he had had a testimonial game and he did have tickets whenever he wanted them, but Shankly felt that he had been offered no more than the minimum that the club would offer any former servant. He believed that not even the club itself could realise exactly what it was that he had given them.

The debate could go on for ever and this book is certainly not about taking sides or creating controversy. On the one hand it could be said that Liverpool did not show appreciation for the man who transformed their club anywhere near as much as Manchester United did for their father-figure – Matt Busby. On the other hand, Shankly, perhaps, allowed his regret at his retirement and the fact that he missed the game so much, to cloud his view and allow it to fester into a mode of blame-apportioning which handed a huge chunk to his former employers.

Shankly had never been a lover of be-suited bosses. He felt that, for most directors, football was just an ego trip, a way of impressing their friends and inflating their own self-esteem. There are many who would support this claim but, in fairness, there are many devoted football directors who don't pretend to be anything more than fans who can afford to invest more in the game than the price of a season ticket.

Shankly now had more time for holidays of course, but he and Nessie had never been jet-setters. Bill's travels in football had been more than enough for both of them, so the Shanklys would pack their bags and head for their favourite holiday haunt – Scotland. One of their really favourite spots was Glasgow, where they would visit the shops, visit old friends and talk about football, old times and more football.

If the Powers of Liverpool had not shown their appreciation in quite the way that Bill Shankly had felt was appropriate, one of his earlier clubs certainly brought him close to tears. Workington invited him to open their new lounge in August 1980, and he willingly obliged, visibly moved when he discovered that it had been named The Shankly Lounge.

There were many individual gifts from supporters during his years of retirement and he continued to receive many letters and phone calls. His biography proved to be a big seller and his presence, in the game he loved, continued to be felt by the people with whom he empathised.

Nobody would have been surprised to open their newspapers and read a headline proclaiming that Bill Shankly had been appointed as the new manager of some club or other. It never happened – and nobody was quite prepared for his last major bombshell.

On the morning of Saturday, 26 September 1981, Shankly rose at his usual early time and had breakfast. Liverpool were away to West Ham and would draw 1-1, with Craig Johnston scoring. Everton were heading for a 1-0 win over West Brom, Mike Lyons the scorer. Huddersfield were going to beat Southend 3-2 at home. Grimsby were going to suffer a 0-1 home defeat by Sheffield Wednesday. Carlisle were to beat Oxford 2-1. Tranmere would draw 0-0 at home to Wigan. Preston were travelling to a 1-1 draw at Newport and Kevin Keegan was going to score twice for Southampton in a 2-4 defeat at Coventry.

Those were probably going to be among the last items of soccer news that Bill Shankly would hear. Just after breakfast he had a heart attack and was hurriedly taken to Broadgreen Hospital where his condition was said to be 'stable'. Never before had that hospital received so much mail as 'get well' cards flooded in by the sackful. Shankly showed a slight improvement on the Sunday but then deteriorated again on the Monday. Nessie remained at his bedside throughout. Half an hour after midnight he suffered another massive heart attack and 50 minutes later he was certified dead.

The entire world of soccer was stunned. Shankly's reputation had become famous wherever football was played. In Liverpool men and women of all ages wept openly in the streets. Newspaper editors could think of nothing more to grip their front pages than the simple banner – 'Shankly Is Dead!' – It said it all.

On Friday, 2 October 1981, the funeral was held at St Mary's Church in West Derby. The funeral cortege travelled past the Everton training ground where players and staff paid their respect. Elsewhere thousands of mourners lined the streets and stood silently outside the church. Ray Clemence, Emlyn Hughes, John Toshack and Ron Yeats were pall bearers, with Ian Callaghan, Kevin Keegan, and Ian St John providing an extra escort.

Many famous names of football were there, including Matt Busby and Tom Finney. The strains of *You'll Never Walk Alone* filled the air as the service drew to a close and then came

Shankly's last journey to the Priory Road Crematorium – only a short distance from Liverpool Football Club in the heart of Anfield.

At the next home game a banner was unfurled on the Kop. 'Shankly Lives Forever'. When the Old Kop was demolished, the Shankly banners once again waved proudly at the last game before redevelopment. The message was loud and clear as it has been ever since his death in 1981 – the spirit of Shankly lives on at Anfield and elsewhere. During his pre-Liverpool career Bill Shankly accumulated a treasure – a wealth of knowledge, experience and instinct. Upon his retirement he had bequeathed it. Upon his death it became quite simply – The Shankly Legacy.

Secrets of Success

BEFORE we look at the effects of the Shankly Legacy, we need to see what exactly that legacy included. One of its prime ingredients was the treasure of wisdom and experience. Just as a loving parent might aim to build up a nest-egg to bequeath to his offspring, so Shankly – quite deliberately – built for the future of Liverpool. Inadvertently he also built for the future of British football.

"I want people to talk about the future Liverpool just as they talked about the old," said Shankly. There is no doubt that he has succeeded in that aim. Since he took them into the top division in 1962, Liverpool have become fixtures there – not only never having been relegated but never having dropped below eighth place in the League tables. Interestingly, that placing has only happened twice. The first time was in the 1962-63 season – the first term after Shankly had restored Liverpool to the First Division. The second time was in the 1993-94 season when Graeme Souness was in charge and had thrown away the Shankly blueprint in favour of a 'big success' spending spree. The Liverpool League record since the 1962 promotion has been nothing short of phenomenal.

But what is the great Shankly secret of success?... It is multi-faceted although so simple and nobody could explain it better than Bill Shankly himself.

"The basic system is what we call collective play. It is very simple but very effective. It is something we learned from the continent – a cat and mouse game that calls for patience and improvisation. Improvisation is the key word. It is a team effort in which everyone helps everyone else. If a player switches position there is automatically someone else there to replace him. No gaps are left. You don't get players saying; 'that's not my job'. Improvisation means that players slot in wherever they are needed. If I'm a full-back and go on a run, you would drop into my place to cover – or someone who was nearer would and you might cover for them. That's improvisation, the ability to adapt at a moment's notice and then adapt back again. Everyone supports everyone else. Terry McDermott was very good at that.

"Playing that way saves energy. When you are playing 50, 60 or 70 games in a season you need to conserve energy. The improvisation system is designed to do just that. Nobody has to work harder than anyone else. It is also confusing for the opposition because they never know who they are supposed to be marking.

"The system involves control – pass – control – pass. It means that players have more space and more time. More options can be created. You don't get people running into no-man's-land. That's nonsense! It's not necessary! If everyone helps everyone else there are always plenty of options and the opposition can't possibly cover everything. That's one of the reasons why Kenny Dalglish was so instantly successful when he joined Liverpool. The system allowed him time to perform, and he was the kind of player who could take great advantage of that. He could rely on having players around who would help play him into scoring positions or were there to help play him out of trouble and into a better opportunity.

"I've seen players turn their backs on their team-mates. They didn't want the ball if they were having a difficult game. Nobody at Liverpool would do that! Other players will run themselves into the ground and achieve nothing. Our approach was to use the ball like a baton in a relay race. You pass it to me, I pass it to him, he passes it on. It's the ball that is covering most of the ground – not the players.

"Not only does that conserve energy and keep efficiency through the game but it helps cut down on wear and tear which means that you get fewer injuries – and that means that you can keep a smaller squad playing together. That then builds confidence and team-spirit which in turn means that the players will even more willingly help each other in a game and the system turns full circle. It works!

"Keeping injuries to a minimum is very important, much more important than simply having a fit player. The more injuries you avoid, the fewer changes you have to make for each game. That builds consistency – very important if you want to win championships. We put a lot of emphasis on that, which is why we took a lot of trouble in making sure that our training was right and also our preparation. Not only were we careful about our match preparation but also in our preparation for the season. A lot of damage can be done if players are not prepared correctly for the rigours ahead.

"If you look at Liverpool's pre-season training as an example, we were always very cautious with the initial pre-season training period. For the first three or four days you don't want to be tearing players to pieces. A lot make the mistake of asking too much too soon and as a result you overtax the muscles and you start problems that will recur time after time throughout the season.

"I believe that the absence of Ray Clemence cost us the championship one season. He couldn't play because of a muscle injury and we dropped several vital points while he was out of the team. I think he would have made all the difference. The cause of his injury was practising kicking dead balls. That's hard work and can cause a lot of strain, especially if you have not prepared yourself properly. He injured a leg muscle as a result. It happens a lot in the game and much of it can be avoided."

Shankly was meticulous in his players' preparation. Perhaps his physio studies had given him a greater appreciation of the workings of the human body than most managers. Whatever the reason few details would escape him and, if he could not find an immediate answer to a problem, he would research and contemplate until he found the right solution.

Bill Shankly liked his players to report back for duty in reasonable condition after their summer lay-off. In his own playing days most of his colleagues took summer jobs which required a fair amount of physical effort. The majority could not afford the summer break's dip in income. For all there was the need to keep in some sort of fit condition – hence they took work as miners, labourers, farm-workers – even grave-diggers – to keep the wolf from the door and lethargy from the muscles.

In his Liverpool days as manager Shankly did not expect his players to become fine-weather grave-diggers. Times and football lifestyles had changed far too much for that. However he did expect them to take care of themselves physically – a jog here, a work-out there – even a walk on the golf-course would help. When they reported back for training Shankly expected them to be ready to go to work – even if they had put on a pound or two.

"The initial period of returning for training is vital. You can make or break your season in that time. Once you have had three or four days of light work, a few exercises, some light jogging, that kind of thing – then we can get down to something a bit more like it.

"I changed quite a bit when I became manager of Liverpool. I didn't like the idea of players going straight to the training ground, having a rigorous session, getting dressed and going home. Your body doesn't react well to that kind of treatment. Training is not just about muscles – your whole body needs attention, inside and out.

We changed the whole thing so that the players met and changed at Anfield, went in a bus to Melwood where they would have their training session, walk around the ground two or three times, have a cup of tea and then travel back to Anfield for a bath, change and something to eat. It made all the difference. The body gets a chance to slow down steadily after it has been made to work hard, every part is able to gradually relax instead of being rushed into work and then rushed out of it, into a bath, followed by a meal. It doesn't work at its best like that, which is why I changed the routine. I'm sure that it helped us to keep a much more reasonable injury list – the players' bodies were toned that much better. It might not sound very much but it was a big factor for us and proved to be a very, very important part of Liverpool's whole approach to training and general fitness."

Of course the Shankly approach to training was not limited to where the players would change or at what stage they would have a cup of tea. His own work in training was unstinting and he expected no less of his players although, again, he had his own ideas of work-rate and how the training should be arranged.

"Liverpool players always went out fit and ready for the game. We trained for the match. It is no good spending hours running and then more hours playing a full game of football for no apparent reason. If you train with the game in mind then you will train to match conditions. Our whole method was based on exhaustion and relax. In a game you are called upon to work really hard for a short burst of time and then you get a breather, another short burst and another breather. That is what it is like to play in a football match and that is how we trained.

"We would maybe have an area of 50 yards by 45 yards as a pitch, perhaps there would be a three-a-side game on it – or maybe just two players, and that was a killer. At the start they would have a short period of intense activity – control – dribble – shoot – sprint. It would start at one minute and gradually increase with relax breaks in between. Those are match conditions!

"We would also have three-a-side games because usually that is the number of players involved in a move at any one time. Training like that gets players used to passing, running, helping each other. There's no hiding or escaping in a three-a-side game.

"Another thing we did was breathing sessions – very important to keep the body working correctly on the inside. We would have players stop, start, twist and turn, making sure that they breathed properly as they did it and during their moments of rest.

"All of this kind of preparation is important in giving you an edge. If players feel right, they'll play right. Our sessions helped their fitness, their style, their confidence in themselves and each other. They were a team.

"I never believed in having two training sessions in a day – or in having really long sessions. What's the point? Even 90 minutes is not that necessary. If you train properly then 35 minutes will do you. Our aim at Liverpool was to get everyone involved in the game as quickly as possible and our training was the same. Even talking is part of training and a very important part at that.

"You want your players to go on for ten or 12 years or more. They can only do that at the top of their game if you don't burn them out with too much unnecessary training.

"We used to have a very light work-out on the morning of a game – just to get everyone toned and in the right frame of mind. If they had been overworked in general training they could not have had a morning work-out and also play a game in the afternoon."

Much happened at Liverpool that was rather different to the policies of other clubs. Shankly would join in the mini-games – and moan if his team lost. The rest of the time he would go from one group of players to another. There would be Bob Paisley in charge of one group, Reuben Bennett in charge of another, Joe Fagan would be training another bunch and there would be Ronnie Moran passing on advice as well as another young man who was still learning the trade himself, encouraging his team-mates on to even greater effort. Yes, current manager Roy Evans was receiving his education at the feet of the master.

"I used to have my team of trainers – coaches as they later became known in the jargon of football. We would sit down and talk almost daily and then we would work in groups and sessions at the training ground. I used to go around and see that everything was being done the way I wanted it. The mis-training at Liverpool had been going on for a long time before I joined the club and I wanted it right. We worked well as a management and coaching team. We freely discussed everything and made sure that the players received the personal attention that they needed."

That was at a time when many clubs left everything to the manager and the 'trainer', who put the players through a few basic keep-fit exercises and carried a bucket of cold water and the legendary magic sponge. As ever, Shankly was ahead of his time by having such a large team of coaches. There was more to it than training though – even diet was important, and the time of eating.

"A classic example of a detail overlooked making all the difference, was when we had a spell of regular trips to London for League and Cup matches. We were not playing particularly well on these trips and we were not getting the results which I felt we should have been getting. I retraced our steps until I found what it was that we were doing wrong.

"We were travelling down by train every time and having a snack on the journey. Then, when we arrived at the hotel, we were having a full four or five course meal as well. It was too much and it was upsetting the metabolism. I changed that. We caught a later train and had a meal on the journey, then later, at the hotel, the players could have something very light – some toast and honey, a poached egg or something like that. The earlier meal had time to be digested properly and when it came to the next day's game there was none of the sluggishness that we had been experiencing.

"Being a manager means that you have to get to the bottom of problems, you have to investigate until you find out what is wrong, then of course you can deal with it, put it right or try something else until you find the cure.

"Eating is very important for everyone – for a professional footballer it can make all the difference between winning and losing. I've always said that moderation is important in everything and I've never changed my mind about it. Work hard in training but don't kill yourself, if you like a beer then have a beer, but in moderation. It's a key factor. When we were having problems on our away trips to London we were eating too much too late – that's why we changed."

Shankly's preparations for a Saturday afternoon game were also revolutionary. He adopted policies that have since been copied to great success by others. The build-up to a game would start on Friday.

"We would have some very light training on the Friday and then we would get together in a little room and discuss what we were going to do. Reuben Bennett would take the reserves for their talk and I would have the 12 or 13 players who had been picked for the first team. We had a table-top laid out as a pitch to show positioning and moves and we would talk the game through. It would be a lengthy talk and we would take in a report on the opposition from one of the staff – mostly on their formation and any negative characteristics of the players. Our real concern, however, was not in who we were playing, but about our own team and how we were going to play.

"I remember once, before a game against Manchester United we had our usual talk and, at the end, someone asked, 'are Law, Best or Charlton not playing?' Now that was music to my ears because I had deliberately not mentioned them. If you started talking about players like that then you'd frighten yourself to death. No, I only wanted us to think about ourselves. Let the opposition worry about what we were going to do – we were not going to waste our thoughts on worrying about them. We were to concentrate purely on us.

"When I gave these talks, I used to throw in a joke every now and then so that it didn't get too serious. If you get too serious then you start to get tense, and then you could take that tension into the game with you. That's no good! At Liverpool we always needed to be relaxed and confident with our game. So I'd drop a bomb every now and then to get a laugh and make sure everyone was relaxed."

Being patient and relaxed was a hallmark of the Liverpool game. The Shankly teams always looked confident when they came out of the tunnel at the start of a game, and had an aura of serenity that must have been quite daunting for the opposition.

"We had two major points in our preparation talks. One was to bring everyone into the game as quickly as possible. Some players can be in a game for 12 or 15 minutes without getting a kick of the ball. The longer that goes on the more difficult it is for that player to perform. He starts to get nervy and his confidence can quickly go. At Liverpool, our policy was to get everyone into the game as quickly as possible so that everyone had had a touch of the ball and felt involved.

"Another of our major policies was patience. A game lasts for 90 minutes, you don't have to do it all in the first ten – or even in the first half. It might take us 80 minutes to break down the opposition but we would keep playing patiently and gradually things would go right. The number of goals that we scored in the last five minutes was unbelievable. It usually takes the heart out of the opposition and then sometimes you can end up with two or three goals – all scored at the end."

That was part of Shankly's Liverpool strategy. Another aspect was the, then, unique ploy of taking players away from home on Friday evenings – even when the Saturday match was being played at Anfield.

"It was an important part of our preparation. We went away from home for all matches. I used to find a suitable hotel for us to stay at and away we would go. As time went by the selection of hotels grew because there were a lot of places opening with good facilities. But even early on we found some nice hotels, somewhere quiet.

"After our chat on the Friday, the players would all go home and spend a bit of time with their families. They would have their main meal at home and then we would all meet back at Anfield at about half past eight to nine o'clock. The cars would all be left there and we would take the coach to the hotel, our hide-out for the night. We would get there at about ten and there would be a light snack available, some toast or whatever, and that was it for the night."

What Shankly did not reveal in his interviews was that, after the players had gone to bed, he would often stand guard for another hour or so in the hotel reception – just to make sure that none of his charges smuggled themselves out, or anyone or anything in. Shanks liked his players to be resting in their rooms from 10.30 pm.

"The next morning we would all have breakfast together.

Again it would be something light – poached egg, cereal, toast, that sort of thing. We would go for a walk, perhaps have a little jog or something and then we'd travel to Anfield together to arrive there about an hour before the kick-off.

"There was not much more you could do at this stage, so we would just try to keep things relaxed in the dressing room. I wanted to keep the atmosphere light so I would be ready to make a joke over something and raise a laugh. I might tell an exaggerated story, or tell them that the opposition had arrived and that half of them were limping and the other half shaking. Bob Paisley and Joe Fagan were good at joining in with it. We didn't want individuals to start worrying. If anyone did have a worry we wanted them to share it. Players had to be assured that it was a team effort. Even players like Roger Hunt or Kevin Keegan were not expected to win the game on their own.

"Having a laugh in the dressing room kept any tension away. I expect the opposition would have been a little dispirited when they heard our lads having the time of their lives before the game. That was a bonus, I wanted our opponents to be nervous. I had the 'Anfield' sign put up to let them know what they were in for when they ran out to face our team. Another favourite joke of mine was to give the doorman a box of toilet rolls and tell him; 'Give these to them when they arrive Charlie!' It was only a joke but it would make them think."

Perhaps there was the danger of Liverpool's mighty men becoming over-confident – but if there was ever any sign of that Shankly immediately discouraged it.

"Over-confidence is not a good thing. It is a form of ignorance and bad manners. If you are over-confident you talk too much and then you crash, you look silly and then you can lose all your confidence if you're not careful. You have to find a happy medium, because you want players to have confidence in themselves and in their team-mates but you don't want them to be over-confident."

Once the players are into the match there is little a manager can do. Although he was undoubtedly a man of great passion, Shankly would most often hide his feelings until the end of a game. Outwardly his face would show utter composure. Inwardly he would be, metaphorically, biting his nails. Always, he played every ball himself.

There were no half-measures for Bill Shankly. Victory was sweet – defeat was bitter. The defeated opponents were usually 'the best team in the country' after they had been beaten. Victorious opponents were given nothing more than a cursory handshake – Shankly's thoughts were already striving to get over such a set-back in time for the next match. He was never one to go crazy in the dressing room though.

"What would be the point. Yes I have lost my temper once or twice – but not very often. The players know the result. They know if they have performed well or not. We never lost that many but you always have to try to find something positive from your set-backs. You can learn much more about yourselves from defeat than you ever can from victory.

"If we had lost a game we would get together in the big lounge at Anfield at about 2 o'clock on the Monday afternoon for a free-for-all discussion. Everyone would have their say and they could say exactly what they felt. If I thought it was going to get out of hand I would step in and say a few things to calm it down – but it rarely got to that. If you've got honest players they will be honest with each other and admit their mistakes.

"We would have a full analysis of how we had lost, when we had lost. Was there a weakness that kept on recurring? Were we conceding goals at a particular stage of the game? We would consider everything to make sure that we were as fully prepared as possible for our next game.

"We didn't just have these talks when we lost. We would analyse our successes as well to learn as much as possible. But we always found that there was much more to learn from a defeat, and in that way we felt that it had not been a complete waste of a game."

The discussions were also a major part of Shankly's psychological approach to the atmosphere in which his players were asked to do their best for Liverpool Football Club.

"At Anfield we train together, eat together, sit in the lounge and talk football together. In fact, this club is a family." Bill Shankly said. And he always wanted the best for his football family, just as he did for Nessie and their daughters and for the rest of their family back in Scotland. He always liked to see Anfield and Melwood providing the best facilities for his football family and he also liked to see everything clean and sparkling.

"You could take the Queen around Anfield without hiding a thing," was one of his proudest boasts. You probably could too but she would have been like a visiting monarch for there was only one King of the Kop.

Shankly was proud of his achievements and did not in the slightest mind giving tips to others, especially after his retirement. Despite the span of time since his retirement in 1974 up to the present day, his wisdom still holds good. The tips given in this chapter were among those given in a number of different interviews both before and after his retirement.

Any manager today, whether managing a Premiership side or a Sunday morning pub side, can learn and gain from Shankly's words of wisdom. They offer the very basics of how to run a successful side. As we shall see later in the book, there are those who learned first-hand from the master and who have now put into operation much of what Shankly gave them. Keegan and Evans are prime examples of that. But in revealing his Liverpool secrets of success, Bill Shankly bequeathed to the entire game, that very special gift – the Shankly Legacy.

Memories of Shankly

ALMOST everyone who was around at the time can tell you a Shankly story – or will have some special memory of an encounter with him. My own first meeting with him was as a teenager working for *Soccer Star* – which was then the weekly football magazine. I had already spoken to many of the great names in the game through interviews with Stanley Matthews, Matt Busby, Tom Finney, Bert Trautmann and many others.

I was strangely apprehensive about Shankly. His team had not long won the FA Cup and they were the biggest thing in soccer at that particular time. From everything that I had heard about this shoot-from-the-hip Scotsman, I did not really know what to expect when I met him. I began in totally the wrong way by apologising for taking up his time and saying that I understood that he must be very busy.

He smiled and put me at my ease immediately.

"My time is football laddie! I'm busy with football, and you're busy with football – so let's talk about football and let the time worry about itself!"

During the years that followed our paths crossed a number of times – all to good effect from my point of view. I only wish that I had realised what those few kind words at the start had done for my own confidence. Bill Shankly had put us on level terms –

something which I have never forgotten since. Be polite, don't elevate yourself but don't undersell yourself either – Thanks Bill!

Many of the Shankly stories have been chronicled over and over again, but they lose nothing by the passage of time or by repetition.

Billy Bremner was an opponent, a fierce opponent with Leeds United, but he recalls fellow Scot Shankly as one of the nicest men that he ever met.

"He was a very unusual man. If his team beat you he would say that you were the best team in the world – simply because that would make his own team the best in the universe. If you beat his team though, he would say nothing. He was not a bad loser in the sense that he would make ridiculous excuses or lose his temper. He would just go very quiet, but you could see that he had been stung by the defeat. Away from all that he was a lovely chap with a marvellous sense of humour and a total dedication to the game. He was football, football, football. That was Bill Shankly."

Shankly was famous for his wit and wisdom, often contrasting – but never overlooked. He once defined courage like this:-

"Courage is the major factor in any player's climb up the football ladder of fame. When I have mentioned this before, some people seem to think that I'm talking about physical ability. Nothing could be further from the truth. Courage is a big word. It covers a multitude of accomplishments – just as much mental as physical, indeed, perhaps more so.

"Courage is more than being able to stand up to a buffeting on the field of play. Courage is also the ability to get up when things are getting you down... to get up and fight back. Never to know defeat, let alone accept it. To have principles – be they of fitness or morality – and stick by them. To do what you feel you must do, not because it's the popular thing to do but because it's the right thing to do.

"Courage is skill, plus dedication, plus fitness, plus honesty, plus fearlessness. It is a big word, but it is one which should hang above your bed if you really want to be a professional foot-baller... and to be one that is a credit to the game and yourself."

Then there are examples of his wit. One of his most famous quotes is this:- "There are two great teams on Merseyside – Liverpool and Liverpool Reserves."

In 1966 he had a favourite joke about Everton lining up at the start of the FA Cup Final. The Everton captain then was Brian Labone – and the Shankly tale went like this:-

PRINCESS MARGARET: But Mr Labone, where is Everton?

BRIAN LABONE: In Liverpool, Ma'am.

PRINCESS MARGARET: Of course! We had your first team here last year!

In 1972, when the championship was a three-horse affair between Liverpool, Derby and Manchester City, Derby and City were playing each other in the April. Shankly sent a brief message to City manager Joe Mercer – 'I hope you both lose!'

When asked if he had really taken his wife Nessie to see Rochdale on their wedding anniversary, he quickly replied:-

"Of course I didn't take my wife to see Rochdale as an anniversary present! It was her birthday. Would I have got married during the football season? And anyway, it wasn't Rochdale – it was Rochdale reserves!"

Larry Lloyd was one of Shankly's players at the end of the 1960s and into the 1970s, with more than 150 first-team games to his credit. He recalls Shankly's sheer love of the game.

"The one thing above all others was his fantastic enthusiasm. He'd been a long time in the game but he was always like a newcomer to football in his intense love and enjoyment of the game.

"I also remember that he would watch a visiting team come in at Anfield. Once they had all disappeared into the visitor's dressing room, he'd burst into ours and say; 'They're midgets – not a big bloke among them. Two points today lads! It's a cert!' That was typical of him. It was also typical that, within Liverpool, he had his own five-a-side soccer team. It was himself, Reuben Bennett, Joe Fagan, Bob Paisley and Ronnie Moran. Guess who was their manager and captain."

When Celtic won the European Cup in 1967 in Lisbon against Inter-Milan, they brought the trophy back to Britain for the first time in its history. Bill Shankly didn't want to watch the game on television, he wanted to be there – to soak up the atmosphere. After the game he was the first non-Celtic person to dash into the dressing room, fling his arms around his old pal, Celtic boss Jock Stein, and yell at the top of his voice, "John! You are immortal!"

After Liverpool thumped Everton in a 5-0 derby match, Shankly surprised the gathered football writers after the game by telling them – "I thought Everton were unlucky today." Pressed for his reasoning, he explained – "Well, they happened to meet Liverpool, didn't they!"

His after-match comments became collectors' items. After a defeat in which Liverpool conceded three goals he was invited to admit that the victors were not a bad team. "Team?" he growled. "They're nothing but rubbish. Three breakaways, that's all they got."

After a 5-1 defeat in Holland by Ajax in the European Cup, Liverpool's spirits were at their lowest when the players reached the dressing room. Within seconds it had all changed as Shankly declared:- "Five-one... Aye, that should help them to make a game of it when they come to Anfield for the second leg."

Then there was the famous Swansea Town victory by 2-1 at Anfield, in the sixth round of the FA Cup, in 1964. Shanks summed that up as – "the biggest travesty of justice in football history – the real score should have been 14-2."

Once, when away with the team, Shankly appeared at breakfast in the hotel wearing slippers. With a voice like thunder he demanded, "Who's pinched my shoes? I put them outside my door last night and someone's left an old pair in their place!"

There was a dead silence around the breakfast table. Shankly looked down at the feet of a director sitting next to him. "You've got my shoes on!" he exploded – they were certainly the same colour, size and style. "I've heard of managers being sacked," Bill went on. "But they've all been able to walk out in their own shoes!"

Another of his famous after-match press sessions was at Chelsea. Liverpool had just had a good win and the news had come through that Everton had dropped a point at home. One reporter asked him how he was planning to spend his Sunday.

"Oh, the usual way when I've nothing better to do," Shankly replied. "I'll pick up my Sunday paper, find the First Division table and look to see where Everton are – working from the bottom of course!"

It is also true that Shankly's barber was an Evertonian and that Bill had once given him some Liverpool match tickets. When asked why, Shankly simply replied, "You can't be too careful – now and then I get him to give me a shave."

Shankly's humour was legendary even among professional comics. Jimmy Tarbuck was often invited to the Liverpool dressing room before a game to tell a few gags and help with the mood.

"It was marvellous to be able to go and meet the lads before major matches. I had been a huge Liverpool fan since childhood and it was a real thrill to be involved. Shanks used to want me to get a few laughs and keep the players relaxed before the game. I don't know why he felt that he needed me – he was more than capable himself. He was a very funny man. It was a pleasure to have known him."

Another fan is lifelong supporter Ken Dodd, who also admired Shankly's unique style.

"What a lovely man he was," said Doddy. "I've never met anyone quite like him. He was a very humane person, totally dedicated to football, but also a man of the people – the people of Merseyside. They thought the world of him up here in Liverpool."

Another comic, Charlie Daze, had more than just a sense of humour in common with Bill Shankly. Charlie rose to fame in Granada Television's *The Comedians* but, before that, he had been a very promising player in Northern Ireland and, but for a knee injury, would almost certainly have been signed by Manchester United. Today he has an FA coaching badge, and coaches young players in Jersey, scouts for Leeds and still finds time to do extensive tours as a comedian.

"I used to do a fair swap with Bill. He would listen to my gags and I would listen to his soccer gems. He had a fantastic sense of humour and what he didn't know about football was just not worth knowing."

Shankly's generosity was also well-known. Once, on a European trip, he met up with a couple of Liverpool fans who had struggled to save the cash for their fare and match tickets. When Bill heard that they had only managed to save enough for their fare one way, he reached into his pocket and gave them £100 – more than enough to get them back home and buy a meal or two.

There are many stories of Bill Shankly dipping into his pocket to help someone out. He never expected repayment either – he was just naturally generous. He wasn't quite the same when he was contacted for FA Cup Final tickets however. He used to find out if they were really Liverpool supporters and, sometimes, he would discover that the person making the request, and claiming to be a lifelong Liverpool fan, had never even been to Merseyside, let alone Anfield. He used to tell them in no uncertain terms that, if he did have any spare tickets, they would be going to genuine Liverpool supporters and not to some fickle long-distance football fan who would probably be supporting a different club next season. Shankly was forthright in all his actions.

Shankly's pre-Liverpool existence seemed almost to have been wiped off the face of football history – such was his unswerving loyalty to the Anfield club.

Jock Stein once said; "I don't believe everything that he tells me about his players. If they were that good, they would not only have won the European Cup but also the Ryder Cup, the Boat Race and the Grand National!"

Shankly, however, was completely unswerving. There was nothing on the planet to touch a game of football, and there was no one to touch Liverpool or any of his players. Leeds manager Don Revie used to get a phone call almost every week from Shankly in which he would have to listen to lengthy descriptions of the wonders of Bill's players. If Bill Shankly happened to stop for breath, Revie would dive in with the name of one of his own players, only to find him dismissed with a well-mannered; "Aye, he's not bad", before Shankly, once again, launched into further eulogy about the brilliance of another one of his players.

Although Shankly specialised in rubbishing the opposition, it was purely to elevate the qualities of his own side. He was blinkered and refused to see anything good unless it was wearing a Liverpool shirt. He even, on one occasion, rubbished a group of reporters who were having a kick-about in the Anfield car-park – sending Bob Paisley to get the coaching team's five-a-side kit so that he could challenge them to a game.

There are many, many stories about Shankly, and many more memories of his quirks and foibles. There are few about the respect that he really had for his fellow professionals – yet he did indeed have great feeling for Matt Busby and Jock Stein and their respective clubs. And there was another whom he respected greatly – an Englishman of whom he once said:-

"That man scored some two-hundred goals in two-hundred and 70 matches – an incredible record. As a manager he has won trophy after trophy. When he talks, pin back your ears."

He was talking about Brian Clough.

Following his own advice, Shankly rarely had a run-in with any referee. He usually gave them a look which said, "You got it wrong – you know it and I know it." But that's where he left it. He warned his players against arguing with the referee and he practised what he preached.

He did, however, once have this to say: "The trouble with referees is that they know the rules but they don't know the game."... Nuff said!

There is the famous tale of the exchange of words between Bill Shankly and tough defender Tommy Smith. Shankly told him to go and make a cup of tea.

"You're not scaring anyone but yourself. You think you're a hardman – you're not! – This is a hardman." With that, Bill Shankly took a picture of Al Capone from his pocket.

Shankly's simple soccer philosophy said it all really. He believed in a frank approach to the game.

"If you are first, you are first. If you are second – you are nothing!"

Everything of his had to be the best. Once on a car journey he produced a bag of boiled sweets from his pocket. "Have one of these," he offered. "They're the finest sweets."

Once, when told to take a rest by his doctor, Shankly went on holiday. When he returned he was asked if he had enjoyed it. "Aye, I had a fine time," he replied. "We got up a team and beat the waiters."

When he heard that a rival manager was unwell, he quickly quipped: "I know what's the matter – he's got a bad side."

One of his young players asked for a day off to get married. Shankly slowly shook his head in despair and said: "We've bred a monster."

There are more memories of Shankly still to come, but let's not forget the famous 'This Is Anfield' sign.

"It was one of Bill Shankly's ideas," said Bob Paisley. "A bit of psychology. Playing here lifts good pros, puts the bad 'uns under pressure. We counted – there are more bad pros than good 'uns – so the sign went up"

Then, of course, there is the Kop – and something else that is synonymous with Bill Shankly... THAT song... *You'll Never Walk Alone*. The Kop choir in full voice is legendary – but it was during the Shankly reign that the song became the Anfield Anthem... How?

Gerry Marsden of Gerry and the Pacemakers recorded the song and well remembers Bill Shankly's response to it.

"The Kop had already taken to singing it, simply because they liked it. It became the official Liverpool song because of Bill Shankly. I was a big Liverpool fan of course and I knew everyone at the club. It was a sheer delight for me to appear on the Ed Sullivan Show in the United States with Bill and the lads and sing *You'll Never Walk Alone*. It came about because I was touring there and Liverpool were also on tour there. The show producers thought it would be a good idea if we all appeared on the Ed Sullivan Show together, and that's how it came about. It brought the place down when we sang and afterwards Bill said to me – "That's Liverpool's song Gerry, that's Liverpool's song." And that was it. From that moment on it became a kind of club anthem.

"I can honestly say that I get a thrill every single time I hear it sung at Anfield or Wembley. I sang it at the memorial service for Bill – and I really don't know how I got through it. He was such a lovely man. I still expect to see him at Anfield, even now. I shall never forget him. You meet many hundreds, even thousands, of people in my kind of life – but Bill was very special. When you were with him you really could hold your head up high, whatever kind of a storm you were walking through. A great, great man.

"A lot of people think that *You'll Never Walk Alone* is my song – but it's not – it's Liverpool's song. Bill Shankly said so and that's good enough for me."

Yes, even that song is part of Bill Shankly's Legacy.

Shankly's Heroes

BILL Shankly was not just a footballer, not just a football manager, he was also a football fan. Just like the rest of us, he had his heroes. Most of them were people that he'd played alongside, had managed, or would like to have managed.

Probably the first name that Shankly would have mentioned is Tom Finney – a team-mate at Preston, and a player whom Shankly rated as the greatest that he had ever seen, bar none. It wasn't just Finney's brilliant skills, it was also his attitude and dedication to the game.

Finney was born in Preston on 5 April 1922, and joined the club's juniors. He became a full professional in January 1940, when, of course, soccer life was rather different in those war-torn years compared to the luxury life of today's professionals. Most footballers in those days, as we have already discovered, had other strings to their bows – a trade to which they would almost certainly return upon retirement. Finney's other string was plumbing, but it was his ability to tap a ball that made him a national figure and a hero of Bill Shankly.

"He didn't just beat people, he gave them thrombosis," said Shankly in one of his many tributes to his former Preston team-mate, who chalked up 187 goals in 433 League appearances through his one-club career which lasted until his retirement in

1959. He had been a first-team player during the war years too and therefore his first-team appearances were probably nearer the 600 mark.

Finney was quite an amazing player because he was really a right winger and played most of his Preston games there. For England he played on the left wing because another player, someone called Matthews, had first claim on the right wing spot. For a time Preston tried Finney at centre-forward, and he was so successful in that position that he was picked to play for England there as well. Finney played 76 games for England and scored 30 goals – which means that he is still among the top goalscorers of all time for his country – bettered only by Bobby Charlton, Gary Lineker and Jimmy Greaves.

"Tommy Finney was grizzly strong," said Shankly. "Tommy could run for a week. I'd have played him in his overcoat. There would have been four men marking him when we were kicking in. When I told people in Scotland that England were coming up with a winger who was better than Stanley Matthews, they laughed at me. But they weren't laughing when big Georgie Young was running all over Hampden Park looking for Tommy Finney!"

Shankly also admired Tom Finney's total dedication to his game.

"He would spend hours behind the stand – just himself, a ball and the wall. He would pass it with his left foot, get the rebound with his right, shield it, dribble it, knock it back to the wall, and keep on doing that sort of stuff long after everyone else had gone home. He loved the game and was dedicated to doing his best. He put in hour after hour to try to perfect his play."

In England internationals, Finney has been credited with more than 50 'assists' – in addition to the 30 goals he scored.

"Tom Finney was the greatest player that I ever saw," said Shankly. "Yes, without a doubt. He was about 5ft 7ins and weighed about 11 stone. He didn't have a big frame but he was very strong with very strong legs which meant he could get off the ground, he was good in the air. But his ball control on the ground was unbelievable, close control and he could face you, just kind of shake himself, and he was gone – he'd just run past you. A lot of players can play with their backs to the goal, or from the side, but he could come up to you, face you and deceive you. It's a difficult thing to do and few people in the game, at any time, have been able to do that kind of thing.

"Peter Barnes was good at it, but Tommy's was closer control than Peter Barnes'. Finney's control was so close that he never lost possession. He was crafty and he always knew where you were. He always had the ball further away from you than himself – always. You had to follow him to get anywhere near it – then he would switch it. Tommy's control was just too close, he was quick, he was elusive. Raich Carter once told me that if he played in the same team as Tommy there was no telling how many goals he would score in a season. He would have filled the net up if he had played with Tommy Finney in the team.

"That was Tommy Finney. He had all the great attributes, all the great awareness. He was always aware of his position and yours – but above all, he was brilliant inside the 18-yard box. He would make a bee-line for that. If you brought him down it would have been a penalty. He had the ability to beat you in the 18-yard box. As you approach goal the pitch gets narrower. When you're inside the 18-yard box it's narrower still, hence the congestion, but he could beat you even inside the six-yard box. No disrespect to any of the great players, George Best, Stanley Matthews – great players, but Finney had even closer control than them. When he had the ball it was his. He would carry it – it was his. I cannot emphasise that any more. Cruyff could play, a great player, but Tommy could puncture a team from the wings. He was more composed than other great players. Many of them were showy and flashy. Tommy Finney could do all that they could do and still stay calm and composed.

"Even in the days of players costing up to £1 million, Tommy Finney would have been worth £5 million. You couldn't begin to talk for less than that – No way! If I was the manager of a club with Tommy Finney at his peak, I would have paid at least £5 million for him. Knowing what I know about him, I wouldn't have hesitated."

It is a measure of Tom Finney's ability and status that he was twice Footballer of the Year in 1954 and 1957 – and in 1979 he was honoured with the PFA Merit Award, the year after it was bestowed upon Bill Shankly.

Tommy Docherty

Tommy Docherty has earned a good living in recent years as an after-dinner speaker and media 'expert'. His sharp wit is acclaimed throughout soccerdom and he has enjoyed himself as a kind of 'clown prince' of pundits.

He was previously a good manager. Of course there are some who might contest that – but there is no doubt that he gave the various clubs that he managed a certain fire and excitement. In the case of Manchester United, he restored their pride and took them into Europe by way of winning the FA Cup and a high placing in the Football League. As a manager he was among the most colourful of characters in a world of characters. During his days as Chelsea manager he was feted by the many celebrities who flocked to Stamford Bridge in the trendy 1960s.

Because of his larger-than-life image, it is easy to forget that he was also an exceptional footballer who was, indeed, rated by Bill Shankly among his all-time heroes.

Tommy Docherty was born in Glasgow on 24 August 1928, and was a kindred spirit of Shankly, in that he came from a soccer-crazy family who lived on the bread-line while maintaining a sharp determination to succeed and a sense of humour that challenged and defeated failure.

Docherty's career began with Celtic. Later he played for Arsenal and Chelsea and was capped 25 times by his country. But it was as a half-back in nearly 400 senior games for Preston that he achieved most of his fame as a player. From 1949 to 1957 he commanded the middle of the field and, during that time, Preston maintained a very high profile in English soccer.

"Preston had paid £4,000 to sign him as a direct replacement for Shankly. Bill could not resist writing to his fellow Scot and congratulating him on joining a fine team. Neither could he resist offering Docherty some mischievous advice. 'Just put the number-four shirt on – it knows what to do,' was the famous line which brought a great laugh from Docherty and became one of his favourite tales.

In truth Shankly knew that Preston could hardly have found a better replacement and he rarely missed an opportunity to say so.

"Tommy Docherty was the same sort of player as me. He came in and did very well for Preston. He was a very good buy for them at £4,000. He was a very good player, a hard man but a very skilful one. I would love to have had Tommy in my team.

"I remember saying to him once that if we had five Tommy Dochertys, five Bill Shanklys and a goalkeeper, we would beat the world. He said to me, 'If we had five Tommy Dochertys and five Bill Shanklys we wouldn't need a goalkeeper!' That was Tommy's joke, but I think he meant it really.

"If I was picking my team to take on the rest, Tommy Docherty would be one of the first on the sheet."

Perhaps Shankly would have wanted Docherty in the dressing room as much for his reports as for his obvious playing abilities. As Docherty once said while he was the manager for Chelsea:-

"I talk a lot – on any subject – which is always football!"

Tommy Lawton
Another of Shankly's heroes was Tommy Lawton. Lawton was probably best-known for his 90 goals in 151 League games for Notts County from 1947 to 1951, but he was already a star centre-forward before he ever arrived at Meadow Lane.

Tommy Lawton was born in Bolton on 6 October 1919. Playing for Castle Hill School he scored an amazing 570 goals in three seasons. His career began with Burnley Juniors. On his 17th birthday he signed professional forms, and just four days later he scored a hat-trick against Spurs. He hit 16 goals in 25 League games and mighty Everton were so impressed that they bought him in January 1937, to replace Dixie Dean. He did not disappoint them, scoring 65 goals in 87 matches.

World War Two intervened in Lawton's career, but when the Football League programme restarted he joined Notts County for £20,000. From 1951 to 1953 he played for Brentford and his tally was 17 goals in 50 games. His final bugle call came when he joined Arsenal in September 1953 and played 35 League games which yielded 13 goals. He didn't quite finish there because he then took his skills to non-League Kettering.

Along the way he scored 22 goals in 23 full internationals for England, a phenomenal record that has never been surpassed pound for pound.

"He was a great player. I played against him several times and he was always trouble. You had to stop the ball getting to him because, if you didn't, it would soon be in the net. He was probably one of the very best goalscorers that England has ever produced. A great centre-forward."

Shankly spoke from experience. After all, Tommy Lawton had scored in that memorable England victory at Hampden Park in April 1939 – and it had been Bill's failure to stop Matthews putting the ball across to Lawton that had sealed Scotland's fate that day.

Matt Busby

Not only were Busby and Shankly team-mates for Scotland, they were also good friends even though they were rival managers. Busby was born in Orbiston, near Bellshill to the north-east of Glasgow, on 26 May 1909. Like Bill Shankly he was from a mining family and was also born into a hard life. His father was killed in World War One.

His soccer career began with local side Denny Hibs but, in 1928, he was invited to join Manchester City. He stayed for eight successful years until signing for Liverpool, where he remained until enlisting for World War Two. Liverpool wanted him back as a player after the war but Manchester United made him a more challenging offer as manager. The rest, as they say, is history.

For a quality half-back who captained his country in war-time internationals, it is quite amazing to see in the record books that Matt officially played only one full international for Scotland – in a defeat by Wales in 1934.

However, it was his career in management and his survival of the Munich Air Disaster that endeared Matt to millions and also earned the very high regard of Bill Shankly, who said;

"Matt Busby is, without doubt, the greatest manager that ever lived. I'm not saying that I think he's the greatest manager, I'm saying that he is the greatest manager. The man was blessed with ability and of course he used that ability. Until Matt got his young boys ready, he used his older players – then, of course, came the Busby Babes. That was Matt's foresight – his ability. Everything that a man needs to become a football manager, Matt Busby has. There is no doubt, he's an inspiration to anyone – always willing to help you.

"What Manchester United is today, is what Matt Busby created at the beginning. Old Trafford was bombed, made derelict, during the war. He rebuilt it – and the club!"

Denis Law
Another of soccer's all-time greats will tell you that he owes a great deal to Bill Shankly – who was his first manager at Huddersfield in 1955.

"It was Bill, if my memory serves me correctly, who came down to the railway station in the Yorkshire town to meet me. And what a shock he must have had!" Said Law. "There I stood, bag in one hand, ticket in the other, a slim – to put it politely – lad. A strange lad in strange surroundings and, to cap it all, sporting a pair of steel-rimmed spectacles.

"I don't know exactly what Bill's feelings were. I seem to remember that he cast an anxious eye up and down and around the entire station, as if he was unwilling to believe that this was the lad who had come down from Aberdeen to join his team on the strong recommendation of their Scottish section.

"Fortunately for them, and me, I was able to prove in my first practice match with Huddersfield that I did possess a bit of ability. I was built up, and I grew up, an operation was performed on my eyes – and the rest you know."

Seen through Shankly's eyes he 'Looked like a skinned rabbit!' Shankly qualified that curious description of a wannabe professional footballer when he explained the early days of his association with Denis Law.

"When he came to us he looked a poor little lad. He was small and very thin. He had legs like a chicken and he wore spectacles because he had a squint. I wasn't sure, at the time, if this was someone's idea of a little joke. But then I saw him play and I knew that this was no joke. I thought, 'yes, we can do something with him'. But we'd a lot to do to build him up. We made sure that he had plenty of steak and milk, and we got his eyes sorted out. He had ability – we had to get him fit and healthy and show him how to use those abilities.

"He was a very good boy though – very polite and willing. He worked hard. He was dedicated and that is so very important."

Denis Law was born in Aberdeen on 24 February 1940. His career has turned him into one of the most famous Scots of all time. After getting his first-team chance at the age of 16, away to Notts County on 24 December 1956, Law had impressed so much that Shankly told reporters after the game that the young boy from Aberdeen was destined to become one of the biggest names in the game. He even predicted that he would get 80 or so caps for Scotland.

Law's career took him to Manchester City in March 1960, followed by a spell in Italy with Torino, which he hated, and then to Manchester United in August 1962 for a ten-year relationship which saw his fame develop into stardom. He ended his career in 1974 after one last season back at Maine Road.

Shankly's prediction of a glittering career had proven to be correct. Law was European Footballer of the Year in 1964 and won many domestic awards as well as medals for both League championships and the FA Cup. And those Scotland caps? Well, Shankly's thought that Law would win 80 caps did not allow for potential injuries. As it turned out, he played 55 times in senior internationals – more than enough to get him into the Scottish FA's Hall of Fame. His 30 goals for his country were equalled by Kenny Dalglish, but have never yet been beaten.

Law points to the role that Shankly played in his career as being the best launching pad that any rising star could have had.

"I worked for two of the greatest managers of all time – Shankly and Busby. I owe everything to those two men. Bill Shankly didn't just give me my first chance but helped me so much more than that. He was a great man and a great manager. He took a personal interest. He had no time for shirkers, but if you gave your all then he would give you everything in return. He was a marvellous, marvellous man. He looked at players for what they could be rather than what they were. He would provide everything for what you could be and the rest was up to you. As a skinny kid arriving at Huddersfield, even though I didn't know it then, I was at the best possible place in the world to help at that time to help my career. Mr Shankly was the best!"

George Best

In the 1960s George Best was simply sensational – not only on the pitch but off it as well. He was the first real pop-star player. He was on an equal footing with stars like the Beatles and the Rolling Stones, commanding front-page headlines every time he sneezed. Perhaps it was with Best in mind that motivated Bill Shankly to issue a warning to all young players.

"Today, as in the past, we have people within the game who believe that one can continue to play fair football while also seeking the bright lights outside the game. I will admit that there have been instances of players doing both. But I will never tolerate the suggestion that one can burn the candle at both ends and still not have it affect your football. Whenever I'm told about a player who does this, I answer; 'but how much better he would be – and for how much longer too – if he'd only finish with the bright lights!' The really honest folk within the game will all agree with me. Looking back over the years we have seen too many examples the other way – of players going downhill into dismal oblivion – because they believed that they were different from the rest and would be able to mix the two You can't!"

If Shankly did have Best in mind – and many other cases could be cited – it may seem a little strange that Bill included George among his favourite players. Whatever he thought about Best's extra-curricular activities he made no attempt to hide his admiration for his breathtaking football talents. He also had some sympathy for him, knowing the culture shock that Best must have experienced when he sampled life in Manchester after an upbringing in a small-time area of Belfast.

Best was born on 22 May 1946. He was barely out of short trousers than he was in them again – well, football shorts anyway. As a gawky kid of 15 he arrived at Old Trafford. Within a few days he was back in Belfast again, having run away from this new frightening environment.

The rest of the Best career has been well chronicled. He spent ten years at Old Trafford, and probably gave Matt Busby more thrills and spills than all the other players put together. His career fizzled out with appearances for Stockport, Fulham and Bournemouth – as well as spells in non-League and American soccer.

For sheer skill and excitement few could hold a candle to him. It was unfortunate that he held the candle himself and did indeed have it well lit at both ends.

But let's not dwell on that aspect of his life. Instead let's join Bill Shankly and rejoice in the talent of one of the greatest footballers who ever lived. He scored 137 goals in 361 League matches for Manchester United in addition to 19 FA Cup goals, six of which were scored in a memorable 8-2 win at North-ampton in February 1970.

During his time at Old Trafford, two League championships were won plus the FA Cup. Then, on that night of nights at Wembley in 1968, Manchester United at last won the European Cup. George Best was in sparkling form that night and hit one of United's four goals.

On the international scene, he scored eight goals in 37 appearances for Northern Ireland. It is unfortunate that he never had the chance to perform in a World Cup finals tournament or the European Championship for he would surely have won even greater acclaim. As it was he was named Footballer of the Year in 1968, and landed a great double when he was picked as European Footballer of the Year just a few weeks later a feat accomplished two years earlier by team-mate Bobby Charlton.

"He was a very special player, a truly great one," said Bill Shankly, when listing Best among his all-time favourites. "He had tremendous skill, he had speed, he had awareness. He could show all the same abilities as others – but he could do it while sprinting. He had magical feet. Marvellous to watch but frightening if you were playing against him. When we played Manchester United, I never mentioned him in my match talk because I didn't want to worry my players. Best was a gem."

Much later there was a verbal clash between George Best and one of Shankly's other heroes – Kevin Keegan. Keegan suggested that Best had done football a disservice because of his well-publicised off-the-pitch activities. But Best was quick to respond.

"To call Keegan a superstar is stretching a point. Skill-wise there are a lot of better players around. He's not fit to lace my boots as a player."

Regrettably, Shankly had died before this scuffle of words. It would have been interesting to ask him for his comment.

Jimmy Greaves
It might perhaps seem a little unusual too that Jimmy Greaves should also be on Shankly's list of greats. An Englishman who was never renowned for diving in where the feet were flying, Greaves had a special talent for scoring goals that earned Shankly's deep admiration.

"He was an efficient goalscorer. He always got the ones that you should get. A lot of players will score spectacular goals and then miss many more that were quite simple. Greaves wasn't like that. He didn't try to burst the net, he was just happy to see the ball cross the line even from the lightest of taps. That's the sign of a cool, calculating, professional goalscorer. That's the sort of player who wins you things."

Jimmy Greaves was born in East Ham on 20 February 1940. It was not far from West Ham's Upton Park ground, and that was where he concluded his League career in 1970. But his glory years had, of course, been well before that. As a 17-year-old he made his first-team debut for Chelsea and between 1957 and 1960 he scored an incredible 124 goals in 157 League matches.

That was just the start. He went to AC Milan for a very unhappy season until Tottenham rescued him in December 1961 for £99,999, just one pound less than Denis Law's record move to Torino six months earlier. With Spurs Jimmy Greaves hit the headlines again – more than 220 times. That's how many League goals he scored in 321 games.

Greaves remained a Tottenham player until his move to West Ham in March 1970. He played for England at Youth and Under-23 levels before making the first of his 57 senior appearances – which resulted in 44 goals. During his Tottenham days, Greaves picked up two FA Cup winners' medals and a European Cup-winners' Cup winners medal.

With a career total of 357 League goals in 516 games, it is easy to see why Bill Shankly had such an admiration for Jimmy Greaves.

"He was up there with the best of them – Mannion, Carter, Lawton. I would put Greaves alongside Law. They were both brilliant finishers – you won't see any better. If Greaves or Law were through with only the goalkeeper to beat, you could get your tea out and drink it – it's going to be a goal, no question. If the goalkeeper comes out they'll go past him. If they're forced out wide they'll put it in from a bad angle. If the goalkeeper stays on his line they'll take the ball round him and tap it in. That's the sort of confidence of Greaves and Law. It's a gift. Jimmy Greaves could score a goal if the ball was a foot off the bye-line... any bye-line, goal-line, or side-line.

"How many times do you see players put through and they fail with only the goalkeeper to beat. They lose possession to the goalkeeper, they put the ball wide or over the bar. They don't know what to do, either because they have not been taught, or because they don't have the instinct. Greaves was well-taught but he was also a natural, instinctive goalscorer. When Jimmy Greaves was in that position he said, 'Thank you very much', because he knew he was going to score a goal."

That was the wonder of Greaves.

Ferenc Puskas

"Please sir, take me to your country and teach me to play football." That was the request from a young autograph hunter at the Cumberland Hotel in London after Ferenc Puskas had led

Hungary to that historic 6-3 win over England at Wembley in 1953. If Bill Shankly had been there he would probably have asked if he could go too. He was a big fan of Hungarian football during the 1950s and especially of Ferenc Puskas.

It is probably difficult for today's younger soccer fans to truly appreciate what exactly all the fuss was about in 1953. Shankly was there at Wembley.

"I was glad I was there. I was very lucky to see it. The skill of the Hungarians was just amazing. I remember one ball coming across from Puskas – and it was just like Jack Nicklaus hitting a golf ball. Puskas put a spin on it and you could watch the markings on the ball as it went, not only perfectly where he wanted it – but actually slowing down to make it playable when it arrived. Puskas could do that."

It was not the only time that Shankly watched the great man with such admiration. He also saw him in action with Real Madrid and also had a much closer encounter some years later.

Another soccer legend was Real Madrid's Francisco Gento who gave a wonderful behind-the-scenes revelation of the skills of Puskas.

"His shooting was unbelievable and his left foot was like a hand, he could do anything with it. In the showers he would even juggle with the soap!"

Ferenc Puskas was born on 2 April 1926, and was immediately nicknamed 'Ocsi', which means 'Kid brother', because he was a second son. He still signs letters to friends with that nickname. He played in the streets of Kispest with a ball made of socks and rags, but he went on to mega-stardom. At 17 he was playing in full internationals for Hungary and eventually won 84 caps, scoring 85 goals. After the Hungarian political problems of 1956 he settled in Austria and later in Spain, where he also played for the national side four times.

As a club player he starred with Honved and Real Madrid and won just about every medal available, as well as winning countless scoring awards. He was in the Hungary side that lost the 1954 World Cup Final but two years earlier had picked up Olympic Gold. In 1960, with Real Madrid, he won the European

Cup in a Final played against Eintracht Frankfurt at Hampden Park. Bill Shankly was there that night too.

"It was one of the greatest games that I have ever seen. It was a spectacle. Real slaughtered Eintracht – and Puskas, together with the great Di Stefano, were in the middle of everything. Real won 7-3 and were in total command despite the three goals scored by Eintracht. It was a night for goals. They were all spectacular and exciting."

Puskas returned to Britain for another European Cup Final in 1971 at Wembley. He was manager of Panathinaikos, who were pitched against Ajax in the Final. The Greek club were beaten 2-0, but not before Shankly had the chance to witness another demonstration of skill by the then 45-year-old Puskas.

"His side used our training ground at Melwood to prepare for the Final and it was a pleasure and an honour to have them with us. They were giving their goalkeeper some extra practice and we all watched. In fact I think that all the Greeks in Liverpool were there. They gave me free fish and chips for the rest of my life because their team was using our training ground.

"Anyway, Puskas put the ball on the 18-yard mark and then shot it with his left foot about a foot inside the post. He did it 12 times in succession. Remember, he had finished playing then so I don't know what he would have done from 12 yards with a penalty. He lashed the ball just a few inches above the grass and into the corner of the net. I wanted to see him doing it. Puskas could play all right – fantastic.

"Hidegkuti was another amazing Hungarian player, absolutely brilliant with Puskas. Then there was Di Stefano, an incredible player. With Puskas and Di Stefano playing together, Real Madrid were one of the best teams I have ever seen. They also had Hector Rial who, like Di Stefano, was Argentinian. Then there were Gento, Didi, Santa Maria – all terrific players. But the pick of them all was Ferenc Puskas."

Eusebio
Bill Shankly willingly acknowledged that one of the best footballers of all time was Pelé. He had no doubt about it.

"Pelé was marvellous. He had terrific skill and he was as strong as an ox. He was a heavyweight in football terms – a big frame, big bones, very hard to move off the ball. He was great, one of THE greatest players of all time – but Eusebio had the edge for me."

Eusebio da Silva Ferreira was born in Mozambique on 25 January 1942, one of eight children. They all lived in a tin shack no bigger than the average caravan. His father died when he was five and he grew up very quickly. Even as a boy he became famous in Mozambique for his sporting prowess. He was very good at basketball, a champion sprinter and, by the time he was 17, he was a professional footballer. When word reached Benfica, they stepped in to sign him. The deal meant security for his family so he could not resist the chance to move to Europe.

The rest is history now. In 1965, Eusebio was European Footballer of the Year and he won many domestic honours as well as the European Cup in 1962. British soccer fans took the Black Panther to their hearts. They saw him heartbroken at Wembley in 1963 when he scored in the European Cup Final, only to see his Benfica side lose 1-2 to AC Milan. He was heartbroken again in 1966 at Wembley when England dumped his Portugal side out of the World Cup and again, in 1968, he was back for another tearful European Cup Final – this time losing 1-4 to Manchester United.

British fans saw him as a man with genuine skills combined with great sportsmanship. He would not have known how to take a dive. Was he the European Pelé? Was he as good as Pelé? or was he better?

"I think he could do all that Pelé could do but I think he was just that little bit faster and, for me, that made him the better of the two. No disrespect to Pelé, who was many people's ideal footballer, but in my opinion Eusebio was even better – and if Portugal had won the World Cup, he would have been given status above Pelé."

Diego Maradona
If Eusebio was a hero to British fans then Maradona was a villain.

He represents the less savoury side of Latin culture to the majority of Anglo-Saxons. The famous 'hand of God' incident in the 1986 World Cup was simply the icing on the cake as far as England supporters were concerned – and despite the plaudits from the pundits, most of them refuse point-blank to regard him as anything more than a cheating Argentinean.

However, Bill Shankly recognised something different in Diego the teenager. The incidents involving drugs, guns and the more seedy side of life, only came to the fore in the Maradona story after Bill had died. He would probably have been dismayed because he saw Maradona as a potential soccer genius.

Diego Maradona was born on 30 October 1960 in Lanus, an area of Buenos Aires. His rise from the mean streets of poverty to the stadia of prosperity has been well recorded but – just to put the record straight – he began with Argentinos Juniors before joining Boca Juniors. Barcelona brought him to Europe and, having stolen the show in South American soccer, he proceeded to repeat his performances under the critical gaze of the crowned football heads of the continent.

Napoli, FC Seville and Newell's Old Boys are among others he has served and, of course, he has been a World winner for his country, both at Under-21 and senior levels. Nicknamed 'Pibe de Oro' – the Golden Kid – he certainly had the Midas touch with his feet. In 1986 he was named World Footballer of the Year. There are few awards or honours that he has not won and, from an unbiased point of view, he has had the skill to rub shoulders with the greatest names in soccer history.

"Maradona, in his early international career, emerged as possibly the best player in the game at the time," said Shankly. "At 19 he has all the natural skills that other players have to work hard for. He also does everything at breakneck speed and he needs to learn to slow down a little bit. He is full of enthusiasm and ability, but he needs to become a little more composed. At 19 he can do that – he is still very young and has time to learn these things.

"He sometimes looks for a penalty when a goal might be easier. A goal is always better than a penalty, he should remember that. He works hard and covers a lot of ground. At the end of a match he must be really tired. He's young and he can use up the energy but he doesn't really need to do all that if he would just slow down a bit and share the work. You can't burn yourself up all the time, you must conserve some energy.

"He could be so lethal and beat people in the box, terrific skill – but he should let others do the fetching and carrying and not try to do everything himself. If he can learn to do that he will be the best in the game."

Of course Shankly made these comments long before Maradona matured into the player who achieved world fame for a variety of different reasons. Shankly's appraisal was right on the mark – for that time. What a disappointment he would have felt if he had still been alive today.

Frank Worthington

Probably there will be a few raised eyebrows when the name of Frank Worthington crops up among Bill Shankly's favourites – but Shankly had such a high regard for Worthington that he tried to buy him.

Worthington was born in Halifax on 23 November 1948. He was destined for a career that was going to take him on a trip from club to club around England and eight full caps for England too.

He began as a trainee with Huddersfield and became a full professional in November 1966. His various transfers then took him to Leicester, Bolton, Birmingham, Leeds, Sunderland, Southampton, Brighton, Tranmere, Preston and Stockport.

Worthington's longest spells with one club were with Huddersfield and Leicester. Having made the Huddersfield first team he played 171 League games and hit 41 goals – a feat that he bettered at Leicester with 72 League goals in 210 games. His eight caps were all won in the mid-1970s and he scored two goals.

In some respects he followed the George Best school of soccer stardom in that Frank enjoyed the more glitzy side of life. He used to sing and might well have achieved showbiz stardom had it not been for his soccer career. On the other hand he might well have achieved soccer immortality were it not for his quest for the life of a pop-star.

Worthington was not just a colourful character though. He was a very good attacking footballer – which is why Bill Shankly was interested in him.

"I wanted to sign him. I wanted to pay £150,000 for him. The reason that I didn't sign him was nothing to do with me. He was turned down on medical grounds. The medical man at Liverpool examined him and said, 'You can't sign him'. So we had no choice. It was out of our hands.

"But I would have signed him and he would have done a job for us. He was an old-fashioned centre-forward type. I liked him. He was strong, he was brave, and he knew how to score goals. That's all I needed to know about him. If he had played for Liverpool he would have become even more famous and won a lot more England caps."

Freddie Hill

Freddie Hill won two England caps in 1963 against Northern Ireland and Wales. That was his claim to fame – but how different it might have been if Bill Shankly had made him a part of the Liverpool super-team as he had intended.

Hill was a Yorkshireman – born in Sheffield on 7 January 1940 – but his career began with Bolton Juniors on the other side of the Pennines. He played for Bolton from 1957 to 1968 and scored 74 League goals in 375 games. Later he played for Halifax, Manchester City and Peterborough.

He was a very clever forward, highly rated by Bill Shankly, even though most soccer fans today would have to research the record books to find out just who he was.

"Freddie Hill was, for me, the best player of his day in England. I remember going to see him play in a Cup-tie for Bolton against West Ham and he just tore West Ham to pieces. He was a marvelously talented player, very skilful. I wanted to sign him. I said 'he's for me'. For £45,000 he was going to be the steal of the century. But once again our medical specialist said no and we couldn't sign him.

"I was disappointed and I knew that Freddie was too. But in transfer cases like that the medical men have the say. I was sorry about that, very sorry. He was an excellent player, good control, great at deception. Ability-wise no one could turn him down – it was just a great shame about the medical."

Hill made 510 League appearances for his clubs and scored 87 goals. With Anfield as his stage, he too might have become one of the most famous performers of post-war English football.

Billy Bremner

A fellow Scot who would have been welcomed into any Shankly team was Billy Bremner, who was as tenacious a player as Bill Shankly himself had been. He was born in Stirling on 9 December 1942, but all of his professional career was in England except, of course, for his many international appearances for Scotland.

Originally an inside-forward, Bremner joined Leeds straight from school after winning Scottish Schoolboy international caps. He became a full professional in December 1959, and thus began an amazing run of 585 League games for the club which he later captained. During his reign Leeds won the League championship twice, the FA Cup, the League Cup and the Fairs Cup.

He was at his best in midfield, tenacious in the tackle – but also quick to attack. Bremner was considered a hard man, just as Shankly had also been. He rarely felt the need to verbally defend his all-action style of play but did once say, "I'm no angel – but I've never kicked anyone deliberately."

At the start of the 1968-69 season, Bremner took over the captaincy of Scotland from John Greig. In all he made 54 senior appearances for his country – another name for Scotland's Hall of Fame, and another name for Shankly's hall of heroes. He knew exactly where Bremner was coming from, what motivated him and what mattered to him.

"We spoke the same language. He was captain of Leeds, I was manager of Liverpool. We were in enemy camps but we understood each other. Billy Bremner was one of the finest half-backs that Scotland has produced. I once told someone that he was so good he could have worn one of my shirts. A great player. They don't make them like Billy Bremner very often."

Bremner's career took him to Hull and Doncaster Rovers during his twilight zone, and later he went into management. By the time he did that, Bill Shankly was ending his days – otherwise the two men might well have spent more time together.

"I would definitely have been on the phone to him for advice. We never had that much to do with each other during my playing days but, if you wanted to know something as a manager, he would have been one of those I would have turned to," said Bremner.

Shankly would certainly have been keen to help, mostly because of his admiration for Bremner the player.

"Bremner was exceptional. I also admired Bobby Collins and Norman Hunter, all three were great Leeds players – but Billy Bremner was outstanding. He was a joy to watch – unless, that is, we were playing against him."

Alan Ball

Bill Shankly considered Alan Ball to be one of the best in the world when he was at his peak. He admired his single-minded competitiveness and would have loved to have seen him in the red shirt of Liverpool rather than the blue of Everton. He was one of only two or three players that Shankly considered having man-marked when he was planning his tactics.

Ball will be forever famous as a leading member of England's 1966 World Cup squad – but his contribution to the game has been so much more than that. He was born on 12 May 1945 in Farnworth, and followed in the career of his father. Alan Ball senior played for Southport, Birmingham, Oldham and Rochdale before going into management. Ball junior began at Blackpool but then moved to Everton, Arsenal, Southampton, Vancouver, back to Blackpool, Hong Kong and Bristol Rovers. He had an amazing career which was topped by 72 full England appearances yielding just eight goals but dozens of bouquets. Later, he too went into management.

"The only thing that stops me becoming a world-class player is that I don't score enough goals," Ball once said. Bill Shankly was among those who disagreed with him.

"Alan Ball was world class, he was my kind of player. Yes sir, Ball was a very special player – I would have paid a high price for him. He had so much energy and he had the skill to match. He could read a game, he could beat players, pass the ball, plan things, carry out things, set people up. He was creative and he had a tremendous will to win. That's my kind of player all right."

A teenager when he made his England debut, Alan Ball joined Everton just a month after the 1966 World Cup when Blackpool received a then British record £110,000.

"If I could have signed him I would have paid much more than that," said Shankly. "Ball was well worth more than just breaking a transfer record for. For me he was one of the greatest footballers of the century."

And the Rest

Bill Shankly rarely admitted that he admired a player until that man was wearing a Liverpool shirt. His Liverpool heroes get their own chapter – but there are one or two other names that have not yet been mentioned. These are players whom Shankly would mention in dispatches, so to speak. Players who he regarded with esteem.

Among them were Paddy Crerand, of Manchester United and Scotland, Dave Mackay, of Hearts, Tottenham, Derby, Swindon and Scotland, and Jim Baxter, of Rangers, Sunderland, Nottingham Forest and Scotland.

"I remember seeing Baxter and Crerand together playing for Scotland at Hampden. It was a bone hard ground but Baxter and Crerand conducted the orchestra. They beat England 2-0 – and it was the first time that I had seen a lap of honour done by a Scottish team – but it was Baxter and Crerand who had masterminded the win. They played the ball with such skill that it looked as if they were playing on a good soft ground instead of such a hard surface.

"It annoys me to think that Scotland have never won anything yet they could put on a display like that with such great players.

"I have seen some marvellous players from all countries through the years and I would have loved to have signed them all for Liverpool. But you can't do that of course. Sometimes it is enough just to have seen."

Liverpool Heroes

THERE were heroes and there were Liverpool heroes! Bill Shankly did not like to single out any one of his players to elevate them above the others, but he did say enough to give us a pretty good idea of which Liverpool players he admired the most. It wasn't just the Reds whom he personally signed either – Shankly also took notice of the Anfield stars who arrived after his departure.

Kenny Dalglish, after being introduced to Bill Shankly by John Toshack, remarked: "It was Tosh who took me to see Shanks. After training one day he said to me that I should come up with him and see Shanks for a little while. It was like a pilgrimage. Tosh had been signed by Shanks and he was obviously still very close to him. I think that all the older, more experienced players at Liverpool were. They still somehow thought of Shanks as the boss because, before he had retired, Bob Paisley had been the trainer.

"It wasn't any lack of respect for Bob – it was just that Shanks had been the gaffer for so long, and had signed so many of them, that they still had this feeling for the man."

That sums up the relationship between Shankly and his players. They were his heroes and he, of course, was theirs. Not theirs alone either! Even in retirement – even in death – Shankly has continued to be the father of Liverpool. Following is a list of some of his favourite sons, many of whom have had a share in the Shankly Legacy and passed on some of that treasure to others.

Ian St John

Bill Shankly twice wanted to sign Ian St John. The first time was for Huddersfield but the board would not provide the cash. As we have already seen, hard-up Liverpool raised the money to make Shankly's second attempt more successful. It was a move that sent St John on the road to stardom, a road that is still winding its way through an interesting life. In his Anfield days, St John pulled a Liverpool shirt over his head, today it is the 'cans' of broadcasting. He has maintained his status as a household name simply by switching from stadia to media. Nothing could have been further from his mind when he was a boy in Motherwell. All he wanted from life, in those days, was to play football.

Ian St John was born in Motherwell on 7 June 1938. He was good at school, both in and out of the classroom, and showed tremendous football ability. Nevertheless he took a job in a local steelworks until Motherwell gave him a full-time professional contract worth £16 per week.

Even at that time he showed an aptitude for coaching and took a keen interest in that side of the game. He even travelled to watch Real Madrid training at Kilmarnock before their European Cup Final with Eintracht Frankfurt.

He enjoyed playing at Motherwell but, for the sake of his family, he felt the need to try to get a transfer to an English club. At first Motherwell refused his request. Newcastle was waiting in the wings and so he asked again. This time Motherwell, realising that it would only be a matter of time before they lost him anyway, went along with his transfer request. Bill Shankly's timing was perfect.

"He came up to see me in a match and I met the great man for the first time. He struck me as a caricature of James Cagney. He had a tremendous aura about him. He asked me about joining Liverpool, but I wasn't that keen since they were then only a Second Division club.

"We went to meet him again the next morning – and the next thing I knew, my wife and I were being driven to Liverpool in a Rolls-Royce there and then. All the way Shankly kept telling me how great Liverpool were, and how they were going to win everything. I didn't take him seriously of course. The first person that I met when we got there was Reuben Bennett, who had coached me when I was a young lad at Motherwell. I think that when I saw him I was convinced.

"The very next night I'm playing for Liverpool at Goodison in the Liverpool Senior Cup – in front of 60,000 people. I couldn't believe it. We lost 4-3 but I got a hat-trick and the whole night was quite an experience.

"It was typical of Bill Shankly to orchestrate everything from start to finish. He was determined that I was going to sign and I'm convinced that he would have had me press-ganged me if I hadn't agreed to go."

Hitting a hat-trick at Everton made Ian St John a Liverpool hero overnight. He remained at Anfield for nine glorious seasons and scored 95 League goals in 336 games. He became a folk-hero. His goals and his assists were the life's blood of the Liverpool fans, especially since he had played such a major part in winning the championship twice, and the FA Cup.

During those champagne days at Liverpool, St John supplied the bubbles – just as Bill Shankly knew he would.

"St John was my first great signing for Liverpool," said Shankly.

We have already looked at the circumstances behind that significant £30,000 record signing, but the whole episode demonstrates Shankly's knowledge and determination. He knew how important Ian St John could be to Liverpool.

"I knew that there was no risk in buying Ian St John. You just know with some players that you could stake your life on them. With St John and Yeats – if I had had the money personally I would have used it to buy them. That's how much I knew they would be a safe investment.

"Ian St John was a great player. He was strong, he had football skills, he could score goals and he'd a good football brain – he could run the show up front. You don't get many players like that. I knew he would do a great job for us – and he did!"

Although he had made the Scotland senior side before leaving Motherwell, the majority of St John's caps came during his Liverpool career. In all he appeared in 21 full internationals and hit nine goals. He is still highly respected North of the Border as, indeed, he is on Merseyside.

In 1970 he left Liverpool and played with Hellenic in South Africa for a while. In September 1971, he joined Coventry and made a useful contribution there for more than a year, until transferring to Tranmere in October 1972, where he ended his playing days in that season.

He had a little dabble in management with Motherwell and Portsmouth and also spent some time as coach at Sheffield Wednesday. But he was in great demand as a media man and decided to pursue that career – which would also give him time to continue with his coaching interests. He and his son, Ian junior, run soccer training camps throughout the year all over Britain – hoping that they can help aspiring youngsters on the way to hearing their own names echo around a stadium as did Ian St John.

Ron Yeats
If Ian St John was the chisel of the Liverpool attack, then Ron Yeats can only be described as the anvil of the defence. He joined the club only a few months after St John and proved to be yet another Shankly 'superbuy'. Ron Yeats himself, however, never really thought that he would rise to such dizzy heights of soccer stardom.

"I didn't come up the usual way, through the junior sides in a club. I did it the hard way," Yeats explained. "I was working in a slaughter-house in Aberdeen for some time after I left school. I just played in youth football until I was 18, when I joined Dundee United.

"There was little doubt in my own mind that I'd never be anything more than an ordinary sort of player. I had no thoughts of greatness or any of that stuff. Bill Shankly changed all that! He arrived on my doorstep one day – it was the first time that I had ever met him – and he said that he wanted to sign me. Quite honestly, I was amazed.

"He said to me, 'Liverpool are going up next season and I'm going to build the side to do that around you and Ian St John'. There I was, expecting to have an average career in the game, when along comes Shankly to tell me that he's building a team around me. Imagine what that did for my confidence."

It was 22 July 1961, that Yeats signed for Liverpool. Dundee United received £30,000, and could probably have got more if only they had realised just how keen Shankly was to sign the 23-year-old former Schoolboy international.

"He would be a good buy at £300,000. This is a great centre-half that I've signed today," said Shankly.

Neither of them knew then, that just a few years later, Yeats would become the very first Liverpool captain to be presented with the FA Cup. However, Shankly had a pretty shrewd idea that he was buying someone a bit special.

"I had seen St John and Yeats play against each other. Yeats was a tower. We went up to Dundee and saw him, but the club turned us down. The next morning they phoned and told us we could have him for £30,000. We met in Edinburgh the next day and he signed. Now they – Yeats and St John – were two of the greatest signings. They were the start of the Liverpool Football Club. Yeats could have played in the Second Division with no other defenders and won it. Fantastic man – 6ft, one and a half inches, but the quickest thing on two legs. Strong as an ox. There were very few in the game in the same class."

Shankly might not like to pick out his players for special acclaim but he did like to express himself from time to time, and he meant what he said about Yeats. In response, Yeats acknowledged the part that Shankly played in shaping his career.

"He gave me a lot of confidence. He made any player feel like a great player. If you feel like one, then you'll play like one. Even when we lost, the boss would prove that it was all a mistake – the winning goal was offside, one of our blokes was fouled – that sort of thing.

"Another thing is that there were no non-triers in a Shankly team. He wouldn't tolerate any lax attitudes – no matter who you were. We didn't have any stars really – everyone was treated the same."

When Ron Yeats finally left Liverpool in 1971, it was to join neighbours Tranmere Rovers as player-manager. He remained until April 1975. During his time there, as we have already mentioned, he was joined by Bill Shankly.

It was his Liverpool career that made him famous. All the fans thought the world of the man that they'd nicknamed 'Rowdy' – after the character in the TV series *Rawhide*. The championship, the FA Cup, and countless other awards came his way.

It seems incredible that he was capped only twice by Scotland – but Yeats himself just shrugs that off. His pride is in having made around 450 appearances for Liverpool and, in 1986, he again became part of the Anfield set-up. He returned as chief scout.

Shankly's knock on his front door back in 1961 had opened the way to more than just a new club – it had flung open the entrance to a completely new life.

Peter Thompson

To buy one of the best left-wingers of all time, Bill Shankly had to retrace his steps. He went back to Preston and found a young man who was born in Carlisle. Born on 27 November 1942, Thompson was 21 when Shankly signed him for £35,000 in the summer of 1963. The newspapers of Lancashire were predicting all kinds of success for the Preston 'find' and, of course, Shankly became very aware of him. He had him watched, took a look himself – and then pounced to capture a player who is still revered at Anfield as one of Liverpool's all-time greats.

"If you get tired in the game boys, just give the ball to Peter and he'll play around with it for ten minutes while you get your breath back," was one of Shankly's favourite sayings. He rated Thompson among the best in the world. When Shankly bought him the fee was £35,000 – today, a player of his class would be in the £8 to £10 million range. He had the sort of trickery that would have players sliding into nothing – he had already gone, even as they made their move.

Moving to Liverpool opened the door to high profile for Peter Thompson. Not only did England wake up to this special home-grown talent, but so did the England management. His Liverpool career took off instantly with the start of the 1963-64 season. Before the campaign was many weeks old he was in the England Under-23 side – and before it closed he had won his first senior cap.

Thompson stayed at Anfield for nearly 11 years and played more than 400 senior games. He finally left for Bolton in January 1974. In total he played 16 times for England and was a member of the successful 1966 World Cup squad.

"Peter Thompson was a grand little player. He was strong and had great balance," said Shanks. "Most of all he was a footballer. I've never believed in over-burdening players, they should not have too much training or responsibilities in a game. I always believe in letting players do what they do best.

"Peter was a classic example. He liked to have the ball at his feet, take defenders on, run at them, frighten them. He had the skill to do that. It was good to watch him and he enjoyed his football because we gave him the freedom to do his best, to do what came naturally to him.

"He was often a match-winner for us even if it was not his foot which put the ball into the net. He could rip defences apart – and often did. A great player. Liverpool made him the complete player and he did a great job for the club".

Geoff Strong

Geoff Strong was one of the most versatile players ever to pull on a Liverpool shirt, having filled eight different positions during his service at Anfield. He was born on 19 September 1937, at Kirkheaton – and emerged as a top amateur with Stanley United. He was still an amateur during his early days at Arsenal, who he joined in 1957, but he soon turned full professional and remained a Gunner until his £40,000 transfer to Liverpool in November 1964. In 125 League games for Arsenal he scored 69 goals.

His tremendous versatility was probably his undoing, since Shankly tended to keep him in reserve to fill whatever spot was found wanting. He made 155 League appearances for Liverpool, and scored 29 goals. He also scored some important Cup goals and played his part in the FA Cup and League championship successes of his time at Anfield.

When his Liverpool days were drawing to a close at the end of the 1960s, he joined Coventry City for £30,000. He played 33 League games in 1970-71 which was to be his last League season. That brought his senior career to a close. One of the greatest puzzles is that this multi-talented player was never considered good enough to play for England.

Although he did not play as many first-team games as he might, Geoff Strong was, nevertheless, highly thought of by his Liverpool boss Bill Shankly.

"When we saw Geoff Strong we knew that he could fit into our system and would probably do better than with the club he was with then. I was very disappointed that Geoff Strong didn't get a lot of caps. He was a very good player. He was a frontman when we bought him, but he finished up as sweeper at the back. We bought him as a football player. We knew he could play and if you've got a good footballer you know you can use him wherever you need him. An all-rounder can be useful wherever you put him.

"Geoff Strong was one of those all-rounders. We used him all over the place and he never let us down. I always liked to have players who were able to fit in and be adaptable. He was one of the most versatile in the game."

He was also a very good shot. Many of Strong's goals were from loose balls and half-clearances at the edge of the box.

"He was very good at that. He could read a situation and capitalise on it. That's the sign of a very good player indeed. That was just one of Geoff Strong's attributes," said Shankly. "He was a very good signing".

Having broken the club transfer record of the time yet again, Bill Shankly would, quite naturally, pour praise upon his man – but all that praise was well justified. Shankly had indeed made a Strong signing.

Peter Cormack

When Geoff Strong moved to Coventry, Shankly needed another utility player. Someone whom he could send into the fray in any department that might need an extra pair of feet. He didn't have to look very far to find a fellow Scot who could fill the bill – Nottingham Forest's Peter Cormack was a Geoff Strong play-alike.

Cormack was born in Edinburgh on 17 July 1946. He joined his local favourites – Hibernian – and quickly progressed to stardom with them. Nottingham Forest signed him in March 1970, but little more than two years later he was on his way to Anfield for £110,000.

Once again Bill Shankly had been talent-spotting – but in the case of Cormack that talent was there for all to see. He had already played for the Scottish Football League and had also been capped for the Scotland Amateurs, Under-23s and seniors. When he joined Liverpool Cormack was an attacking inside-forward, but Shankly used his abilities in various positions and he settled into the midfield where he could add to either the attack or defence as required.

"Peter Cormack was in the team that won both League and the UEFA Cup, two medals in one season, that's a great achievement for any player. He was a good player, a good lad and a good buy. We bought him because we had a job for him to do, a team role and he was good at it.

"He was good in the air – similar to St John in certain ways... not in all aspects of the game but in his defensive work. Before we signed him I felt that we had a particular role for him – as we did – and he was successful too."

Cormack spent just over four years at Anfield and made 125 League appearances in which he hit 21 goals. He was still there when Bill Shankly retired, but in November 1976 he left for Bristol City, where he remained a key player until 1979. Later he went into management with Hibs back in Scotland, ending his career where it had started.

During his soccer life Peter Cormack worked for both Bill Shankly and Jock Stein – an education that money could not buy.

Emlyn Hughes

It must be very rewarding for a manager to sign a young player and see him develop all the way to captain of his club AND his country. That is the story of Emlyn Hughes – who was born in Barrow-in-Furness, not too far away from the famous bus station, on 28 August 1947. He has a Welsh-sounding name and a Rugby League upbringing – his father having starred as a professional in that rough, tough sport.

Hughes shared his father's interest in rugby but his real love was soccer. When he left school he immediately became an apprentice with Blackpool. He was still a teenager when he made his First Division debut. In those days he used to wear a number-three shirt, although he showed all the signs of being a forager, capable of moving with the ball and feeding his forwards.

Shankly well remembered going to see him make his debut for Blackpool against Blackburn Rovers at the end of the 1965-66 season.

"It was a nothing kind of a game. Blackburn were already relegated and Blackpool were safe from going down. It was one of those matches that had to be played but would have no bearing on anything. Matt Busby and Jimmy Murphy were also at the game – they had gone to watch someone else, Mike England I think. Bryan Douglas was playing for Blackburn, another good player with lots of experience.

"Douglas was in the Finney class, one of the all-time greats, and here was this 18 or 19-year-old boy having to mark him. Well, he had an incredibly impressive match. There was nothing at stake but Emlyn Hughes turned it into a Cup-tie. There was even a player sent off for retaliating against him. I tried to buy him after the match – after just one game. I tried to buy him from Blackpool. I knew he was a winner."

Shankly's bid was unsuccessful but the following season the ambitious Hughes sought a transfer and, of course, one of the first to hear about it was Bill Shankly. Once again it meant breaking the Liverpool transfer record but, even at £65,000, Shankly was convinced that Hughes would be a bargain.

"I finally got him early in 1967. There was no risk involved. I knew that he was a very good player and that he would get even better".

Shankly's confidence in his new teenager was such that, at a press conference, he even predicted that Hughes would one day captain both his club and England. The gathered media men laughed – Shankly's vivid imagination and flair for a good quote had gone into overdrive – or so they thought. He turned out to be absolutely correct.

After England Under-23 games, Hughes was called up for the first team. The proudest spectator at the game in Amsterdam against Holland was Emlyn's dad – who nearly missed the game because his tickets had been left at the wrong gate – Emlyn's fault, as he later admitted. England won 1-0, and it was a great debut for the young man from Barrow – the first of 52 caps, many of them as team skipper.

His Liverpool career blossomed and he became captain of the club too. In a little over 12 years he won just about everything that was going, including four League championships, the FA Cup, the European Cup twice, and the UEFA Cup twice. On a personal note he was Footballer of the Year in 1977 and was later awarded an OBE.

One of the points about Hughes that endeared him to Shankly was his undying enthusiasm for playing football. Kevin Keegan summed up the Hughes approach when he said: "Emmo lived the game 24 hours a day. If a match went to 900 minutes he probably wouldn't notice because he gets so involved."

In 1979 Hughes left Liverpool for Wolves, where he played the the last three of his England games and won the League Cup – the only domestic honour that had thus far eluded him. Rotherham signed him in September 1981, and in March 1983 he moved to his penultimate club, Hull. Finally, in September 1983 he joined Swansea and afterwards hung up his boots.

Hughes tried his hand at management but did not enjoy it and so concentrated on his media demands – which is where we still find him today.

Possibly his finest games for Liverpool were against continental opposition, as Shanks explained:-

"Hughes came in to replace Milne, and I remember that we went to play Cologne and Overath was playing – the great Overath. Roger Hunt came in at half-time and said that he was doing a terrific job. Hughes was the man. He never gave Overath a kick – and Overath was one of the best German players, one of the best in Europe in fact.

"Overath was a special player so we had to give him special treatment. When we had the ball Hughes had freedom but, if we didn't, Hughes had to pick him up immediately and mark him close.

"Another time we played Bayern Munich in the UEFA Cup. We beat them 3-0 here and then went to Munich. I put him directly against Franz Beckenbauer and he kept Beckenbauer out of the game. He was a destructive centre-half when we wanted him to be.

"I didn't like to use him like that, but we only ever did it against two players – Beckenbauer and Alan Ball of Everton – two of the greatest players in the world. Emlyn Hughes had the beating of them – he was some player for Liverpool."

Tony Hateley
The name Hateley means different things to different generations. In the 1980s and '90s, Mark Hateley has been one of the most exciting forwards in the game for England and for clubs like Glasgow Rangers, AC Milan, Monaco, Coventry, Portsmouth and Queen's Park Rangers. But, for the generation of the late 1950s to the early 1970s, it was his father, Tony Hateley, who rampaged through defences.

Born in Derby on 13 June 1941, Tony Hateley began with Notts County Juniors and graduated to the first team in 1958. He remained there until Aston Villa signed him in 1963 – and thus began a nomadic career that took him to Chelsea, Coventry, Birmingham, back to Notts County and finally to Oldham where he finished in 1973. In the midst of this wandering he spent 14 months at Anfield, from July 1967 to September 1968.

Hateley was a very dangerous centre-forward, brilliant with his head and the scorer of spectacular goals. In his early career with County and Villa, he hit 145 goals in 258 League matches – no mean feat. When Bill Shankly paid a record £100,000 for him, he was expecting a goal explosion. He was not disappointed at first – especially when Hateley hit three in a 6-0 drubbing of Newcastle in only the third match of the 1967-68 season. But Hateley was injury prone and he never fully realised his obvious potential.

"We got Tony Hateley for a specific purpose. If we had had Tony Hateley as a boy we would have made a better player of him, because we would have given him a job to do. We would have had someone alongside him who would have taken advantage of his abilities. Tony Hateley was one of the best headers of the ball of all time.

"He was brilliant in the air and we used to utilise him for that. He could distribute the ball with his head like other people use their feet. It was a great shame that we didn't have him earlier. He would have won many England caps and, with our training early on, I don't think he would have had all the injury problems that kept interrupting his career."

Shankly felt genuine sympathy for Hateley, for whom he had an obvious high regard. When Tony was at Liverpool, Mark Hateley celebrated his sixth birthday. Perhaps he was too young to benefit from the Shankly magic – or was he? Certainly some of the experiences his dad had at Anfield were passed on and probably did have a part in his son's success, and his vast array of caps, cups and medals, in his glittering career. Has the Shankly legacy no boundaries?

Tommy Lawrence

Tommy Lawrence was already a part of Anfield when Bill Shankly arrived. He was reserve goalkeeper and came from the same neck of the woods as Shanks, having been born in Dailly, Ayrshire on 14 May 1940. He was brought up in Lancashire and Liverpool had found him with non-League Warrington as a teenager, more than holding his own with hardened adult players.

Lawrence was a Red from October 1957, but it was not until Shankly gave him a first-team chance that his prospects seemed really worthwhile. He was a stocky character but at around five feet ten inches he was fairly short for a goalkeeper. He had a very safe pair of hands and when Shankly gave him his chance to replace Jim Furnell in October 1962, he soon endeared himself to the fans – even though his nickname, 'The Flying Pig', does not sound much like a term of endearment.

Under the guidance of Shankly he won Scottish Under-23 caps and then played three times for Scotland seniors. In his eight years in the Liverpool side he also shared in the League and FA Cup honours. Lawrence was never a spectacular goalkeeper, but he was very safe and had great presence and command in the penalty box. He was also quite unique for the time as Ian St John explained:-

"Tommy was the very first sweeper-goalkeeper. It was something which Bill Shankly himself conjured up – using the goalkeeper to launch counter-attacks. Before that, it was traditional for a goalkeeper to gain possession and then hold on to the ball until everyone was ready for a big boot up the field. It was almost like a goal-kick every time the goalkeeper had the ball. Shanks introduced the quick delivery from the goalkeeper – rather like the role of the centre-half. Liverpool have used the system ever since and so have other clubs. Manchester United have perfected it in recent years with Peter Schmeichel. Tommy Lawrence was the first."

Although Shankly later brought in Ray Clemence – who became his favourite goalkeeper – he really appreciated the role that Lawrence had played during his Anfield days.

"He was very solid – you need that. He didn't fling himself about but he always knew where to be and when to be there. He gave the defence confidence – and that's an important part of a goalkeeper's job!"

After more than 400 first-team appearances with Liverpool, Tommy Lawrence signed for fellow Merseysiders, Tranmere Rovers, in September 1971. He spent two seasons there before retiring from League football at the comparatively young age, for a goalkeeper, of 33 with an armful of mementos from a successful career.

Larry Lloyd

When Shankly knew it was time to replace Ron Yeats he also knew that he would be having to replace an institution. He found his new defensive pivot at Bristol Rovers and, in April 1969, Larry Lloyd was on his way to Liverpool. Bristol Rovers received £50,000 for a player whom they had nurtured from his junior days.

Lloyd was born in Bristol on 6 October 1948, and had achieved England Youth status before Shankly took a look at him. He was similar to Yeats in size and style and was readily accepted by the Liverpool fans although, years later, they were to groan as he became a thorn in the side of their team after he had joined Nottingham Forest.

Larry Lloyd nearly didn't try for a career in soccer. During his early days with Bristol Rovers he was also serving an apprenticeship as a constructional engineer. He reached a crossroads at which he had to decide which career was for him. Soccer won, but it was a close call as he never expected to get beyond the lower reaches of the Football League. It wasn't long before Bill Shankly approached Bristol Rovers boss, Bert Tann.

"I understood that Liverpool wanted me after I had played only 30 games," said Lloyd. Tann believed that he needed more time. Shankly continued to watch, especially when Rovers narrowly lost a Cup-tie at nearby Goodison, 0-1.

Yeats was still first choice when Lloyd arrived, and he encouraged the new arrival in training. Lloyd recalls a reserves game in which it could be said that goalkeeper Ray Clemence and himself gave a knock-out performance.

"Ray and I became very close pals – but in that reserves game we got too close for comfort. A high ball was coming in. I went for it and so did Ray. He gave the ball an almighty punch. Only problem was that that my head was between his fist and the ball. It's not every day that your mate knocks you out! But that was Liverpool – life there was unlike any other club I have ever known."

Lloyd stayed long enough at Liverpool to play around 200 first-team matches and win a League championship medal as well as the UEFA Cup. His England career continued with Under-23 caps and then three senior caps. When he was sold to Coventry in August 1974, for £225,000, eyebrows were raised. He suffered injury problems during his two years at Highfield Road and he certainly seemed to be on the slippery slope when they allowed him to go to Nottingham Forest for £60,000 in October 1976. But the inspirational Brian Clough restored his fitness, his confidence and his first-team status. Liverpool fans winced at Wembley when Lloyd was in the Forest side that beat his old club in the 1978 League Cup Final.

At Forest, Lloyd won the League championship, the European Cup twice, and the League Cup twice. He was also recalled to the England side for one final cap. In March 1981 he became player-manager of Wigan, but today he is more at home behind a microphone as a regional radio co-commentator.

"Larry Lloyd was the ideal replacement for Ron Yeats. He came into the reserves first and learned how we do things. Then, when his time came, he was ready. He was big and strong and commanding in defence – a very good player", said Shankly.

Gordon Milne

Gordon Milne was one of Bill Shankly's early Liverpool signings. He was the son of Jimmy Milne, one of Bill's team-mates at Preston. Shanks had watched Milne junior grow up – from the first days of being able to walk to reaching the Preston first team. He thought that Milne would be a good investment at £16,000 – and, once again, he proved to be right.

It was in August 1960 that Milne joined Liverpool as a 23-year-old wing-half, or midfielder as they are now known. He was given his first-team debut that season and went on to make 277 first-team appearances for Liverpool before moving to Blackpool at the end of the 1966-67 season for £30,000. He was in the 1964 League championship side and he also won 14 senior caps for England.

He was immensely popular with the supporters and his team-mates. His success was no surprise to Shankly, who rated him very highly.

"Gordon Milne was a message courier. He could take a ball from our defenders and pass it on to our front men – that was his role, and he did it very well – among the best. He could take it from his own players, he could dispossess the opposition. He could think, he had a good brain and played a very important part in the centre of the team," said Shankly. "You need someone to fetch and carry on the pitch and he was the best man for the job. He did all that was asked and more. Yes, Gordon Milne was a hard worker and a very good player for Liverpool Football Club."

After his two years at Blackpool, Milne went into management and coaching, first as player-manager of Wigan, but later as boss of Coventry and Leicester before taking his talents abroad and playing a major part in the rise of soccer standards in Turkey. He became manager of Besiktas in 1986 and among his players there, for a lengthy loan spell, was Les Ferdinand, who later went on to benefit even more from the Shankly Legacy with Kevin Keegan at Newcastle.

"Working for Bill Shankly was a major experience," said Milne. "He knew just how to get the best from his players. The word 'inspirational' is the nearest I can get – but it is still not saying enough."

Ian Callaghan

Nobody has played more times for Liverpool than Ian Callaghan! He played 641 League matches in 21 years at Anfield, but when you add the various major Cup games that total of appearances swells to an unbelievable 850. Yet Bill Shankly did not sign him – he was inherited when Shanks joined the club.

Callaghan was born in Liverpool on 10 April 1942. He joined Liverpool as a junior and was still a reserves player when Shankly first met him. By the end of the 1959-60 season, Callaghan was a first-team player having made his debut against Rotherham in April 1960.

During the next 20 years, Ian Callaghan – Callie as he was affectionately known – became a part of Liverpool soccer history. He not only won every domestic honour, but also the European

Cup and the UEFA Cup. In 1974 he was Footballer of the Year and he was awarded the MBE. His international career spanned 12 years since he was first capped for England in 1966, and played in the World Cup tournament of that year, and then made his final appearance in 1978. Although his international career spanned all that time, he only actually won four senior caps, two of them at the beginning and the other two at the end of those 12 years.

Ian Callaghan was a very clever player, a great winger, fairly small with a slight build. He was extremely fast and could cross a ball with fine accuracy. He easily adapted from being a traditional right winger to an attacking midfielder as soccer tactics and formations changed during his career. Kevin Keegan once said:-

"We call him the 'ageless wonder'. He was playing for the club while most of us were still at school. He is so fit that I reckon he'll still be in good class football at 40. He can give us all a few years yet none of us would care to challenge him to a hundred yard sprint."

Keegan's tribute was well-founded because Ian Callaghan was, indeed, still in League soccer at the age of 40. It was his last season and he was with Crewe. He left Liverpool in 1977 and had a short spell in the United States with Fort Lauderdale. Swansea then signed him in September 1978 and he made 76 League appearances for them before moving to Cork Hibs in Ireland. Crewe brought him back in October 1981 for his League swansong.

He had been a tremendous servant to soccer and especially to Liverpool. He epitomised all that is good in soccer – relying on skill and athleticism. Never once did he get sent off, and at all times he conducted himself as a true professional sportsman, aware of setting a good example to his legions of fans of all ages – among them Bill Shankly.

"Callaghan had incredible industry. He could change the whole formation of your side. You'd maybe start off with 4-2-4, but he would play in such a way that you would be into 4-3-3 before you or your opponents realised it. He would quietly change your game and thereby create gaps before anyone was aware of them. He could drop back and play deep too, pulling opponents with him which then stretched their formation out of shape.

"Callaghan was a crucial man in the set-up because he had great stamina and the skill to match. He played at his peak for a long time because he was not over-burdened when he was younger. It made all the difference to his career and to the service that he gave Liverpool. He was a wonderful player and deserved his great success."

If Shankly was a model manager, Ian Callaghan was his model professional.

Gerry Byrne

Gerry Byrne was one of Shankly's Liverpool heroes for his sheer bravery as much as anything else. It was Byrne who broke his collarbone after just a few minutes of the 1965 FA Cup-Final at Wembley, yet played on throughout the game – including extra-time – to help Liverpool to victory. His performance earned many bouquets from Shankly who rarely, in those days, singled out players for special praise. Byrne was different – he was made from the same granite as Bill Shankly himself.

Born in Liverpool on 29 August 1938, Byrne was a Reds fan from birth and there was never another club for him. He joined straight from school and was already in the first team at the age of 19. Shankly was impressed enough to keep him there, perm-anently occupying the left-back position. He was a part of the Anfield furniture and during his career he played more than 300 senior games for the club.

To those outside Liverpool he was just a left-back – but on Merseyside they appreciated his skill. He was quick in the tackle, quick to recover and quick to launch a counter-attack. The only thing that surprised the Liverpool faithful was that he played only twice for England.

Byrne himself was just happy to play for Liverpool – anything else was a side issue.

"It was Liverpool, Liverpool, Liverpool for me. I had loved the club for as long as I could remember, and my only real ambition has been to play at Anfield. I never wanted to go elsewhere – I was happy."

To Shankly, of course, all that was pure music. Guts and loyalty together in one player was, and still is, a rare commodity in the game and a real treasure to managers.

"Gerry Byrne was one of my favourite players. You don't hear many talk about him but Gerry was a fantastic player," said Shanks. "Gerry Byrne did what no one else in the world could have done when he played for nearly two hours with a broken collarbone at Wembley. Nobody but Bob Paisley and me knew until after the game. The fact that nobody knew just shows how well he played. Gerry Byrne should have received all the medals for the match. He was incredibly courageous. But that was Gerry Byrne – a truly great Liverpool player."

Byrne never did play for anyone else. At 29 he stopped because of injuries. Even his great bravery could not exempt him from succumbing to one injury too many. He stayed on as coach for a while but eventually left and returned to being a Liverpool fan.

On his first-team debut in 1957 he had scored an own goal – a nightmare! By the time he left he had fulfilled all his dreams.

Chris Lawler

Another home-grown Liverpudlian who played a major part in Shankly's re-creation of the club was right-back, Chris Lawler. He was born in the city on 20 October 1943, and recruited to the Anfield juniors. When he made the England Youth team, it became obvious that he was destined for a great soccer future as, indeed, it turned out to be – with more than 500 senior appearances for the club, from his debut in 1962 to his departure in 1974. He was capped four times by England and, once again, had it been a different time in soccer history he could well have made ten times as many appearances for his country.

Kevin Keegan said: "Chris was not only a superb defender, but he also doubled as an attacker. He got overlapping down to a fine art. I wasn't a bit surprised to see that he scored more than 60 goals for the club – quite a total for a defender. I don't ever remember seeing an opposing winger get the better of him – and he kept near-enough injury free apart from one spot of cartilage bother."

Lawler did not stop playing when his Liverpool career ended. He had won the League championship, FA Cup and UEFA Cup but still felt that he had something to offer at the age of 32 when he joined Portsmouth – where former team-mate, Ian St John, was the manager.

"He played about 40 matches for us in a season and a half. Not only did he perform well but he was also a great teacher and it is a loss that he didn't go into more serious coaching," said St John.

But Lawler wanted to return north and, in August 1977, he joined his final club, Stockport, where he played a further 36 League matches before retiring. He did coach in Norway for a while, and at Wigan before he rejoined Liverpool to coach under Joe Fagan. When Kenny Dalglish took over as player-manager in 1985, Lawler decided to call it a day and left to pursue his other business interests in North Wales.

His Liverpool team-mates always said that he was the quietest man in the team – both on and off the field. They also remember his very dry sense of humour when a sudden remark by him would dissolve the whole dressing room into hysterics – just the way Shankly liked it.

"Lawler was a great right-back. He would quietly get on with his job but he was so very effective. He was a great team player. He didn't seek the limelight, but he was never out of the game. In the dressing room he was a solid team member – you need great players like Chris Lawler."

Tommy Smith

Loved by Liverpool fans, maligned by others, Tommy Smith was one of the most uncompromising defenders the game has ever seen. Those for the prosecution called him 'dirty', those for the defence said he was tough but fair. You pays your money and you takes your choice – but one thing is certain. Not much got past him and his express train tackling was one of Liverpool's greatest assets during his 15 years at the club. Here again was a player who made 632 appearances for his club in both domestic and high-profile European games and yet only once pulled on an England shirt.

Shankly thought he was tremendous – and didn't mind saying so.

"Forget about the hard-man image – that's trash. Tommy Smith could play," said Shanks. "Yes, he was tough when he tackled but he was never a dirty player. He was a winner that's all. He gave all he got, even in training. It was his enthusiastic approach and style. When he was a teenager he used to come to me after every session and ask when he was going to be in the team.

"In one training session he tackled Chris Lawler and injured Chris's ankle. He didn't do it deliberately – it was just one of those things. But he came up to me straight after and said, "Does that mean I'm in the team now Boss?" That was Tommy Smith. He lived to play football. He was a Liverpool man and he wanted to be in the first team. He was a fantastic player right from the age of 16. He was ready for the big team when he was 17."

Smith was, indeed, a Liverpool man. He was born there on 5 April 1945, and is still the Scouser through and through – with all the natural wit and the charm of a well-used crowbar. What you see is what you get with Tommy Smith – and his team-mates liked what they saw.

"The King of 'em all – the best pro I've ever met. He must have played about two million six-a-sides in his day, but he'd still fight his best mate over a throw-in," said Emlyn Hughes.

"Sure, Tom was a hard man to beat," agreed Kevin Keegan. "When he went for the ball he was determined to win it, but he was fair. I've never seen him deliberately chop anyone down. And I don't think it's true that he trained by tackling lamp-posts!"

Smith had his own view.

"People have accused me of being a rough player, but that wasn't so. I have never deliberately fouled anybody and when I had my name taken it was usually for arguing with the referee. I feel that players like myself and Nobby Stiles were usually more sinned against than sinners. Not that I'm complaining – football has been good to me and I was with the greatest team in the world."

To Bill Shankly, Tommy Smith was priceless. "He did a tremendous job for Liverpool. Don't let anyone be fooled. Tommy Smith was a great player. He could play football all right."

When his Liverpool career came to a close, he joined up with his former team-mate, John Toshack, at Swansea, but not before heading the winner in the European Cup Final of 1977. A year after that he went to Swansea and spent most of the 1978-79 season there, before returning to Anfield for a brief spell as coach.

Smith was capped once by England – but his Anfield collection more than made up for his lack of international honours. He was involved in four League championships, two FA Cups, two UEFA Cups and the European Cup – not a bad haul from his 630 plus first-team games – and certainly not bad for someone often dismissed as all boot and no skill.

Tommy Smith still laughs at that image. He is still in great demand by the media and for after-dinner talks. He remains as chirpy as ever – an out and out Scouser.

Alec Lindsay

It's amazing to think that there are many so-called soccer fans today who have never heard of Alec Lindsay – yet he played more than 240 appearances for Liverpool, and was rated high among the list of Bill Shankly's Liverpool heroes.

Lindsay was a Lancashire lad, born in Bury on 27 February 1948, and his career began with Bury, where he was an apprentice before signing professional forms in March 1965. He won England Youth caps while he was there and when Bill Shankly needed a replacement for Gerry Byrne, Alec Lindsay was just the young man for the job. He signed in March 1969, just after his 21st birthday, for £67,000 – and soon came of age when he was thrust into first-team action.

At Bury he had already played 150 first-team games and, in the next eight years at Liverpool, he was to add another wealth of experience before moving to Stoke in August 1977 for his final senior soccer season. Along the way he picked up four full England caps, as well as FA Cup, UEFA Cup and League championship medals.

But it was his style that earned him the most praise. He was incredibly cool at all times, which accounts for him being one of Liverpool's main penalty takers.

"I rate Alec Lindsay as the best man in Britain playing in that role at the time," said Kevin Keegan. "He'd have won a string of England caps if Sir Alf Ramsey hadn't preferred to move our team-mate. Emlyn Hughes, out of position and give him the number-three shirt.

"Alec's left foot kicking is so accurate that we used to say he could place the ball on a sixpence. He and I used to share the penalty responsibilities – but I'm not saying which of us had the most success."

For Bill Shankly, Lindsay was one of his best-ever players, and he wished that he had perhaps had him at Anfield a little earlier in his career.

"Alec Lindsay was full of skill, a real class player. He'd been at Bury a long time and he found our training hard because it was so different from what he had been used to. It was sometimes necessary to needle him a little to get the right motivation – but he was well worth the effort. He was marvellous to watch. He took everything in his stride and often kept things together under pressure. A wonderful footballer."

Steve Heighway

If you want break-neck, thrill-a-minute soccer – then Steve Heighway was the man for you. Here was an Irishman who not only played great football but had a University degree as well. Heighway was a Dubliner, born on 25 November 1947. In England, he was expecting a career as a teacher, but Liverpool scouts saw him playing for non-League Skelmersdale and tipped off the boss.

Heighway could have started his Liverpool career much earlier but his studies were important to him. It was May 1970 when he finally signed professional forms at Anfield. It was the start of a ten-year career that brought him fame with both his club and his country. He was capped a total of 34 times for the Republic of Ireland between 1971 and 1982 – his last cap being awarded after he had left Anfield to sample the delights of soccer in the United States with Minnesota Kickers.

Heighway's 'full house' collection of medals came as a result of more than 375 first-team appearances at Liverpool, where he was the hero of the fans because of his swashbuckling style – sprinting down the wing to meet all challenges. He was also a hero to Bill Shankly.

"Stevie was a great signing. He was at Warwick University in Coventry. I went to the University to see him. There were a lot of clubs trying to sign him. One even phoned him while I was there talking to him. He was approaching his 23rd birthday and he wanted to complete his studies before he became a full-time professional footballer.

"Well, I signed him and he came to Liverpool. He was a revelation, a breath of fresh air – electric quickness and clever with it. We were lucky to get him. Stevie came in when Peter Thompson was injured and that was that – we couldn't take him out. It would have been a terrible thing not to play him because he had pace, the ability to beat men and a good attitude. So Stevie was a player who came in and made an impression straight away. Marvellous footballer."

Heighway's University education also paid off later on. He returned to Anfield and put his teaching skills to good effect as Liverpool's Youth Development officer. He has always kept a fairly low profile as far as publicity is concerned. He once told a soccer journalist, "I've no confidence in any soccer reporter." He didn't need it – his skill spoke for him.

Ray Kennedy

Ray Kennedy was the very last signing ever made by Bill Shankly. He bought him in July 1974 for what was also Shankly's record transfer fee of £200,000.

It is difficult, perhaps, to think of Kennedy among Shankly's

Liverpool heroes, but it was the great man who signed him and watched his progress during the years that followed. Kennedy was still at Anfield when Bill Shankly died.

Born on 28 July 1951, Kennedy was an apprentice at Arsenal and played almost 160 League games for the Gunners before joining Liverpool. He came hoping to repeat his 1971 League and Cup double that had been achieved with the Highbury club. The Liverpool double came after his departure, but Kennedy won a batch of domestic and European honours with the club.

A switch to midfield from striker proved to be the making of Ray Kennedy, who was to play a similar role for England in 17 appearances.

"We bought Kennedy as a footballing professional to do a particular job," explained Shankly. "He adapted well and did what was asked of him, and he turned out to be an even better player than we had hoped. I had a special interest because he was the last player that I ever signed and he did very well for the club."

Swansea bought Kennedy in 1982 for £160,000 after more than 300 games for Liverpool. He stayed with the Welsh club for nearly two years before moving back to his native North-East and Hartlepool in November 1983, finishing his playing career at the end of that season.

Later it was discovered that he had Parkinson's Disease, and a special testimonial game was arranged between Liverpool and Arsenal to help raise cash for his treatment. Kennedy dedicated himself to raising the profile of the disease so that there was more awareness about the illness and more fund-raising activity to help in the battle against it. Just as on the soccer pitch, Ray Kennedy was not a man to be beaten.

John Toshack

If Ron Yeats and Larry Lloyd had been the towers of the Liverpool defence during Shankly's reign, John Toshack was certainly the tower of the attack. He joined Liverpool in November 1970, from Cardiff for £110,000, and he proved to be one of the best attackers ever seen at Anfield.

Toshack was born in Cardiff on 22 March 1949, and was an

apprentice with his local club before making the first team as a teenager. He was a prolific scorer and hit 75 League goals in 162 games before Liverpool found that they could resist him no longer.

He was a typical Welshman, with a strong accent and the ability to write poetry. In just over seven years at Anfield his accent had developed a definite Scouse ring and his poetry had become progressively worse. His football improved though and he struck up a great partnership with Kevin Keegan. They both scored goals aplenty – but Toshack was also a great provider with his head, meeting long clearances with a determined head of the ball, often to the feet of Keegan who had rushed into a goal-scoring position.

There is a nice story about the day John Toshack travelled to Liverpool to sign for the Reds. Shankly met him and his wife at Lime Street Station and was visibly shocked to see Mrs Toshack wearing a coat that was in Everton blue.

"Never mind love," he said. "We'll get it dyed red!"

During his Liverpool career, Toshack scored 74 League goals in 172 games – and he probably supplied the passes for at least that many more. In March 1978, he returned to Wales as player-manager of Swansea, beginning a whole new career as a soccer boss that has taken him to the top division in the country and to various awards in Spain, where he settled in well to earn respect as a great coach.

Toshack even had one game as manager of Wales – but he resigned immediately after that one game because he felt that he would miss the day-to-day running of the club.

Shankly helped him with his later management career, but was primarily concerned with Toshack the player – the big, strong star that he'd plucked from Wales.

"John Toshack was about skill and strength. He was a big man but he was quick and had a brilliant head. There were few in his class when I signed him – and we made him better."

Roger Hunt
Without a doubt, Roger Hunt held a very special place in Bill

Shankly's personal hall of fame. He had great admiration for any player who won the World Cup, even if he was an Englishman. Hunt was born on 20 July 1938 in Golborne, not too far from Liverpool.

He was spotted playing for a junior club in the Warrington area and became a Liverpool professional in May 1959. Shankly saw his potential as soon as he took over as boss at Anfield and Hunt became a first-team player for the next ten years, scoring a record 245 League goals in 404 appearances.

"Roger Hunt was a brilliant player," Shankly recalled. "He could leather them in, or he could score with a simple tap in or a nod of the head. But he much preferred to batter them in – he liked to make sure."

Not that Hunt was without critics. There were those who thought that England manager, Alf Ramsey, had made a mistake in selecting Roger Hunt rather than Jimmy Greaves but, in the end of course, Hunt scored one of the four goals that won England the World Cup.

Shankly backed his men to the hilt and once replied to one of Hunt's critics: "Of course he misses a few – but he gets in the right places to miss them."

In the 1961-62 season, Hunt had scored 41 League goals to create a record that still stands today – 35 years on. In addition to his 34 caps he has won many domestic medals for Liverpool and was one of the nation's favourite players. When he chose to retire from the game in 1971, it was after two seasons with Bolton whom he had joined in December 1969 for £31,000.

His soccer skills were lost because he turned down many coaching offers and went instead into the family haulage business. He still appears now and then, especially during World Cup anniversary years, when fans still clamour to shake his hand or seek an autograph.

When Hunt won his World Cup medal, Shankly was one of the first to congratulate him. He was proud that a Liverpool player had made such an achievement.

"Ian St John had helped Roger along during his early Liverpool days and we were all pleased for him," said Shanks. "He was a

Liverpool player of the highest order and fully deserved the highest honour."

The Kop agreed – which is why they dubbed him 'Sir' Roger Hunt!

Ray Clemence

If there was a single flaw in Bill Shankly's make-up, it was his lack of understanding of goalkeepers – they made him nervous. He had very little confidence in the man in the green jersey – multi-coloured as it is now – which is why Ian St John was able to tell us such a great story about Ray Clemence and his early days in the Liverpool first-team squad.

"I remember we were playing TVS Munchen 1860, in the Fairs Cup, and we beat them 8-0 in the first leg at Anfield. Bob Paisley thought it would be good experience for Ray to play in the second leg – and suggested it. Shanks looked at him aghast. "I don't know about that Bob," he said. Ray was on the bench for the second leg and we scored after 20 minutes, so we're 9-0 ahead. Bob again suggested that it would be a good time to put Ray on – but, again, Shankly looked at him as if he had suggested abandoning the game. The same thing happened at half-time. Then, with 20 minutes to go, Shanks turned to Bob and said, "What do you think of sending young Clemence on?" Bob threw the sponge into the bucket in frustration. It was typical of Shanks – goalkeepers frightened him to death."

Clemence was born in Skegness on 5 August 1948. As a boy he used to be a deckchair attendant in the summer – but dreamed of being a professional footballer. His dream came true in a big way. He began as a junior with Notts County but, in August 1965, he was allowed to leave and join Scunthorpe. Two years later he was on his way to Liverpool for a bargain £18,000.

"We liked to sign young players from lower divisions and give them time in our reserves. It gets them used to our ways and develops the habit of winning matches. It's a good habit to get into," said Shankly.

Once he had broken into the first team, there was no shifting Ray Clemence, other than for the occasional injury. He was once out of the side for a few weeks with a pulled muscle and Shankly was convinced that his absence cost Liverpool the League championship.

"If the 1960s team had had Ray Clemence in goal they would have won the European Cup and all the trophies under the sun. I say that because Ray Clemence was one of the greatest goalkeepers of all time. If he had been in that 60s side, I don't think anybody could possibly have beaten us."

Clemence played 656 first-team games for Liverpool and won three European Cups, two UEFA Cups, five championships, the FA Cup and the League Cup. Then he moved to Spurs for £300,000 in April 1981, chalking up more than 250 further senior games. In all, he won 61 England caps, at a time when the 'keeper's jersey was in constant contention between himself and Peter Shilton. Later he was also awarded the MBE. Probably there was nothing that meant quite so much to him as the praise that he received from Bill Shankly.

"Ray was probably the biggest single factor in the success of Liverpool. You have to have a great goalkeeper – and he was the best. The things he did, the goals he saved during the course of a season – the ones that might have sneaked in. He changed the whole course of matches and won us many games and points. Brilliant Ray Clemence."

Clemence has been actively involved in coaching and management since he retired in 1987. Perhaps the best of that aspect of his career is still to come – but one thing is for certain – he was the goalkeeper that Shankly learned to trust. Shanks became confident that the Liverpool goal was in very safe hands.

Kevin Keegan

Arguably, the star of the Shankly Show is the young man who has since become one of the most inspiring managers in the game today. We speak, of course, of Kevin Keegan. We shall be looking at his managerial prowess a little later on but, first of all, let's take a look at Keegan the player – the player for whom Bill Shankly predicted great things.

Stan McDonald, now art editor with IPC's soccer magazines,

was a photographer in 1971. He went along to Liverpool in early May of that year to take some shots of Steve Heighway with an award. He could not get in at first and had to climb over a wall. Shankly spotted him and bawled him out – until he realised why he was there – then he became very hospitable. The whole episode was watched by a kid sitting on a dustbin. That kid was Kevin Keegan on the very day that he was to sign for Liverpool.

Keegan was born in Doncaster in February 1951. His early soccer aspirations were hampered by his height – or rather his lack of it. Doncaster were not keen and Coventry turned him down, simply because they considered him to be too small. Scunthorpe had no such reservations and he became a professional in December 1968. It was a wise move for the club and Keegan soon chalked up more than a hundred first-team appearances while he was still a teenager.

Scunthorpe manager, Ron Ashman, broke the news to Keegan that Liverpool wanted him and he drove him to Anfield personally. Shankly welcomed the new recruit, they negotiated a weekly salary of £50, and he signed on the dotted line. Scunthorpe were the richer by £33,000.

"I was indebted to Ron Ashman for the start he gave me at Scunthorpe. He advised me and guided me. When I went to Liverpool I changed from one great manager to another. Bill Shankly was brilliant. He was like nobody else that I ever met and I owed him a great deal for the part that he played in my career."

As for Shankly, he had no doubts that Kevin Keegan was going to be a very big star.

"Kevin Keegan is down as European Footballer of the Year twice, bracketed as one of the greatest footballers of all time – which he is," said Shanks. "And his exploits will never be forgotten – and his guts and his twisting. I tell you, he's some man. He makes you proud to know him. Kevin Keegan went into the unknown and did it all himself."

Keegan's career has been well chronicled – but briefly... He spent six years at Anfield before joining Hamburg, who paid £500,000 for him. A year earlier Real Madrid wanted to sign him but he wanted another season at Anfield. When he returned to

England in July 1980, it was to Southampton in a blaze of publicity. Two years later he joined Newcastle for his final season as a player. He entered the St James' Park arena as a hero and departed as a King. Little wonder that he was so rapturously welcomed back when he became manager of Newcastle in 1992.

In more than 300 games for Liverpool he won the European Cup, two UEFA Cups, three League championships and the FA Cup. He was also named Footballer of the Year. With Hamburg he won the German championship and reached the European Cup Final.

His adventures for his country included 63 senior caps and also the England captaincy. There's not much more you can ask from a soccer career, but almost all the success that Keegan has experienced was predicted by Bill Shankly.

"I found out about Kevin Keegan from Andy Beattie, who was doing some scouting for us then. He was watching Keegan for nine months and he was talking about him incessantly. Preston were also interested so we made our move. When Keegan came here for his initial training he was first in everything, a fantastic little fella. We had to simmer him down because he was working too hard at everything. He wanted to be in front all the time. I had to explain that he was only doing preparatory training. I said to him, 'that's only the shadow boxing that you're doing'.

"I've never seen such enthusiasm. You could see from the start that he was out to prove a point. He had had a humble background. I understood him because we both came from mining villages. He was a little sad sometimes, quiet, keeping out of the way in the corner of the dressing room. He isn't that kind of a person really. He's a good speaker. Not only is he a good player but he can talk as well. I think he'll maybe get a job with the television one day. It will improve the television if he does. He'll get a job as an orator of some kind – maybe the Prime Minister, who knows?

"The first time I really watched him play was in a final practice match between the reserves and the big team. He made a competitive game of it. His attitude was fantastic in everything he did.

"From the very beginning of his training at Liverpool, Kevin Keegan was a winner."

He still is!

Liverpudlians

To Shankly, Liverpool's army of supporters were members of his team, and each and every one of them are counted among his heroes.

"I knew before I joined Liverpool that the crowd was fantastic. The noise from the Kop was amazing – and it went from strength to strength as we made progress. The Kop is unmatched in noise and humour. It is world famous. Their sayings, their chants, everything is marvellous. They could be very funny.

"I remember Leeds playing here and Gary Sprake was in goal. He made a dreadful mistake and, instead of rolling the ball to one of his own players, he rolled it into the goal. The Kop sang 'careless hands' to him – it was their instant humour. One night we were playing in the fog and we scored at the Anfield Road end. The Kop roared out, 'Who scored?' – and from the other end they chanted back, 'Tony Hateley!' The Kop is something special.

"I enjoyed it when I stood on the Kop after I had retired. It wasn't just the Kop though, all the supporters in every part of the ground played their part. Liverpool is not just a club – it's an institution! My aim was to bring people close to the club.

"Men died, and the women brought their ashes to the ground to be scattered on the pitch. There were some very sad occasions. One family brought the ashes to be buried and our groundsman dug them deeply into the ground just inside the right-hand post of the goal facing the Kop. People didn't just support Liverpool when they were alive – they continued even after death.

"There's no hypocrisy about Liverpool, but there is always humour. Whenever the ball hit the post where that chap's ashes are buried, we would always say that he was playing a blinder. It was not meant to be disrespectful. It was just a joke within our great Liverpool family. That's how close the people were to the club, they wanted to remain a part of it when they died.

If I had a business and I wanted a workforce – I would pick it up from Merseyside. All they need is handling. We would wipe the floor with anyone. I would pick my workforce from Merseyside and anyone else can pick theirs from anywhere else and we'll have a go with them. We'll be successful because there is such a big spirit here. I know that with them on my team, I'll win."

He did!

Those That Followed

THERE have been very many Liverpool stars through the years, far too many, unfortunately, for us to be able to mention them all here. Shankly continued to watch over them, even from a distance, and we have his opinion on these. To help us with a few of the others I have asked the man who, as a player, had great insight on the heart and mind of Bill Shankly.

Ian St John was the first major Liverpool signing by Shanks and he remained in touch with him right up to his death, sharing opinions and anecdotes. St John provides us with the most likely view that Shanks would have had, on players who he never saw pull on the famous red Liverpool shirt.

First though, we look at a player whom he did know and did regard very highly – a player who was brought in to replace Kevin Keegan and became as much a part of Anfield history as Shankly himself.

Kenny Dalglish

The chant of, 'Dalglish – Dalglish', by the Kop choir was almost a war cry – but it was really a spoken salute to the man who achieved 'mission impossible' by filling the gap left by the sale of Kevin Keegan. Possibly he was the only player in Britain at that time with the style and skill to climb such a mountain.

Kenny Dalglish was born in Dalmarnock, on the Celtic side of

Top, left: Ian Callaghan, one of the greatest servants in Liverpool's history. "Callaghan had incredible industry," said Shankly. "He could change the whole formation of your side."

Top, right: Tommy Smith was portrayed as something of a hard man but Shankly said, "Forget about that trash, Tommy Smith could play. Don't let anyone be fooled. He could play football all right."

Bottom, left: Steve Heighway – "When I signed him for Liverpool he was a revelation," said Shankly, "A breath of fresh air, electric quickness and clever with it. We were lucky to get him."

Bottom, right: Roger Hunt – "He was a brilliant player," said Shankly, "He liked to batter them in best of all. Of course he missed a few, but he was in the right place to miss."

Top: *Manager John Toshack talking to his Deportivo La Coruna players. "There were few in his class when I signed him – and we made him better," said Shankly, whose influence later helped Toshack in his managerial career.*

Bottom, left: *"If the 1960s team had had Ray Clemence in goal, they would have won the European Cup and all the trophies under the sun," said Shankly. "I don't think anyone could possibly have beaten us."*

Bottom, right: *Kevin Keegan and Terry McDermott on the Newcastle United bench as the Magpies go for the 1996 Premiership title in attacking style. "He's some man," said Shankly, "He makes you proud to know him." McDermott was the first player to join Liverpool after Shankly resigned, but it was Shankly who lined him up.*

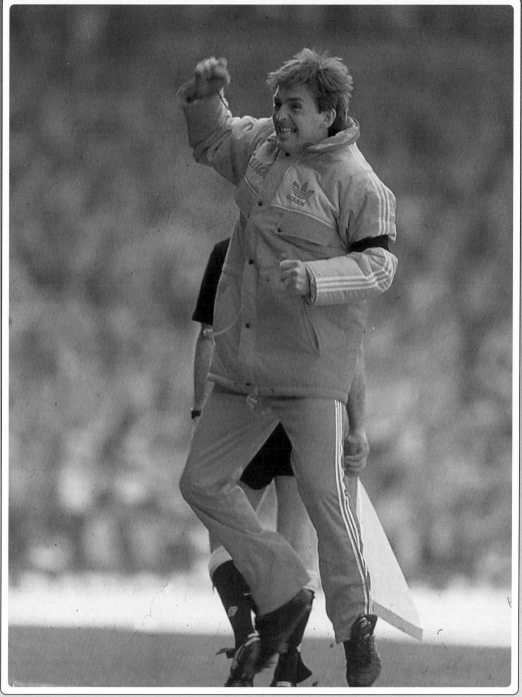

Former Liverpool star Kenny Dalglish jumps for joy as the Reds' manager. "He came to a club where he would get help. The Liverpool system meant that he was not expected to go it alone," said Shankly.

Left: Alan Hansen joined Liverpool three years after Shankly had left but the great man said, "He showed real class when he first joined. When I saw him I knew he was going to be a great player once he had settled in."

Top, right: Bruce Grobbelaar – "If he'd slept at all, Shanks would have had nightmares knowing that Bruce Grobbelaar was going to keep goal for him the following day," says Ian St John. "He already thought that goalkeepers were from a different planet."

Bottom, right: Ian Rush – "He would definitely have been a Shankly player, although in his early days Shanks would probably have agreed with Bob Paisley and told Rushie to be more selfish in front of goal," says Ian St John.

Top: Robbie Fowler – "Shanks would have been very hard on him, especially in training. He would have been delighted with his ability and attitude but he didn't like to praise individuals."

Bottom, right: Steve McManaman, who Shankly would have loved in the same way as Peter Thompson and Steve Heighway, two of his favourite players. Says St John, "He'd have given him the freedom to play his own game and just said, 'Run at them'."

Bottom, left: David James – "Goalkeepers filled Shanks with dread. He would definitely have kept David James in the reserves for a while to let him get used to life at Anfield. And he would be telling him to use the box better. He liked his goalkeepers to be mobile."

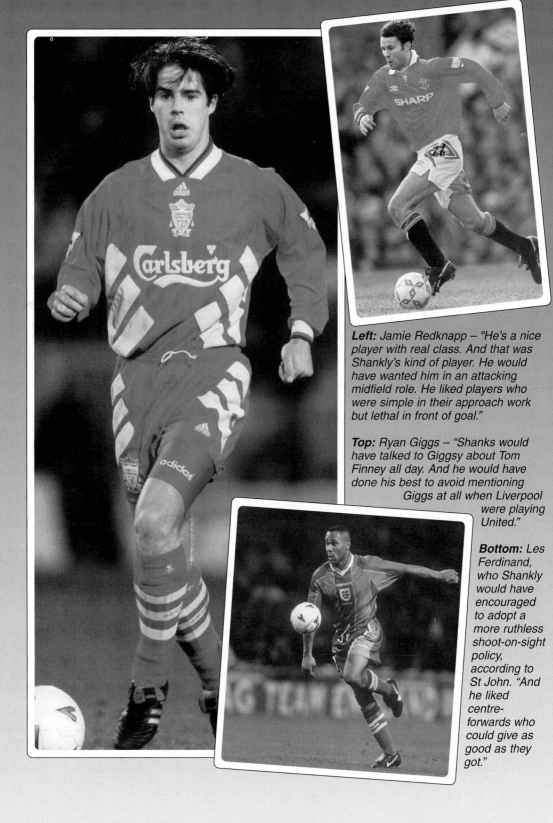

Left: Jamie Redknapp – "He's a nice player with real class. And that was Shankly's kind of player. He would have wanted him in an attacking midfield role. He liked players who were simple in their approach work but lethal in front of goal."

Top: Ryan Giggs – "Shanks would have talked to Giggsy about Tom Finney all day. And he would have done his best to avoid mentioning Giggs at all when Liverpool were playing United."

Bottom: Les Ferdinand, who Shankly would have encouraged to adopt a more ruthless shoot-on-sight policy, according to St John. "And he liked centre-forwards who could give as good as they got."

Eric Cantona – "Shankly would probably have said to him, 'You are aggravating people enough with your skills. You don't need to do anything else.' He would have been a big fan of Eric Cantona – especially if he could have got him into a Liverpool shirt."

Alan Shearer – "Shanks could not have resisted buying Shearer if he had been on the market. He liked old fashioned centre-forwards who could score any type of goal."

The current Liverpool management team of Roy Evans, Doug Livermore and Ronnie Moran, carrying on the Shankly Legacy.

Geoff Twentyman in his Liverpool playing days. Shankly brought him back to Anfield as a scout and he has repaid the favour many times over by unearthing many fine players who have helped Liverpool's cause, not least of them being Ian Rush.

Glasgow, on 4 March 1951. When he was still a boy he moved to the Rangers side of the city. He performed well in school soccer and, at the age of nine, was a school regular – as a goalkeeper! A trial at Celtic in his mid-teens led to him signing up for the Bhoys. He began an apprenticeship as a joiner – but that ended when his soccer career took off with a rather different aspect of woodwork in mind.

His Celtic career was a story all of its own. From his debut in 1969 against Raith Rovers, to his midnight departure for Liverpool in 1977, Dalglish was a star. He won five Scottish championships, four Scottish Cups, one Scottish League Cup, hit more than a century of League goals and won a regular place in the Scottish international side. He had learned much under his first boss, the late Jock Stein, who said:-

"I don't think you could have a better player to handle than Kenny Dalglish. His strength has always been his enthusiasm for the game. For Celtic and Liverpool he gave his best all the time. He is exactly the type of player you always want in your side."

Dalglish, with his total of 102, has played more games for Scotland than any other player. It was Tommy Docherty who first picked him for a full international.

"I consider myself lucky to be the one who had the chance to give him his first cap for Scotland. Quite honestly there was no way that I could ignore him. He had a terrible habit – he just kept on getting goals!"

Much was expected of Dalglish when Liverpool paid, what was then a British record, £440,000 for him. He did not disappoint. In his Anfield playing career he made nearly 500 appearances and won five championships and four League Cups at home, in addition to three European Cups. By the time he had finished playing, he had an incredible haul of English, Scottish and international medals and awards. Then there was a final twist, of course, when he was appointed player-manager of Liverpool in 1985

When you add to his awards, two Footballer of the Year titles, the PFA Player of the Year award and an MBE, Kenny Dalglish really does seem to have been the dream player with the dream career. Bill Shankly kept his feet on the ground by talking of his role in the Liverpool set-up.

"Kenny Dalglish became so successful at Anfield because he fitted in immediately. The Liverpool system meant that he was not expected to go it alone. He came to a club where he would get help. If you get the ball at Liverpool you immediately had options, players were there to help you. Kenny Dalglish was an instant success at Liverpool Football Club because he had the kind of skill to take advantage of that. He had choices and he was the kind of player to use them. He was a great signing for Liverpool, he could have been made for the job."

Shankly and Dalglish were two of a kind. Everything revolved around football and Dalglish enjoyed his meetings with Shanks.

"He was more than just a character – he knew what he was talking about, and you could listen to him for hours – a marvellous man!" said Dalglish.

Terry McDermott

They don't come much more Liverpudlian than Terry McDermott and yet he managed, somehow, to begin his career well away from Merseyside and when Liverpool wanted him they had to buy him from Newcastle. He was Bob Paisley's first signing and the first player to join Liverpool after Shankly had resigned. He had been in the Newcastle side that had lost to the Reds at Wembley in the 1974 FA Cup Final – and he had impressed both Bob Paisley and Shankly.

McDermott was born in Kirkby on 8 December 1951. Although he played for his school, Liverpool's network of spies had failed to haul him in and he became an apprentice at Bury – which is where he broke into senior football. He was in the Bury first team consistently, until Newcastle saw him and then in February 1973, he was on his way to the North-East for the first of three times.

He immediately became a first-team squad member at Newcastle and he maintained that status – which is how he found himself in the Wembley FA Cup Final line-up of 1974.

That day was Liverpool's day but both Shankly and Paisley earmarked McDermott for further attention.

"He looked like he could do a job for Liverpool, so I thought it would be a good idea to make some enquiries," said Shanks. It was, of course, Bob Paisley who made those enquiries. "He struggled a bit at first because he had to adapt to the Liverpool way of doing things, but when he had settled he turned into an excellent player and a great team member, working hard for Liverpool Football Club."

McDermott's contribution during his nine years at Anfield is beyond question. As well as being an energetic part of the midfield engine room, he also had a penchant for scoring spectacular goals. He helped the Reds to four League championships and three European Cups. He also helped himself to 25 England caps and three goals. He also had a unique 'first' in 1980 when he was named Footballer of the Year and PFA Player of the Year – the first time anyone had received both awards for the same season.

Newcastle bought him back in 1982 and he stayed for two years before taking his skills to Cork, followed by Cyprus with Apoel. He has since linked up with former Liverpool and Newcastle team-mate, Kevin Keegan, to form a formidable management duo at Newcastle.

Terry McDermott was one of the many Stars of the Seventies who benefited from the Shankly system that was still in operation and also from being able to talk to Shanks on his visits to Anfield.

"We used to see him quite often," said McDermott. "He would always have something to say – although you could see that he didn't want to interfere. He would just give you a few words of encouragement – or perhaps tell you a tale from his playing days. Whatever Shanks had to say, you just listened. It was enough just to be there."

Phil Thompson
Strictly speaking, Phil Thompson was one of Shankly's own products – but it was really after Bob Paisley had taken over that

he made his mark as a first-team player, and ultimately as captain of Liverpool.

He was born in Liverpool on 21 January 1954, and was almost immediately cast in the role of a Reds fan as his family were all Liverpool supporters. Thompson was not many years old before he was taking his place on the Kop to cheer on Shankly's men. Imagine then if you will, what it must have meant to him when he became part of Anfield when he gained a place as an apprentice.

Phil Thompson was given his debut by Shankly and had convinced him that he was worth regular selection during Shanks' last season. Shankly then looked on with delight as he watched Thompson steadily shouldering more and more Liverpool responsibility, finally culminating in his captaincy. He was also delighted to see him win an England international call-up that led to 42 caps.

"It's always good to see a young player come through. When they listen and learn," said Shankly. "You watch them making progress, you share in their successes and their disappointments. Phil Thompson was a classic example. He began as a Liverpool fan – and that was the best possible start. Then he joined the club and he was prepared to be taught. He would take in what you were saying and then do it. That's a good example for all young players. He was Liverpool all through and he still is. He came to the club as a little boy and he became a professional footballer."

In December 1984, Thompson moved to Sheffield United and remained there for the rest of that season – then he joined Liverpool again, this time as a coach. He held the post until 1992 when he became a victim of the new regime of Graeme Souness.

Phil Thompson's list of medals would be the envy of many a war hero. Of the major competitions, he won the European Cup twice, the UEFA Cup, the FA Cup, the League Cup twice, and the League championship no fewer than five times. Add to that his England caps and captain's armbands from Liverpool – and on one occasion from England – and you have, what can only be described as, quite a haul and a tribute to a player who learned things the Shankly way as a lad – and used that education wisely.

Alan Hansen

Now a part of the *Match of the Day* furniture, Alan Hansen's playing career was second to none. He was certainly noticed by Bill Shankly, even though he did not join Liverpool until three years after the great man had departed. Shankly believed that Hansen was capable of a glittering Anfield career – and he proved to be absolutely right once again!

"Alan Hansen showed real class when he first joined Liverpool. He lacked nothing except confidence. When you are a defender you need complete confidence, otherwise you make mistakes and it is a bad position for anyone to make mistakes in. More goals are scored from defensive errors than anything else. When I saw Alan Hansen I knew he was going to be a great player once he had settled in."

That was the Shankly verdict a couple of years after Hansen's arrival at Anfield. It was completely accurate. Hansen joined Liverpool in a £100,000 transfer at the end of the 1976-77 season. He was born in Alloa on 13 June 1955, and joined Partick Thistle as a teenager – enjoying his first success when the Jags won the Scottish First Division championship in the 1975-76 season.

At Liverpool he developed into a commanding central defender and captain. In time-honoured Anfield style he was allowed to settle into his new club by means of the reserves, but gradually his performances demanded regular first-team football. By the time he had drawn the final curtain on his career he had played well over 600 first-team matches for Liverpool.

Hansen won just about every possible honour with Liverpool including an amazing collection of eight League championship medals. The first of his Scottish caps was won in 1979 against Wales, and he collected a total of 26 caps during the following eight years.

Ian St John provides another of Shankly's views of Alan Hansen.

"He really rated Alan. He liked his attitude and his temperament. I think he saw another Ron Yeats in the side. He spoke about Alan's growing confidence and how he had become an immovable obstacle in the centre of the field. Yeats looked bigger because he was broader, but Hansen had the same sort of height and a finesse that Shanks enjoyed. He knew that he was going to be hugely successful. If Shanks said that about someone you could put your shirt on it."

Today Alan Hansen shows that same finesse in front of the television cameras, breaking down the matches he watches, and passing comments to his team-members. Same job – different kit!

John Barnes

It is doubtful if Bill Shankly ever saw John Barnes in action – and he certainly never saw him perform for Liverpool – but Barnes has become a part of the Liverpool legend and Ian St John is able to provide us with the likely thoughts of Bill Shankly on a player who is close to celebrating a decade in the Reds shirt.

Barnes was born on 7 November 1963 in Jamaica. His birth was during the season in which Liverpool won the League championship for the first time in 40 years. A Watford fan spotted him playing for Sudbury Court in the Middlesex League and recommended him to the club. His father was on a five-year posting in London for the Jamaican Government at the time. In just another month or two, the family would have been returning to Jamaica and John Barnes would probably have remained an unknown.

Watford took him on in July 1981 and he stayed for an exciting six years, scoring 83 goals in 292 games. While at Watford he made his debut for England in a 0-0 draw in May 1983 and then, a year later, scored a sensational individual goal in a 2-0 win over Brazil in Rio that elevated him to household name status.

It was Kenny Dalglish who took the gamble on signing Barnes for £900,000 in June 1987 – the word 'gamble' being used purely because of media criticism at the time. Dalglish knew that it was not really a gamble at all – he had Shankly's eye for quality players.

"I joined Liverpool because I wanted to win things," said Barnes. "But the events since I have been at Anfield have exceeded my greatest expectations. I did feel a certain curiosity at first, as to how I would fit into the Anfield system – but I can honestly say that I didn't have any problems on that score and I settled into the side much quicker than I had anticipated." It was just as Shankly had said – the simplicity of the Liverpool system could quickly absorb a new player and help him to settle into his new environment with a minimum of teething problems.

Barnes did indeed settle quickly and was soon putting on the sort of display that confirmed Dalglish's wisdom in signing him. In the years that have followed, John Barnes has earned a reputation as an entertainer. His skills with the ball have, at times, been breathtaking, and he has certainly played a major part in the two championships, two FA Cup wins and the League Cup win that have been achieved since he arrived at Anfield.

On the international scene, his England career continued to the 1995-96 season and, when he hit the 80-caps mark, he placed himself among the most-capped England players of all time. He played several times in the England 1990 World Cup squad that finished in fourth place.

As he has lost a little pace, John Barnes has played more of a deep midfield role for Liverpool, the young legs of the front-runners capitalising on his superb distribution. He has maintained the Liverpool tradition of quality football, meeting the standard set by Shankly almost 40 years ago.

"He would have been a Shanks player," said Ian St John. "He is a class act and Shanks admired that. He has great imagination. Shankly used to preach improvisation – and John Barnes is a master of that. Shanks would have encouraged him to take people on. He would have said, 'Go on son, Show them what you can do'. That's the sort of encouragement he would have had from Shanks. Like Dalglish, Shankly would have bought him with confidence and, when you look at John Barnes' Liverpool record, it is easy to see that Kenny's decision was exactly right."

Peter Beardsley
For Peter Beardsley read Peter Pan! There has been little sign of the Newcastle gem losing his sparkle and perhaps some Liverpool fans are still wondering why he was allowed to leave in August 1991. Especially as it was to rivals Everton for a knock-down price of £1 million. That would never have

happened if Shankly had still been the boss – he did not believe in handing gifts to the opposition. It was a decision taken by Graeme Souness and was possibly one that he later lived to regret.

Beardsley was born in Newcastle on 18 January 1961, so it is perhaps fitting that the twilight years of his glittering career have been spent back on Tyneside. But he was in the palm of Liverpool's hand for four years after Kenny Dalglish paid, what was then a British record, £1.9 million for him in July 1987 – not bad for a lad who had had more rejections than a bent coin in a telephone box!

"I tried several clubs, including Newcastle," Beardsley explained. "But nobody wanted to know, so I thought I would have to do my best in non-League football. I went on the dole when I left school and then, after a few weeks, I got a job. I worked for a company who made valves for ships. My responsibilities included, sweeping the floors, cleaning the machines and running errands such as fetching the lunch from the chip shop."

It was Carlisle who gave him his first chance. He became a professional in August 1979, and stayed until 1 April 1982, when he was bought by Vancouver Whitecaps for £275,000. It was no April Fool's joke, Beardsley enjoyed life in Canada. After just five months, Manchester United paid £300,000 and at last he was in the big-time – or was he? Six months and just one appearance in a League Cup-tie later, he was on his way to Canada again. Vancouver signed him on a free transfer this time.

Peter the nomad continued his travels six months later, when the Whitecaps sold him again. This time the price was £150,000 to, of all people, Newcastle – who had turned him down about seven years earlier.

From September 1983, he was a Newcastle player and proud of it. He appeared 164 times and scored 61 goals. Liverpool were watching and Kenny Dalglish liked what he saw and so, in July 1987, Beardsley began four years at Anfield that wowed the Liverpool fans.

In January 1986, while his Newcastle career was in full swing,

Beardsley made his debut for England in a 4-0 win over Egypt in Cairo. He was substitute for Gary Lineker. It was the start of an England career that has since taken him beyond the 50-cap milestone.

Almost every striker that he has played alongside has paid tribute to Peter Beardsley. He is one of the most creative Englishmen of recent years. At Liverpool, his partnership with John Barnes was a winner from the start, and Beardsley collected two championship medals and an FA Cup winners' medal while he was at Anfield.

All good things must come to an end and, in August 1991, Graeme Souness shocked Merseyside when he sold Beardsley to Everton for £1 million. In the 1993 close season, Everton made a profit when they sold him back to Newcastle for £1.5 million. He was given a great welcome home.

Would Shankly have broken the British transfer record to buy Peter Beardsley? – You bet!

"Knowing Shanks, he would not have hesitated," Ian St John believes. "He would have recognised Beardsley as one hell of a talent. He would not have wanted him to play so deep. He would have wanted him to play in, or around, the penalty area, conserve his energy and be a constant threat to the opposition. I can just hear Shanks saying, 'I don't want you back son, go at them Peter – terrorise them!' That would have been his pre-match pep talk to Peter Beardsley."

Beardsley has been back to terrorise Liverpool a number of times since his departure – but he is always given a warm welcome. They like talent at Anfield and, for a while, Peter Beardsley was one of their own.

Bruce Grobbelaar
At this stage, reader, it is time for a brief aside. When I asked Ian St John what Bill Shankly would have made of Bruce Grobbelaar, it took him quite a while to stop laughing.

"I could just picture Shanks on the night before a game knowing that Brucie was going to be in goal – he would have been pacing the floor in his slippers. If he slept at all he would have had nightmares. As I said before, Shanks was not a goalkeeper person – he thought they were from a different planet. Once, he turned down a goalkeeper who wore contact lenses because he thought he wouldn't be able to see properly under floodlights. I can just imagine what he would have made of Bruce Grobbelaar."

As it happens, Grobbelaar might well have been seen by Shankly since he made his Liverpool debut in August 1981, just over a month before Bill died. There is no record of him having made any comment if he did happen to have seen him – and probably, at that stage, Bruce was no more eccentric than most other goalies.

The Grobbelaar story began on 6 October 1957 in Zimbabwe – or Rhodesia as it was then known. He tried his hand at a soccer career in England but, like Peter Beardsley, he found more joy in Canada with Vancouver Whitecaps. Also like Beardsley, Grobbelaar had two spells with the Whitecaps. A move to Crewe in December 1979 was a kind of half-time between his bouts in Canada. While with Crewe he played 24 League matches – AND SCORED A GOAL!

In March 1981, Liverpool decided that he could be another piece in the jigsaw of that time and paid Whitecaps £250,000 for him. For nearly 13 years he was the people's choice between the sticks at Anfield. He played more than 500 games and won just about everything that was going. His antics during matches became more and more bizarre. His famous 'jelly legs' of the 1984 European Cup Final is still shown on television around the world – and his attempts at trying to add to the goal he scored for Crewe drew cheers and loud applause from everyone except those reaching for the Valium on the Liverpool bench.

A much-loved and respected international goalkeeper for Zimbabwe, Bruce spent some of his young adult years as a jungle soldier. Not much got past him then either! In the summer of 1994 he was released by Liverpool and had a new lease of life at Southampton. Two years later he was released from the Dell, probably due to the court case that was then pending concerning allegations of match-rigging. A sad end to a truly colourful career.

"I truly would love to have seen Bruce under Shankly," said St John. "Shanks would have gone mad if he had seen him doing all that dribbling stuff out of his area. Shanks would have respected Bruce's ability, but he would never have stood for all that eccentric stuff."

Ian Rush

The greatest Liverpool record breaker of them all is no longer with the club but, in a career of around 15 seasons at Anfield, Ian Rush became the top Liverpool scorer of goals in one season with 47 in all major competitions. His five goals against Luton in October 1983, equalled the club record for a one-match haul. He is Liverpool's top scorer of FA Cup goals, biggest transfer sale, Liverpool's most-capped Welsh player – and Rush also holds his country's record as top-scorer of all time. Exhausting reading isn't it?

Amazingly, Ian Rush actually turned down Liverpool when they first tried to sign him. Rush was born in St Asaph in North Wales on 20 October 1961, during Liverpool's last season as a Second Division side. His family was almost like a club since there were six boys and four girls born to Mr and Mrs Rush. Ian had trials with Wrexham before joining Chester. He had the choice but preferred the family atmosphere of Chester.

After making his senior debut for Chester he hit the goal trail immediately. Within a year he was offered the chance to join Liverpool.

"I turned them down because I just didn't fancy a move at that time," said Rush. "I felt that I still had plenty to learn and that I could do it at Chester while still getting first-team football. I knew that a move to Liverpool would probably mean a spell in the reserve side. Besides that, I couldn't really imagine surviving at such a big club among so many star names.

"A couple of months later they came back and this time they just invited me to take a look around Anfield. They must have known that would swing it. I spent only a few hours at the ground – but once I'd seen the place, I knew I couldn't pass up such an opportunity. Everyone at Chester was very good about it and the supporters were great. I had lots of goodwill letters from them."

Rush signed for Liverpool on 1 May 1980, and thus began something of a dynasty. In the mid-80s he spent a season with Juventus but, apart from that, he was a permanent fixture until he was freed in the summer of 1996 to join Leeds.

Ian Rush has won the lot. There is not a domestic medal that he has not won several times over. He has won the European Cup and countless personal awards for his goal-scoring feats. Liverpool fans place him in the same category as Dalglish, Keegan and St John – and there was a special tribute from the young man who has taken his mantle, Robbie Fowler.

"Playing alongside Ian Rush is the best education that I could have had. He is a brilliant, natural goalscorer whose record speaks for itself. There could never be another Ian Rush. I have lined up alongside a legend."

But what of the Shankly view? Would Rushie have been among Shankly's heroes? Ian St John tells us:-

"Rushie would definitely have been a Shankly player. He would have loved Rushie's great appetite for the game and for goals. Shanks loved great team players, people who would graft for the good of the whole side. Rush was in the Roger Hunt mould and that was exactly the sort of player Shankly liked.

"When Ian was in his early days at Liverpool, Bob Paisley told him to be more selfish in front of goal. I think Shanks would have said the same. When Rushie appeared for the last time in a Liverpool shirt at the end of the 1995-96 season, everyone – including his team-mates – stood and clapped. You could almost hear Shanks leading the applause."

Perhaps Shankly was there when the Deeside Primary School won each of their 33 games in one season, and little Ian Rush scored 72 goals. Or, maybe he was there in the 1983-84 season when Rush hit 48 goals in 64 first-class games. Then again, perhaps he was at Wembley in 1986, when Rush scored twice in the FA Cup Final to beat old rivals Everton and secure Liverpool's 'double'.

In reality, of course, Shankly wasn't there, but, when he hears about it, he'll wish he had been!

Today's Heroes

WHAT would Bill Shankly have made of today's new generation of Liverpool Stars – or, indeed, some of their more illustrious opponents? It has been more than 20 years since Shankly retired and soccer styles and attitudes have changed quite a bit. But, basically, the game is still about scoring more goals than your opponent. No doubt, Shankly would have held his head in disbelief at some aspects in today's game but, there again, he was a man ahead of his time so let's, once more, enlist the aid of Ian St John to give us the Shankly view of the pop-star players of the 1990s.

Robbie Fowler

The new goal-king of Anfield is a local lad who was an Everton fan but still turned them down to join Liverpool. Robbie Fowler is the man of the moment, the kid with the 'goalden' touch. He was born in Toxteth, a notoriously rough area of the city, on 9 April 1975.

Fowler's rise to fame began at school – he was a prolific scorer even then. Playing for a Sunday League side while still a schoolboy, he once hit 18 goals in one game. His success at Liverpool is partly due to Graeme Souness, who was in charge when Robbie made his debut and what a debut! Liverpool were away to Fulham on 22 September 1993 in the Coca-Cola Cup.

They won 3-1, and Fowler scored one of the goals. What came next was totally 'Roy of the Rovers' stuff – in the return leg he hit five goals. In a League match he scored three against Southampton, and then hit the winner against Everton in his first Mersey derby.

His run of 15 goals in 24 matches came to an end when he was side-lined with a hairline shin fracture. Once over that, he picked up where he had left off and has been Liverpool's top scorer for two seasons in succession. Playing for England Under-21s he scored on his debut and could not be ignored by Terry Venables as Euro'96 approached. Fowler made his England senior debut in the matches leading up to the championship and did enough to secure his place in the squad.

"I called him into the England set-up on merit," said Venables. "He is a remarkable young player with great ability. I was very happy with his attitude and I am sure that he'll be an England player for many years to come."

No greater tribute could Fowler have than that given by the man he replaced as Anfield's hottest hit-man, Ian Rush – who not only played alongside him, but also helped him learn the trade.

"Robbie has shown that he can take on the best defences in the country and still score goals. His strike rate, at any level, is a great achievement but for a young lad to do it in the Premiership is astounding."

Fowler himself is thrilled with the way his soccer career has gone so far and pays tribute to Ian Rush and, significantly, his boss Roy Evans.

"Rushie was brilliant for me. When you play alongside the best, some of that skill has to rub off. He was quick to help me improve my game and he certainly played a great part in my goalscoring. The boss has also been great to me. He is always there to point out improvements, to encourage and to chat to you if you need it. He has been a big help to me."

When someone so young has so much success so soon, there are obvious pitfalls. He has a lively sense of humour and fun, and likes to play hard.

"I'd have to say that I like a laugh," said Robbie, "and as I'm still very young, I like to be one of the lads. We play a few tricks on each other at Liverpool. I've been known to stick a label on myself and and go around the conveyor belt when we're passing through an airport. It's just to let off steam by having a little fun."

Would he be getting away with it if Bill Shankly was his boss? Ian St John has the answer.

"Shanks would be very hard on him – especially at training. Because of all the adulation he would have given him very little praise, so that he kept his feet firmly on the ground. Shankly didn't like to praise individuals so that nobody would get carried away with their own publicity. Of course, he would have been delighted with Robbie's ability and his attitude to the game, but he would have kept a tight rein on him off the pitch. Shanks knew everything about each individual player. If you were a minute late getting into your hotel room, he knew about it – and he would want to know the reason. That's how he would be with Robbie Fowler – appreciative of his talent, but hard on discipline."

Steve McManaman

Steve McManaman is another Scouser who is proud of it. He is so heavily into Merseyside that he even sings his favourite Beatles songs on Karaoke nights. Funnily enough, like Fowler, McManaman was also an Everton fan and also had trials at Goodison. Like Fowler he turned them down because he liked the Liverpool set-up better.

One of his early jobs at Anfield was cleaning the boots of John Barnes – now he shows opposing defenders a clean pair of heels of his own. Steve puts much of the credit for his own success at the feet of John Barnes.

"I owe him a lot. I only cleaned one player's boots as an apprentice and they were his. That was when he was in his prime and Liverpool won the double. Now, he helps me all the time. He's got 70-odd caps, and it's great to learn from someone like him."

Steve was born on 11 February 1972 and, as mentioned previously, he was heavily into Everton before joining Liverpool. His favourite players, however, were both foreign, and it is not difficult to see how and why he tried to model himself on them. If you can get close to emulating Marco Van Basten or Pelé, then you're not doing too badly.

Terry Venables must have thought he was doing pretty well, which is why McManaman, too, was in the Euro '96 England squad.

"He's been playing better than when I first picked him. He's getting more consistent by the week. He has this ability to go by people and unsettle defences."

McManaman was actually into England reckoning even before he had established himself as a regular in the Liverpool side. Before he made his full debut for his club, which was on 15 December 1990 in a 2-0 win over Sheffield United, he had already made his debut for the England Under-21 side. Even before that he had played for the England Under-18s against Spain at Wembley.

As well as having great skill with the ball, Steve McManaman has speed and stamina – commodities which he put on show when he was still at school and won the North-West School's cross-country championship. But there is also something else – as team-mate Steve Harkness explained.

"Macca's the coolest person at the club. He never gets flustered and he never loses his temper. He's just dead calm and cool."

Yes temperament, one of the most important ingredients, something that can make all the difference between a good footballer and a great footballer. What about the Shankly view? Ian St John had no hesitation.

"He'd have loved him. McManaman is in the same mould as Peter Thompson and Stevie Heighway – two of Shankly's favourite players. He just loved players like McManaman, who were prepared to take people on. He'd have given him the freedom to play his own game and just send him out with simple instructions – 'Run at them, Run at them'. That's all he would have said and he'd have been delighted with the result."

David James

The critics scoffed when Liverpool paid a million pounds for David James in the summer of 1992. They put it down to another example of the eccentricity of Graeme Souness. James had little time to settle in before he was in the first team and being bombarded by the cream of English forward lines. Needless to say, he was dropped after a fairly short time because he was losing confidence. It is fair to say that he was thrown in at the deep end without much of a defensive life-jacket.

That was then, however, and this is now – David James was a key factor in the recent Liverpool revival. He has grown in stature, experience and confidence. At last the promise that he showed at the start is now beginning to be fulfilled.

David James was born on 1 August 1970, in Welwyn Garden City. He was a big lad at school and just grew and grew. He joined Watford straight from school as a trainee and was soon in the first team – making his debut on 25 August 1990, when Watford lost 1-2 to Millwall. He was only a few weeks past his twentieth birthday – which is very young for a first-team goalkeeper.

England selectors were keeping an eye on his progress. He played for the Youth team and then the Under-21 side. More recently, he has been in the England 'B' team but, as yet, his name has not fitted into the senior squad.

Since joining Liverpool, David James has become a high-profile young star. He won his first senior medal when Liverpool won the Coca-Cola Cup in 1995. He is one of the biggest goalkeepers in the game at six feet five inches and 15 stone. His ability to sketch and cartoon is well-known, and his modelling work has seen his photograph plastered across billboards and glossy magazines. He has the whole world in his hands.

"I know I still have a lot to learn, but I am enjoying life at Liverpool and I don't think I could be at a better club to make career progress. The place has a special atmosphere all of its own. When you come to Anfield, you know you are joining history. Also the squad and the coaching is so great."

Former Liverpool captain, Ian Rush, knows a thing or two

about goalkeepers, and he is impressed by David James' progress.

"Nobody ever questioned his ability, but I now think that he believes in himself a lot more," Rush explained. "He has realised that he can go to the very top of the game and enjoy a long and successful career at Liverpool – and perhaps even for England. I would think that he's worth a try."

Whether or not Bill Shankly would have paid a huge fee for him we shall never know, but Ian St John helps us to get a clue.

"I think I mentioned before that goalkeepers filled Shanks with dread. If he had bought David James he would definitely have kept him in the reserves for a while to let him get used to life at Anfield – just like he did with Ray Clemence.

"David is developing into a very good goalkeeper, but I think Shanks would be telling him to use the box better. He has started to move about more as he has gained in experience whereas, before, he used to be rooted to the line for crosses. Now, he is taking command and Shanks would have encouraged that. He liked his goalkeepers to be mobile and act as another sweeper. That's what he would be wanting from David."

Jamie Redknapp

When the daughter of your boss is one of your biggest fans you can't go far wrong! Incidentally, Jamie Redknapp is quite a good footballer as well. Of course it might seem that a little point like that is merely a bonus, when you are talking about a young player who receives more fan-mail in a week than most players get in a season.

Redknapp was born in Barton-on-Sea, on the South coast, on 25 June 1973. At that time, his famous dad, Harry, was playing for Bournemouth. Jamie could have started his career with West Ham or Bournemouth, if he had wanted, but he decided upon Tottenham and was a schoolboy there until Bournemouth signed him on as a trainee in June 1990. Spurs protested that he was contracted to them but eventually gave up their claim.

Harry Redknapp was manager of Bournemouth at the time. Jamie had not been at Dean Court quite seven months, when the Redknapps took a family outing to Liverpool for a special occasion. It was for a meeting with Kenny Dalglish and the signing, by Jamie, of a new contract with Liverpool. It was a successful mission and Bournemouth received £350,000.

Jamie Redknapp began sampling first-team football when he made his senior debut for Bournemouth in a 4-1 win over Hull – on 13 January 1990. By the time he was 21 he had been named Liverpool's Player of the Year. He has played for England at Youth, Under-21 and senior levels, and was also in the Liverpool side that won the Coca-Cola Cup in 1995 at Wembley.

"Shanks would have enjoyed having Jamie in the side," said Ian St John. "He liked players who could really play. He is a nice player with real class – that's Shankly's kind of player. Shanks would probably have wanted him to play in an attacking midfield position and would have encouraged him to play more balls that penetrate the opposing defence. He liked passes to be accurate and incisive when they were sent through. Shanks liked players who were simple in their approach work but lethal in front of goal – that's Jamie Redknapp!"

Redknapp has had a couple of worrying injury spells but now seems to be fully recovered and fast approaching his best-ever form. He is also something of a team prankster, one of his favourite jokes being to phone up his team-mates pretending to be a journalist and persuading them to moan about other members of the Liverpool squad.

"Jamie is a great passer of the ball," said John Barnes. "The future of Liverpool revolves around players like him. With the goals that he is cracking in now, it can only add to Jamie's confidence."

Perhaps the final word should come from the sentiment expressed earlier on. Liverpool boss, Roy Evans, once said: "If my daughter had her way, Redknapp would be in the team for every single game – Perhaps she knows more about him than I do!"

The postman who delivers all that Jamie Redknapp fan-mail every day knows his stuff too. That fan-mail isn't getting any lighter.

Although Shankly did not dwell on opposition players, he

would have them secretly watched and then form his own opinions. What would he have thought about some of Liverpool's opponents of today? Ian St John provides the answers.

Ryan Giggs

The young Welsh Wizard has taken the Premiership by storm since Alex Ferguson put him in the first team as a tremendously talented teenager. He has since grown up a great deal in football terms, even though he doesn't seem to have aged at all. Put simply, Ryan Giggs is a brilliant young player and Bill Shankly would have done his best to ignore mentioning him when Liverpool were playing Manchester United.

"Shanks would have enjoyed his skills but he probably would have castigated him about his final ball. He would have talked to Giggsy about Tom Finney – all day! But he would have loved to have seen Giggs beating players and setting up attacks."

Les Ferdinand

Working for Kevin Keegan at Newcastle has given Les Ferdinand an insight into doing things the Shankly way. He progressed with Queen's Park Rangers and has matured at Newcastle. Ferdinand was a record buy at six million pounds when Keegan signed him in August 1995. He proved that he could live with that price-tag and has since scored some brilliant goals for both Newcastle and England.

"Shankly went through a phase of concentrating on his front-runners and he would certainly have been pleased with Les Ferdinand's progress. He liked centre-forwards who would both receive and give as good as they got. He would probably have asked Ferdinand to adopt a more ruthless, shoot-on-sight policy."

Alan Shearer

Is Alan Shearer the best centre-forward in England? The debate goes on and on. Shearer's track record is amazing. He is a record-breaker, has a reputation for scoring on his debuts and is generally one of the most feared forwards in the game. Shearer is real class. He has his critics – who hasn't? – but, surely, he would have been high on a Shankly shopping list?

"Yes, Shanks would have loved him. He liked old-fashioned centre-forwards who could seize on any opportunity, get stuck in and score any sort of goal – tap-ins, headers or blasters. Shearer is a real handful and Shanks would not have been able to resist buying him if he had been on the market."

Eric Cantona

Talking about legends, what about Manchester's favourite Frenchman? The Cantona story is simply out of this world and you always get the feeling that there are still twists and turns in the plot yet to come. Any player who can win so many medals almost single-handedly, and be taken care of by Alex Ferguson, must be something special. We all know that Eric Cantona is very special. He has been called a genius. If there is such a thing in the world as a genius, he must be. Eric Cantona the brilliant and Eric Cantona the abrasive – the two go together somehow!

"Shankly was a great fan of skilled players. He used to love talking about Finney, Mannion and Docherty. He would have appreciated Cantona's qualities. He would have tried to calm him down earlier on – probably saying something like, 'Ignore people – you are aggravating people enough with your skills, you don't need to do anything else.' Yes, definitely, Bill Shankly would have been a big fan of Eric Cantona – especially if he could have got him into a Liverpool shirt."

The Unsung Hero

GEOFF Twentyman's former claim to fame was that he was one of the most popular names on cigarette cards. His soccer career began with his local side, Carlisle, and he moved to Liverpool at the end of 1953. He stayed for six years and played around 160 games for the club before moving to Ireland as player-manager of Ballymena United. That wasn't the end of his Liverpool career however – far from it. Reds fans have much for which to thank Geoff Twentyman.

When Shankly brought Twentyman back to Anfield, he gave him a simple brief – to head a scouting network that would bring the cream of talent to Liverpool. When you look at a list of the players who pulled on a Liverpool shirt as a result of his endeavours, it is plain to see that Geoff did exactly what Bill Shankly required of him – and continued to do so, even after Shanks had retired.

"I wasn't looking for the finished article, nor was I concentrating on very young potential at schoolboy level," Twentyman explained. "I had to keep an eye out for, and check on, the slightly older players, generally out of their teens, who were capable of going into Liverpool reserves and eventually into the first team."

Geoff Twentyman used contacts from all over Britain to unearth players who could ultimately do a job for Liverpool. His travels would take him all over the country to watch about five matches every week. Who did he find? Well, here's one of Twentyman's discoveries – and he had to keep a low profile to watch this one.

"Ian Rush was a case in point. A lot of big clubs were sniffing around and Liverpool did not want anyone to know that they were interested. I used to pay at the turnstiles at Chester and watch him from the terraces. As we now know, it worked and Rushie became one of the biggest names in the club's history.

"Another time I had to secretly watch a player was when I was pursuing Steve Heighway at Skelmersdale. I arrived at the ground and noticed a few other scouts hanging around. It was a case of pulling the coat-collar up as far as I could, hoping that they would not notice me."

Sometimes a manager will ask his chief scout to look for someone for a particular position – almost like a shopping list.

"I recall Bob Paisley asking me one day, to watch out for a right-back, because he was expecting to have to replace Chris Lawler. I hadn't anyone in mind, but the very next game that I went to was a Northampton Town match. It was there that I first saw Phil Neal. I watched him a couple of times soon after that, and the more I watched him the more I realised that we'd have to get in very quickly if we wanted to snap him up without any opposition.

"Bob Paisley signed Phil within a few weeks and the needy position was sorted. He went on to play for England and, by the time he left Anfield to go into management, he had won more medals with Liverpool than anyone else in the club's history."

Geoff's travels also took him to Scotland where he found two more of the big names of Liverpool history.

"The late Jock Stein tipped me off about Steve Nicol. I went up to Scotland to see him playing for Ayr and, although he was a fit lad, he looked very ordinary at first sight. I watched him on and off for a season and gradually he began to develop. Eventually he started to look a bit special and so we signed him.

"One of the jobs I had to do was meet schoolboy trialists off the train at Liverpool's Lime Street Station and see them settled in at their digs. I remember that there was one kid who came down and, quite frankly, he was no better than any of the kids we had at the time.

"About three years later, he was a regular in Partick Thistle's first team and I went to have another look at him when I heard that quite a number of clubs were interested in him. This time, when I saw him, I knew that he had what it took. We signed him and he had a great Liverpool career. The next time you see Alan Hansen, ask him about it."

Another tip-off was to see a foreign player who was on loan to Crewe from a club in Canada. Sure enough, when Geoff Twentyman went to see him, the player was at his most entertaining. He went on some great runs upfield – and eventually scored from the penalty spot. The only alarming thing was that the player was Crewe's goalkeeper!

"I took Bob Paisley along with me the next time, and when the goalie started dribbling the ball upfield, he did it so well that both Bob and I were hooked. The fact that he put on a great performance between the sticks helped a lot as well. Before long there was a new goalkeeper in the Liverpool side – Bruce Grobbelaar."

Bruce was not the only goalkeeper to be given the thumbs up by Geoff Twentyman. Another was Ray Clemence – and we all know what happened to him. Brian Hall was another of Twentyman's successes and, before he gave up his post as chief scout, he encouraged the club to buy two more players whom he felt would have some impact at Anfield. One was John Barnes and the other was Peter Beardsley... Wonder what happened to them?

Geoff Twentyman served Liverpool Football Club well, and he

helped to create one of the most enviable and successful scouting set-ups of recent years. Indirectly, he helped to land many a trophy at Anfield. His experienced eye for talent and potential meant that Liverpool could maintain a flow of top players without the investment of tens of millions of pounds.

Like most scouts, he is rarely mentioned in the honours lists – Bill Shankly, though, would definitely have said that Geoff Twentyman was one of his unsung heroes – one that poured gold into the Shankly Legacy.

The Shankly Legacy

HOW do you follow an act like Bill Shankly? You try not to. In the case of Liverpool, Bob Paisley stepped into Shankly's shoes, but he always did his very best to avoid moving out of the assistant manager's chair of comfort to the boss's hot seat.

"I got down on my knees and begged Bill not to go," admitted Paisley. "I didn't want the job, and I only took it for fear of the consequences for the rest of the back-room staff if someone from outside was brought in."

Paisley's reluctance certainly didn't reflect in his commitment to his new job. History proves that he became the most successful Liverpool manager of all time – and there are few in the world who could match his incredible list of honours.

Bob Paisley was as different as chalk is from cheese in his manner, compared with that of his pal and colleague, Bill Shankly. While Shankly was brash and extrovert, Paisley was quiet – almost shy – and certainly more of an introvert. Yet they shared a sharp wit and a passionate knowledge of football.

Paisley was born on 23 January 1919, in a little North-East village called Hetton-le-Hole. He played for local amateur giants, Bishop Auckland, and enjoyed tremendous success with them before joining Liverpool in May 1939. His League soccer career did not really start until the end of World War Two, by which time his peak was probably gone for ever. Between 1946 and 1953, however, he still managed almost 300 senior appearances for Liverpool, picking up a League championship medal along the way.

He stayed on after retirement and proved to be a great assistant to Shankly and, later, an even greater replacement. He was shrewd in the transfer market, had learned the lessons of man management and, as a qualified physiotherapist, he had expert knowledge of football injuries, their treatment and the psychology of players. Probably the most important aspect was that he changed almost nothing.

"Bill Shankly put the foundations down and built the walls," he said. "I just put the roof on!"

He adopted all the training and preparation methods that had been initiated by Shankly.

"Our system was the best. Of course there had to be refinements – Bill himself improved things as he went along – but fundamentally, it was still Shankly's Liverpool."

Ian St John still frequented Liverpool, as he does now, and saw at first hand how things were after Shankly's final bombshell.

"There was very little difference. Bob stuck to the Shankly style and we can see how well it worked. Make no mistake, Bob was his own man, but he had been there since the start of Shanks' time at Anfield. He had seen how it all came together and he knew the reasoning that lay behind Bill Shankly's decisions. He inherited the Shankly Legacy and he used it wisely."

He did indeed. He has a fair claim to being the most successful manager of all time, because he inherited a winning style and system, polished it to make it shine, and then cashed in on the value of such a treasure.

Just how much value there was is certainly no secret. Paisley almost won the League championship in his first season. Phil Neal and Terry McDermott had been added to the squad, Ray Kennedy was deployed in a midfield position and the title race went to the wire. There were no trophies to show off that season but it had ended with Paisley having asserted his authority. The horse was the same but there had been a change of jockey.

The 1975-76 season was probably the turning point. Three more names appeared in the first-team squad – 'Supersub', David Fairclough and Jimmy Case had been elevated from the reserves, and Joey Jones was bought from Wrexham. The training and preparation remained the same. The trophies began to flow – thick and fast. By the end of the season, Liverpool had repeated their success of 1972-73 by winning the League championship and the UEFA Cup.

"Bob had finally proven his point," said Ian St John. "Nobody doubted him and Shanks had kept out of it so that no one could say that he was still pulling the strings. But Bob wanted to win something in his own right and, at the end of that season, he had a grin from ear to ear."

It was nothing compared to the grin at the end of the following season. David Johnson was bought for £200,000 from Ipswich and battle was joined. The League championship was won for a tenth time and Liverpool had also reached the FA Cup Final. Were they on for the double? No, it was actually the treble! In an incredible season of European Cup football, Liverpool had also reached the Final of that competition. Manchester United were the FA Cup opposition and proved to just have the edge on the day – beating the Reds 2-1.

Paisley rallied his troops to face Borussia Moenchengladbach in Rome for the 1977 European Cup Final. With hundreds of millions of television viewers worldwide, Liverpool were about to become famous for more than just the Beatles. The game had everything – thrills and skills, ploys and joys, not forgetting cheers and tears. Liverpool won 2-1 and were champions of Europe for the very first time.

Kenny Dalglish arrived following the departure of Kevin Keegan in the summer of 1977. Alan Hansen had been bought a few months earlier. In the seventh minute of his Liverpool League debut, Dalglish scored at Middlesbrough. The goal heralded the start of another era in the club's history. Midway through the season another face was bought from Middlesbrough – Graeme Souness.

The League championship eluded Liverpool as Brian Clough's Nottingham Forest kept up a blistering pace and ultimately took the title, pushing the Reds into second place. To add insult to injury, Liverpool reached the Final of the League Cup for the first time – but it was Forest who pipped them again with a single goal, from a penalty, in the replay!

All was by no means lost though. As reigning champions of Europe, Liverpool were determined to keep their crown. They fought their way to the Final, which had already been allocated to Wembley Stadium. FC Bruges, from Belgium were in the opposite corner. In the end there was only one goal in it – from Kenny Dalglish (who else?). Liverpool had become the first English club to retain the European Cup.

The 1978-79 season started with something less than a bang. The Reds could not believe that the first tie of their European Cup campaign was to be against the team who had been such a bogey the year before – Nottingham Forest. And they did it again! This time, Clough's men won 2-0 on aggregate. Liverpool turned the tables on Forest, however, in the League – and ended the season with only four defeats. Ray Clemence remembers it well.

"We only conceded 16 goals – and there were 27 games in which no goals were conceded. My job was easy because we had such a great defence."

Before the 1979-80 season started, Emlyn Hughes moved to Wolves. Avi Cohen arrived from Maccabi and proved to be a lively, unpredictable joker in the pack of the defence. He added an international flavour to the side but struggled to get a regular slot in such an excellent line-up. Once again the European Cup was a stumbling block, with Liverpool falling at the first fence. The League Cup went the same way and the FA Cup hopes were dashed in the semi-finals when the Reds were beaten 1-0 by

Arsenal – in the THIRD replay! But there was the League championship and, once again, Bob Paisley steered his men to the title and another crack at Europe.

In all this time Paisley had continued to run the ship along much the same lines as Bill Shankly. It was almost as if Shankly had left a treasure chest of jewels and, whenever the side had to dig deep, there was another sparkling gem to see them through. That does not, in any way, detract from Paisley's brilliant management. He was a great driver and mechanic – but it was Shankly who had built the car.

Paisley brought in two more new faces in 1980. One was bought from Chester toward the end of the 1979-80 season. The other came from Ireland's famous Home Farm, and he was drafted into the side in the latter part of the 1980-81 season. Both were then aged 18 and they were going to grow up together as members of the Anfield family. They were, of course, Ian Rush and Ronnie Whelan.

The League championship was well out of sight in the 1980-81 season with Liverpool finishing fifth. The FA Cup also faded when they lost to Everton in the fourth round. But, for the first time, Liverpool lifted the League Cup when they beat West Ham in a replay 2-1 – the Reds goals coming from the Scottish ambassadors, Dalglish and Hansen.

Then there was the European Cup Final and a dream match in Paris against the mighty Real Madrid. The game did not, in fact, live up to its billing, but that didn't matter very much to the Liverpool fans as skipper Phil Thompson received the trophy at the end of a 1-0 victory.

It was a significant moment for Bob Paisley when he held the European Cup for the third time – no other manager had ever achieved such a hat-trick.

"In all that time we knew we were playing for Bob, but we also couldn't help thinking of Bill who had set this terrific ball rolling more than 20 years earlier," said Ray Clemence. "We were still doing things along the lines set down by Bill Shankly. A Legacy is a good description of it."

The Paisley reign continued to the end of the 1982-83 season and, at the end of it all, he was surrounded by the hallmarks of success – six League titles, three consecutive League Cup victories, the UEFA Cup and, of course, three European Cup triumphs. He was also Manager of the Year no fewer than six times, awarded the OBE and had the rare distinction of being the first manager to climb the steps of Wembley to be presented with the trophy his side had just won. That happened at the end of the 1983 League Cup Final, when Manchester United were beaten 2-1 and skipper Graeme Souness insisted that Paisley take the trophy and the honour.

Perhaps Brian Clough summed it up best when he declared: "He's broken this silly myth that nice guys don't win anything. He's one of the nicest guys you could meet in any industry or any walk of life – and he's a winner."

It's true! Bob Paisley was a nice guy. He took everything in his stride, always remained approachable and had a preference for fireside slippers over and above the all-clubbing Del-boy Trotter image adopted by some of his fellow managers and coaches.

Whatever else, he always enjoyed a joke and sometimes would even pretend to be less modest than he was.

"I've been here during the bad times too," he once said. "One year we came second!"

Bob Paisley remained upstairs at Liverpool after he had resigned as manager and it was his assistant who took over. Joe Fagan was Liverpudlian by birth, but his chief claim to soccer fame was more than 150 appearances for Manchester City, including a spell as captain. He joined the Liverpool coaching team before Bill Shankly arrived, he had previously coached at Rochdale, moving to Anfield in 1958.

Eyebrows were raised when it was announced that the then 62-year-old assistant manager was to be the new boss. The Shankly Legacy remained as Joe Fagan had also been a member of the famous Boot Room, and once again that treasure chest proved to be a gold-mine. The FA Cup was soon dismissed but there were other fish to fry. The League Cup Final was a bit special because it was an all-Mersey affair between Liverpool and Everton. It went to a replay but a Graeme Souness goal settled the matter.

The League championship brought an extra slice of history to Anfield as Liverpool won the title for the third consecutive season – the first time that they had achieved such a hat-trick, and only the third club to have done it – Arsenal and Huddersfield being the others.

Then there was the European Cup Final. Back to Rome to play AS Roma was the task if Liverpool were going to win the Cup for the fourth time. The odds were heavily stacked in favour of Roma, who were playing on their home ground. After 90 minutes it was 1-1. After extra-time it was still 1-1. Penalties and nerves of steel had to settle it. Joe Fagan's furrowed brow gave way to a beaming grin as the Liverpool lads won the duel.

The 1984-85 season was going to see more drama and scenes best forgotten. The FA Cup looked to be on the cards until Manchester United put the Reds out at the semi-final stage. Spurs dumped them out of the League Cup – and in the League championship, Liverpool 'slumped' to second place. There was just the European Cup left and Liverpool did, indeed, reach the Final – although afterwards they wished they had not. The Final was against Juventus at the Heysel Stadium in Brussels. Joe Fagan had announced his retirement and the Liverpool board had quickly added that he would be replaced from within the fold of Anfield – by Kenny Dalglish. But those headlines were overshadowed by the events of the Final. Juventus won 1-0 – but the result escaped almost unnoticed in view of the events on the terraces, in which 39 people were killed. It was a sad night for Joe Fagan and a nightmare for football.

When Kenny Dalglish took over, he was the first appointment from outside the Boot Room since 1959. But if he had not actually been in that famous room, Dalglish had been listening at the door. He was also given some official guidance by a man specially appointed to be his guardian angel. Bob Paisley was back – the Legacy was safe.

The 1985-86 season was exciting to say the least. European soccer was out of the question because of a ban by UEFA – and that meant that Dalglish was free to concentrate solely on the domestic competitions. The League Cup run was halted at the semi-final stage by Queen's Park Rangers, but the championship race was still very much alive. Dalglish not only ran the side but he continued playing – and more often than not he ran the entire game as well. Liverpool won the title for the 16th time, many more than their nearest rivals. The season's highlight was yet to come though as both Liverpool and Everton reached the Final of the FA Cup.

A Mersey derby in the FA Cup Final was unheard of and Wembley was awash with blue and red. An entertaining game ended with a 3-1 win for the Reds. Liverpool had done the double at last and the man who had made it happen was only in his first season as manager.

Success followed success with another championship in 1988 and again in 1990. Wimbledon pulled off a surprise FA Cup Final win in 1988, otherwise the Reds would have achieved the double again. The 1989 Final was a repeat all-Mersey affair. Liverpool won again, this time beating Everton 3-2.

The fans at Anfield were still on a high, but they dropped with a mighty thump when Kenny Dalglish announced his resignation in February 1991. It came as a complete shock but the board did not hesitate in giving Ronnie Moran the job on a temporary basis – the Boot Room was still in business.

Moran is still going strong at Anfield and has been with the club since he joined as a 17-year-old in 1951. He played nearly 400 games for Liverpool until retiring in 1964 to take up a place on the coaching team. He has been a fantastic servant to Liverpool Football Club and is totally versed in the Shankly system.

"I just continued to run things the way Shanks had, and then Bob and Joe and, of course, Kenny. It was the Liverpool way and I wasn't going to make changes that were not necessary."

At the end of the 1990-91 season, Liverpool had narrowly missed the League championship. Ronnie Moran had kept the seat warm while the board negotiated with their would-be new manager. It was no secret that they were after Graeme Souness, who was enjoying a controversial, but successful, time as boss of Rangers. He was finally appointed just a few weeks before the end of the season. Ronnie Moran went back into the Boot Room – and the lid was slammed shut on the Shankly Legacy.

"It was quite sad to see really," said Ian St John. "Graeme was a great player, a great Liverpool player. He had also made his point as a manager, but when he arrived back at Anfield, he came back with a new agenda.

"When Kenny had taken over as manager he had continued the pattern. Like Shanks he is football daft. He could tell you almost every player of every club, both at home and abroad. He is a total football nut. He thought Shanks was great and always remembered Shanks giving him the advice, 'Keep fit and don't lose your accent.' Kenny didn't try to change the system, he simply kept it alive and adapted his players to it.

"Graeme was completely different. He changed the whole approach to the game – the training – everything! I think that everyone except the tea-lady ended up with Achilles problems. He thought it was time to change and he set about it with great gusto.

"Shankly's players were rarely injured. You can see from the teams that, very often, the same 11 players would be out there week after week. He was able to do that because of his training methods. He couldn't believe the injury problems he saw at other clubs. Souness had completely different training and playing styles and, quite frankly, they just didn't work at Liverpool."

Souness managed with the same breakneck approach as he had played – a style that had led Frank Worthington to comment: "He's the nastiest, most ruthless man in soccer. Don Revie's bunch of assassins at Leeds were bad enough – but there is a streak in Souness that puts him at the top of the list."

Frank was never slow to tickle the ears of the press, but even allowing for his well-selected choice of words, we can get a picture of Souness that spilled into his management career – with tales of doors kicked off their hinges, and other dressing room demolition displays of temperament.

The Souness bring-and-buy times at Anfield produced the worst League placings for nearly 30 years. There was a respite when Liverpool won the FA Cup with a 2-0 win over Sunderland in 1992, but the writing had been on the wall for some time when, in January 1994, Souness became the first manager to be sacked by Liverpool since Don Welsh departed in 1956.

The board had no hesitation in naming his successor. They unlocked the Boot Room again and out came Roy Evans. The Legacy was open again.

"Roy joined Liverpool from school," Ian St John explained. "He doesn't mind telling you that he owes everything to Bill Shankly."

Evans was born in Bootle and, after joining the club as a trainee, he made his debut as a full-back in 1970. It was obvious though that Evans was never going to consistently be a part of the first team. He played in the USA for a while with Philadelphia Atoms and returned with a championship medal. Shankly gave him the choice – he could either have a free transfer, or he could forget about playing and join the Boot Room coaches.

"I didn't hesitate. I just wanted to be a part of the club. I felt that it was not so much that I was ending my playing days early, but more that I was starting my coaching career early."

Roy Evans reverted back to the old style of preparation and training.

"Roy was a Shankly disciple and under him the whole Shanks way of doing things has returned," remarked Ian St John. "Everyone is happier, healthier and more confident. In his first full season, Roy won the Coca-Cola Cup. In his second season, he took Liverpool to the FA Cup Final, and to third place in the Premiership. It is like the Shankly days all over again. The system still works, and I'm sure that there will be great success in the years ahead for Roy Evans, Liverpool, and the Shankly Legacy."

The Shankly Legacy, inevitably, did not remain the sole property of Liverpool Football Club. Kevin Keegan took time out from soccer after he had hung up his boots but, when he returned suddenly in February 1992, he quickly demonstrated that he had forgotten nothing of the education that he had received under Bill Shankly.

"At Liverpool, success was a gradual thing. It took time. It's the same here, and Newcastle could be an even bigger club than Liverpool. It won't happen overnight, but it gives me pleasure to go abroad and see kids wearing Newcastle shirts. Okay, there still aren't as many as are wearing Liverpool shirts, but in ten years..."

That was Keegan's view after just a couple of months in his new job. It smacks of Shankly's style – the patient enthusiasm, the positive outlook, the psychological refusal to see boundaries.

Within a few months Keegan had saved Newcastle from probable relegation. The following season – 1992-93 – he took the Geordies on a joy-ride to promotion. At last they were back in the big time. What a difference in such a short time. When Keegan arrived, Newcastle were just one place off the bottom of the table, the ground was in decay and the crowds were on the decline. All of that was amazingly similar to the situation into which Shankly had walked at Anfield in 1959.

As we know, the Newcastle revival continued in the Premiership and it seems to be only a matter of time before the trophies start to roll in at St James' Park. Keegan has no qualms about discussing the inspiration for his success. He even has a photograph of Shankly on his wall.

"I can hear him even now. If I have a problem, or need to take a decision on something, I sit and try to picture what Shankly would have done or said. It helps tremendously!" Keegan said. "Bill Shankly was a most important man in my life. I consider it my good fortune that I had his help, advice and instruction to draw on during my career. He was one of the game's great characters and one of the game's great achievers. He made his vision and dreams of Liverpool Football Club come true. He put his character into the club in every facet, from the bottom to the top. For me, possibly his greatest asset was his ability to put all his knowledge and experience into a language that could motivate me.

"My respect for him knows no bounds. His most priceless gift is that he had the human touch – with no pretence. He was the most genuine man that I've ever met!"

Alongside Keegan at Newcastle is former team-mate, Terry McDermott. Together they have created a management team reminiscent of the Shankly-Paisley double-act – a fact that is not lost on Ian St John.

"Their training and preparation follows exactly in the style of Liverpool. There is the same kind of organisation in training, the same kind of game plan and the same kind of preparation for it.

"Shanks believed in letting players express themselves, play their own game and sort out any problems themselves during the game. He would just sit on the bench and watch. Keegan does much the same. But he is very upbeat, very positive, and his team talks will be much the same as Shankly's were. It works doesn't it?

"McDermott keeps morale high. He is the joker of the dressing room and his specific task will be to keep the players happy and relaxed. Kevin and Terry are a good team and they have already performed wonders at Newcastle. It is a different club, just as Liverpool was a different club within a similar time-span, following the arrival of Shanks.

"Their share of the Shankly Legacy has worked for them!"

Ray Clemence is also using some of his Shankly education to further his career. At Tottenham he partnered Doug Livermore, another former Liverpool stable-mate, and together they helped get Spurs to Wembley for the FA Cup Final of 1991, in which Spurs beat Nottingham Forest 2-1. Look in the record books and you will find that Terry Venables was manager at the time – but the day-to-day coaching was chiefly handled by Clemence and Livermore.

During the upheaval at White Hart Lane following the exit of Venables, both men went their separate ways. Livermore returned to Liverpool at the invitation of Roy Evans and has, ever since, been a member of the Evans Boot Room team.

Ray Clemence became manager of Barnet. His appointment came too late to prevent their relegation to Division Three, but the 1995-96 season saw the team only narrowly miss out on a place in the Play-offs.

"I have certainly tried to put into practice some of the things that I learned from Bill Shankly," stated Ray Clemence. "At Tottenham, we trained for fitness without stress and I have tried the same at Barnet. If you can keep the same side together you will get consistent performances and confidence. It was a great education with Shanks. All of us who worked with him took something of him away with us."

Ian St John rates Clemence as one of the best goalkeepers that he has ever seen, but makes a point about management.

"Ray was a fantastic goalkeeper – none better – but how many great managers were goalkeepers? I know that Ray is a great coach and, if anyone can be a successful manager, he can. He has the experience, the common sense and, of course, his share of the Shankly Legacy."

John Toshack has made quite a name for himself as a manager/coach in Spain, but his first management job was at Swansea in February 1978. His initial record was incredible as he took Swansea from the old Fourth Division all the way to the First Division in successive seasons. It was a fantastic achievement and, had there been a little more money to spend, Swansea might have been able to consolidate. As it was, they hit a decline, Toshack left in 1983 and moved to Spain.

"Toshack followed Shankly to the letter at Swansea," said St John. "He was always on the phone to Shanks for advice. If Swansea were playing anywhere near Liverpool, he used to get Shanks to go along and give the Swansea players a pep talk in the dressing room before the game.

"He is still following the same pattern that he learned all that time ago – and it has worked for him. John knew that Liverpool were very special under Shankly, and his ambition is to continue winning trophies the Shankly way."

John King learned from Shankly without going to Anfield. Shanks visited him at Tranmere. Actually it was Shanks who went to Tranmere – at the invitation of Ron Yeats who had become manager of the club.

"Ron already had great experience from his days at Anfield," said John. "But he also learned from Shankly's visits to Preston Park – and so did I. Years afterward, our training and approach have remained much the same as when Shanks first came to see us. We still feel the benefit of his visits."

Tranmere are still the poor relations of Merseyside, but they have the many soccer riches that were bestowed upon them by Bill Shankly.

Kenny Dalglish kept up the good work for Liverpool but then surprised the soccer world for the third time when he agreed to become manager of Blackburn Rovers. If eyebrows had been raised when he was appointed manager of Liverpool, they positively shot off the dome when he suddenly resigned. His third surprise was taking over the reins at Ewood Park.

He was appointed on 12 October 1991, with Ray Harford as his assistant. Blackburn were improving after a poor start and Kenny's first match in charge was a 5-2 home win over Plymouth, which took them to seventh place in the old Second Division. At the end of the season they finished sixth, and were in the Play-offs. A Mike Newell penalty was enough to see off Leicester at Wembley, and Blackburn were promoted to the new Premier League.

Dalglish had spent £6 million to strengthen his squad. The 1992-93 season saw Blackburn finish in a creditable fourth place. The following season they finished second and then, on 14 May 1995, Blackburn Rovers became champions of the Premiership. Dalglish and the club were criticised by many for having spent mega-millions on buying talent. Jason Wilcox put it into perspective.

"It's all right having loads of money to spend, but you still have to buy the right players to fit into your style of football and get-together. Kenny managed to do that and, although the side had some great individuals, they all fitted into a team pattern that proved to be successful."

There was a strong element of Shankly about Dalglish in his treatment of his players. To the public and the press, Kenny presented a dour, monotone exterior. In the dressing room it was a very different story – with the grins and gags reminiscent of Bill Shankly.

Mike Newell commented: "He gets the best out of people

because he knows how to treat players differently. He shares a joke and a laugh with his players and that's what makes him tick."

Mark Atkins confirmed Newell's view.

"He was always talking to the players and explaining what he wanted from them. He always found time for a laugh and a joke with the lads. The only time he got serious was just before a game. He turned us into a team by letting us go out as individuals. He put down guidelines, but mostly he just wanted us to play football."

Does that ring any bells? For Dalglish read Paisley. For Paisley read Shankly.

One of the secrets of Liverpool's success was that nobody ever knew who the manager's favourite players were. Shankly made a point of not picking out particular players for praise until years later. Dalglish learned to adopt the same policy.

"Everybody at Ewood Park simply plays for Blackburn Rovers," said Dalglish. "All the players are treated the same – those I signed, those signed by the previous manager, and those who worked their way up through the ranks. Once we get behind the dressing room door, nobody is considered to be more important than anyone else. The only condition is that they all do their best for each other and the club."

Kenny's fourth surprise was in handing over the hot seat to Ray Harford after Blackburn won the championship. Unlike Shankly, Dalglish moved upstairs to a directorship – but the shock move was as sudden as the departure of Shankly from Anfield.

"You can see great similarities between Kenny and Shanks," said Ian St John. "Kenny was an experienced young player when he joined Liverpool from Celtic. While he was at Anfield he learned a new trade. As a manager, he became only the third boss this century to manage two different clubs to the League championship. In a sense he out-Shanklyed Shankly... but never forget where he did his management apprenticeship and who built the college!"

The Shankly Legacy has invested much in the game. At the end of the 1994-95 season, Kenny Dalglish, Roy Evans, and Kevin Keegan, were in charge of three of the top six clubs. A year later Dalglish had moved upstairs at Blackburn, while Evans and Keegan remained at their respective posts. Their clubs filled three of the top seven places.

Some Legacy, eh?

Tips From The Top

SO you want to be a footballer? Sounds like the title of yet another coaching manual doesn't it? – and yet there are millions of kids who would yell, 'Yes!' to such a question. Hopefully, the chapter on Shankly's methods will have given a few pointers to managers and coaches, but, before he departed, Bill Shankly also left a portion of his Legacy to young hopefuls and to those in charge of them – parents, schoolteachers, youth coaches, in fact to anyone entrusted with sculpturing raw talent into professional potential.

Bill Shankly used to receive hundreds of letters asking how young players can break into big time soccer, and one of the most important points that he made was that players at any level, from childhood to veteran, have to be at the maximum fitness that they can achieve. Here's how Shankly did it.

"As the first step to fitness, I set myself a target which, even today, is considered rather unusual. I set out to be able to jog my way through, at least, an entire match. Even in today's fast-moving games it is reckoned that, if a footballer is in actual contact with the ball for three minutes out of the entire game, he is going some. More than actual contact he must, of course, do a lot more of what we call 'running off the ball'.

"This means, in effect, running to be in a position to take a pass from a colleague, or to be in some other position of assistance to him. In turn this means that, during a match, any one player has to be fairly mobile – more often without the ball than with it.

"Even so, players do get 'rest' periods. These are not, of course, predetermined. The manager does not say to a team before they take the field that player so-and-so will have a rest at a certain time – that would be ridiculous. What does happen, in fact, is that a player will get time to take it easy for a spell simply by the natural ebb and flow of the game. In short, he's not constantly on the move.

"That's where my plan was different. I set out to get myself into such a state of physical fitness that, once the referee's whistle blew to start the game, I could start jogging about the field, taking in sharp bursts, tackles, distribution, long runs on the way, and still be jogging at the final whistle. Having achieved this level, I ensured that, through my football career, I kept fit enough to meet the demands that would be made upon me."

That supreme fitness not only lasted Shankly through his playing days, but also well into the days after retirement when he would play five-a-side games even though he was well into his sixties. He achieved the fitness in the first place by a gradual build-up. Shankly always stressed the need for patience with young players and felt that many potentially great future internationals had given up because of over-training.

"Whether we are talking about boys or grown-up professionals, I have never believed in overdoing things. Of the many really talented young boys, who sign or have trial periods with clubs, very few make the grade and I believe that much of it is because they are overburdened. It is not that they lack the ability, it is that too much is expected of young legs. Coaches have to be patient and give close attention to the capabilities of each individual.

"For instance, I have never believed in training twice a day. You can tire your players or kids – or you can bore them. A lot of coaches will have young boys training in the morning and then training again in the afternoon. By halfway through the second session they are bored and you're doing them no good at all.

"Young schoolboys can be coached out of the game. They are physically taxed, mentally bored and then confused as coaches dazzle them with science. They start talking about this system or that formation. It's like a foreign language to them. How can they do what you want when they don't understand what you want? Coaches mustn't do that! It doesn't impress anyone and every year it loses the game a lot of young talent.

"To young players themselves, I always say that as well as your fitness, practice your skills. A player of any age can do that for himself. Get yourself a wall or practice boards and just keep kicking the ball, passing it, heading it, shooting, juggling, everything. You get out no more than you put in. But use a wall or boards because the ball comes back. If you use a goal the ball doesn't come back unless you hit the woodwork, and you waste time and energy if you keep on having to retrieve it.

"I always urged my professional players to do that. It is also great for young players. If you have fitness and skill you are well on your way. The next thing is dedication. If you really want to be a professional footballer and employ your skills to the best of your ability, then you must also be dedicated. That means that your football comes first. There have been some bad examples of professional footballers who could have done so much more with their careers if they had not allowed their social lives and smoking and drinking to dictate to them. The really honest folk inside the game will agree with me."

So the correct training, fitness, skill, attitude and dedication are all major ingredients. Bill Shankly also listed courage among the necessities for a career in the game. But even if you have, or are developing, all these assets, how do you actually get a career in the game?

"I've been asked this countless times. You can write to the big clubs and ask them for a trial. You may get one, but perhaps you're aiming too high to start with. I know that the big clubs hold the glamour and that their facilities are often better than those of their less financially sound brethren, but don't let that fool you into thinking that there's no future with the smaller clubs.

"It was difficult in my early days. Then, we were hard put to find any gear to train in, and when we did find some tatty old strip to climb into, it was only to lap the field in seemingly never-ending routines.

"It's not like that in modern times. Even the smallest, most financially restricted clubs, manage to put on a brave front for their players – and the coaches are often every bit as good as those you'll get at the larger clubs. Often the only real difference is that there are more of them at the Liverpools and Manchester Uniteds and the rest. There again, of course, the bigger clubs have more players on the staff and so those extra coaches are needed.

"Another good point then, about the smaller clubs, is that with fewer players on the staff, a lad often finds his chance of breaking into the senior side arising faster than if he was with one of the bigger clubs.

"Anyway, it might be worth a try at sending letters but, really, you need to have someone else recommend you. If you're a young lad and you want to get a game, join an organised junior club in an organised league. A club like that will have kit and you will get a number on your shirt – that's important. If you are playing well, someone will ask about 'number-four' or 'number-seven'. So you want to be playing in an organised match with a proper referee. It doesn't matter what league you are playing in. It can be a small local league or a bigger regional league. Get a team that's organised – get your place in that team, and keep it. No matter what game you play in at football, there's always someone watching. The opposition are watching you, the opposition officials are watching you, your own officials are watching you, the referee is watching, and the linesmen are watching you. There will also be a few spectators watching you too. Even for a junior team, a non-League team, a Fourth Division team. No matter who it is there is always someone watching you – and he might be a scout.

"So if you can't get into a senior club, then get into a local side playing organised matches and I'll tell you something – if you can play, someone will see you play. There are many scouts around and some of them are very, very good. If one of these gifted men sees you, he'll not forget you. So I cannot stress enough that you need to get into an organised team, playing at whatever level. You never know who is going to see you.

"If you have a problem in getting in touch with local teams, contact your local Football Association. They will soon be able to put you in touch with your nearest teams and leagues. You can write to the local league secretary and explain that you are wanting to join a team locally – you'll find that they'll help you. Go along and see some of these teams playing. Even if it's on a sports ground with many football pitches and lots of teams playing, go and take a look, find out who is in charge of a team and put your case to him. He'll probably invite you to train with his team.

"If you put yourself out, you'll be successful. I never saw anybody win anything while they're sitting down. You have to get around and make contacts.

"It's a hard job if you're just going to write to the big clubs and then just hope that you'll get a reply. The clubs listen to their scouts first. So try your local sides, get a game, get the jersey on and then you'll have no one to blame but yourself.

"I'm sorry for all the boys and all the trouble they've got to get a career. I know it's hard to break into – but if you can play you'll be spotted. Take it from me, the big clubs are looking for players, but they have their own way of finding them. The way that I've just suggested is the best way – and that's a tip from the top."

And that is your personal share of the Shankly Legacy.

The Shankly Years

AS player and manager, Bill Shankly's career spanned 42 years with, of course, the tragic interruption of World War Two. He had an impressive array of honours, won both with and without his boots on. Shankly was about winning. His priority really was to win the next match – the silverware was hardly on his shopping list. He looked upon trophies and awards as the sort of bonus gifts you get when you've accumulated enough points at a local supermarket or petrol station.

Nevertheless he was a much decorated man. His chief honours are listed here, followed by a season-by-season account of whichever club he was involved with at the time. For statisticians it is another set of figures to compute. For Shanklyites it is the story of his years, every point and every medal the glorious result of honest toil – every defeat a stab-wound.

INTERNATIONAL CAPS
9 April 1938 v England at Wembley, won 1-0
8 October 1938 v Ireland in Belfast, won 2-0
9 November 1938 v Wales at Tynecastle, won 3-2
7 December 1938 v Hungary at Hampden, won 3-1
5 April 1939 v England at Hampden, lost 1-2
Plus seven appearances in Wartime internationals for which caps were not awarded

PLAYING HONOURS
CARLISLE; 31 December 1932 senior debut v Rochdale, drew 2-2
PRESTON; 2 February 1938 v Liverpool, scored first professional goal.
1933-34 Second Division runners-up Promoted
1936-37 FA Cup Finalists v Sunderland, lost 1-3
1937-38 FA Cup winners v Huddersfield, won 1-0
19 March 1949 v Sunderland, final playing appearance

MANAGEMENT HONOURS
LIVERPOOL; 1961-62 Division Two champions
1963-64 League champions
1964-65 FA Cup winners
1965-66 League champions & European Cup-winners' Cup finalists v Borussia Dortmund, lost 1-2
1970-71 FA Cup finalists v Arsenal, lost 1-2
1972-73 League champions & UEFA Cup v Borussia Moenchengladbach, won 3-2
1973-74 FA Cup winners v Newcastle, won 3-0

PERSONAL HONOURS
1973 Manager of the Year
1974 Awarded OBE
1978 PFA Merit Award

And this is a season-by-season account of where his teams finished from his debut playing season with Carlisle, to his farewell campaign in charge of Liverpool:

1932-33 DIVISION 3 NORTH

	P	W	D	L	F	A	W	D	L	F	A	Pts
Hull C	42	18	3	0	69	14	8	4	9	31	31	59
Wrexham	42	18	2	1	75	15	6	7	8	31	36	57
Stockport Co	42	16	2	3	69	30	5	10	6	30	28	54
Chester	42	15	4	2	57	25	7	4	10	37	41	52
Walsall	42	16	4	1	53	15	3	6	12	22	43	48
Doncaster R	42	13	8	0	52	26	4	6	1	25	53	48
Gateshead	42	12	5	4	45	25	7	4	10	33	42	47
Barnsley	42	14	3	4	60	31	5	5	11	32	49	46
Barrow	42	12	3	6	41	24	6	4	11	19	36	43
Crewe A	42	16	3	2	57	16	4	0	17	23	68	43
Tranmere R	42	11	4	6	49	31	6	4	11	21	35	42
Southport	42	15	3	3	54	20	2	4	15	16	47	41
Accrington S	42	12	4	5	55	29	3	6	12	23	47	40
Hartlepools U	42	15	3	3	56	29	1	4	16	31	87	39
Halifax T	42	12	4	5	39	23	3	4	14	32	67	38
Mansfield T	42	13	4	4	57	22	1	3	17	27	78	35
Rotherham U	42	14	3	4	42	21	0	3	18	18	63	34
Rochdale	42	9	4	8	32	33	4	3	14	26	47	33
Carlisle U	**42**	**8**	**7**	**6**	**34**	**25**	**5**	**0**	**16**	**17**	**50**	**33**
York	42	10	4	7	51	38	3	2	16	21	54	32
New Brighton	42	8	6	7	42	36	3	4	14	21	52	32
Darlington	42	9	6	6	42	32	1	2	18	24	77	28

1934-35 DIVISION 1

	P	W	D	L	F	A	W	D	L	F	A	Pts
Arsenal	42	15	4	2	74	17	8	8	5	41	29	58
Sunderland	42	13	4	4	57	24	6	12	3	33	27	54
Sheffield W	42	14	7	0	42	17	4	6	11	28	47	49
Manchester C	42	13	5	3	53	25	7	3	11	29	42	48
Grimsby T	42	13	6	2	49	25	4	5	12	29	35	45
Derby Co	42	10	4	7	44	28	8	5	8	37	38	45
Liverpool	42	13	4	4	53	29	6	3	12	32	59	45
Everton	42	14	5	2	64	32	2	7	12	25	56	44
WBA	42	10	8	3	55	33	7	2	12	28	50	44
Stoke C	42	12	5	4	46	20	6	1	14	25	50	42
Preston NE	**42**	**11**	**5**	**5**	**33**	**22**	**4**	**7**	**10**	**29**	**45**	**42**
Chelsea	42	11	5	5	49	32	5	4	12	24	50	41
Aston Villa	42	11	6	4	50	36	3	7	11	24	52	41
Portsmouth	42	10	5	6	41	24	5	5	11	30	48	40
Blackburn R	42	12	5	4	42	23	2	6	13	24	55	39
Huddersfield T	42	11	5	5	52	27	3	5	13	24	44	38
Wolves	42	13	3	5	65	38	2	5	14	23	56	38
Leeds U	42	10	5	6	48	35	3	6	12	27	57	38
Birmingham	42	10	3	8	36	36	3	7	11	27	45	36
Middlesbrough	42	8	9	4	38	29	2	5	14	32	61	34
Leicester C	42	9	4	8	39	30	3	5	13	22	56	33
Tottenham H	42	8	8	5	34	31	2	2	17	20	62	30

1933-34 DIVISION 2

	P	W	D	L	F	A	W	D	L	F	A	Pts
Grimsby T	42	15	3	3	62	28	12	2	7	41	31	59
Preston NE	**42**	**15**	**3**	**3**	**47**	**20**	**8**	**3**	**10**	**24**	**32**	**52**
Bolton W	42	14	2	5	45	22	7	7	7	34	33	51
Brentford	42	15	2	4	52	24	7	5	9	33	36	51
Bradford	42	16	2	3	63	27	7	1	13	23	40	49
Bradford C	42	14	4	3	46	25	6	2	13	27	42	46
West Ham U	42	13	3	5	51	28	4	8	9	27	42	45
Port Vale	42	14	4	3	39	14	5	3	13	21	41	45
Oldham A	42	12	5	4	48	28	5	5	11	24	32	44
Plymouth A	42	12	7	2	43	20	3	6	12	26	50	43
Blackpool	42	10	8	3	39	27	5	5	11	23	37	43
Bury	42	12	4	5	43	31	5	5	11	27	42	43
Burnley	42	14	2	5	40	29	4	4	13	20	43	42
Southampton	42	15	2	4	40	21	0	6	15	14	37	38
Hull C	42	11	4	6	33	20	2	8	11	19	48	38
Fulham	42	13	3	5	29	17	2	4	15	19	50	37
Nottingham F	42	11	4	6	50	27	2	5	14	23	47	35
Notts Co	42	9	7	5	32	22	3	4	14	21	40	35
Swansea T	42	10	9	2	36	19	0	6	15	15	41	35
Manchester U	42	9	3	9	29	33	5	3	13	30	52	34
Millwall	42	8	8	5	21	17	3	3	14	18	51	33
Lincoln C	42	7	7	7	31	23	2	1	18	13	52	26

1935-36 DIVISION 1

	P	W	D	L	F	A	W	D	L	F	A	Pts
Sunderland	42	17	2	2	71	33	8	4	9	38	41	56
Derby Co	42	13	5	3	43	23	5	7	9	18	29	48
Huddersfield T	42	12	7	2	32	15	6	5	10	27	41	48
Stoke C	42	13	3	5	35	24	7	4	10	22	33	47
Brentford	42	11	5	5	48	25	6	7	8	33	35	46
Arsenal	42	9	9	3	44	22	6	6	9	34	26	45
Preston NE	**42**	**15**	**3**	**3**	**44**	**18**	**3**	**5**	**13**	**23**	**46**	**44**
Chelsea	42	11	7	3	39	27	4	6	11	26	45	43
Manchester C	42	13	2	6	44	17	4	6	11	24	43	42
Portsmouth	42	14	4	3	39	22	3	4	14	15	45	42
Leeds U	42	11	5	5	41	23	4	6	11	25	41	41
Birmingham	42	10	6	5	38	31	5	5	11	23	32	41
Bolton W	42	11	4	6	41	27	3	9	9	26	49	41
Middlesbrough	42	12	6	3	56	23	3	4	14	28	47	40
Wolves	42	13	7	1	59	28	2	3	16	18	48	40
Everton	42	12	5	4	61	31	1	8	12	28	58	39
Grimsby T	42	13	4	4	44	20	4	1	16	21	53	39
WBA	42	12	3	6	54	31	4	3	14	35	57	38
Liverpool	42	11	4	6	43	23	2	8	11	17	41	38
Sheffield W	42	9	8	4	35	23	4	4	13	28	54	38
Aston Villa	42	7	6	8	47	56	6	3	12	34	54	35
Blackburn R	42	10	6	5	32	24	2	3	16	23	72	33

1936-37 DIVISION 1

	P	W	D	L	F	A	W	D	L	F	A	Pts
Manchester C	42	15	5	1	56	22	7	8	6	51	39	57
Charlton A	42	15	5	1	37	13	6	7	8	21	36	54
Arsenal	42	10	10	1	43	20	8	6	7	37	29	52
Derby Co	42	13	3	5	58	39	8	4	9	38	51	49
Wolves	42	16	2	3	63	24	5	3	13	21	43	47
Brentford	42	14	5	2	58	32	4	5	12	24	46	46
Middlesbrough	42	14	6	1	49	22	5	2	14	25	49	46
Sunderland	42	17	2	2	59	24	2	4	15	30	63	44
Portsmouth	42	13	3	5	41	29	4	7	10	21	37	44
Stoke C	42	12	6	3	52	27	3	6	12	20	30	42
Birmingham	42	9	7	5	36	24	4	8	9	28	36	41
Grimsby T	42	13	3	5	60	32	4	4	13	26	49	41
Chelsea	42	11	6	4	36	21	3	7	11	16	34	41
Preston NE	**42**	**10**	**6**	**5**	**35**	**28**	**4**	**7**	**10**	**21**	**39**	**41**
Huddersfield T	42	12	5	4	39	21	0	10	11	23	43	39
WBA	42	13	3	5	45	32	3	3	15	32	66	38
Everton	42	12	7	2	56	23	2	2	17	25	55	37
Liverpool	42	9	8	4	38	26	3	3	15	24	58	35
Leeds U	42	14	3	4	44	20	1	1	19	16	60	34
Bolton W	42	6	6	9	22	33	4	8	9	21	33	34
Manchester U	42	8	9	4	29	26	2	3	16	26	52	32
Sheffield W	42	8	5	8	32	29	1	7	13	21	40	30

1937-38 DIVISION 1

	P	W	D	L	F	A	W	D	L	F	A	Pts
Arsenal	42	15	4	2	52	16	6	6	9	25	28	52
Wolves	42	11	8	2	47	21	9	3	9	25	28	51
Preston NE	**42**	**9**	**9**	**3**	**34**	**21**	**7**	**8**	**6**	**30**	**23**	**49**
Charlton A	42	14	5	2	43	14	2	9	10	22	37	46
Middlesbrough	42	12	4	5	40	26	7	4	10	32	39	46
Brentford	42	10	6	5	44	27	8	3	10	25	32	45
Bolton W	42	11	6	4	38	22	4	9	8	26	38	45
Sunderland	42	12	6	3	32	18	2	10	9	23	39	44
Leeds U	42	11	6	4	38	26	3	9	9	26	43	43
Chelsea	42	11	6	4	40	22	3	7	11	25	43	41
Liverpool	42	9	5	7	40	30	6	6	9	25	41	41
Blackpool	42	10	5	6	33	26	6	3	12	28	40	40
Derby Co	42	10	5	6	42	36	5	5	11	24	51	40
Everton	42	11	5	5	54	34	5	2	14	25	41	39
Huddersfield T	42	11	3	7	29	24	6	2	13	26	44	39
Leicester C	42	9	6	6	31	26	5	5	11	23	49	39
Stoke C	42	10	7	4	42	21	3	5	13	16	38	38
Birmingham	42	7	11	3	34	28	3	7	11	24	34	38
Portsmouth	42	11	6	4	41	22	2	6	13	21	46	38
Grimsby T	42	11	5	5	29	23	2	7	12	22	45	38
Manchester C	42	12	2	7	49	33	2	6	13	31	44	36
WBA	42	10	5	6	46	36	4	3	14	28	55	36

1938-39 DIVISION 1

	P	W	D	L	F	A	W	D	L	F	A	Pts
Everton	42	17	3	1	60	18	10	2	9	28	34	59
Wolves	42	14	6	1	55	12	8	5	8	33	27	55
Charlton A	42	16	3	2	49	24	6	3	12	26	35	50
Middlesbrough	42	13	6	2	64	27	7	3	11	29	47	49
Arsenal	42	14	3	4	34	14	5	6	10	21	27	47
Derby Co	42	12	3	6	39	22	7	5	9	27	33	46
Stoke C	42	13	6	2	50	25	4	6	11	21	43	46
Bolton W	42	10	6	5	39	25	5	9	7	28	33	45
Preston NE	**42**	**13**	**7**	**1**	**44**	**19**	**3**	**5**	**13**	**19**	**40**	**44**
Grimsby T	42	11	6	4	38	26	5	5	11	23	43	43
Liverpool	42	12	6	3	40	24	2	8	11	22	39	42
Aston Villa	42	11	3	7	44	25	5	6	10	27	35	41
Leeds U	42	11	5	5	40	27	5	4	12	19	40	41
Manchester U	42	7	9	5	30	20	4	7	10	27	45	38
Blackpool	42	9	8	4	37	26	3	6	12	19	42	38
Sunderland	42	7	7	7	30	29	6	5	10	24	38	38
Portsmouth	42	10	7	4	25	15	2	6	13	22	55	37
Brentford	42	11	2	8	30	27	3	6	12	23	47	36
Huddersfield T	42	11	4	6	38	18	1	7	13	20	46	35
Chelsea	42	10	5	6	43	29	2	4	15	21	51	33
Birmingham	42	10	5	6	40	27	2	3	16	22	57	32
Leicester C	42	7	*6	8	35	35	2	5	14	13	47	29

1939-40 DIVISION 1

	P	W	D	L	F	A	W	D	L	F	A	Pts
Blackpool	3	2	0	0	4	2	1	0	0	1	0	6
Sheffield U	3	1	0	0	2	1	1	1	0	1	0	5
Arsenal	3	2	0	0	6	2	0	1	0	2	2	5
Liverpool	3	2	0	0	5	1	0	0	1	1	2	4
Everton	3	0	1	0	1	1	1	1	0	4	3	4
Bolton W	3	1	0	0	2	1	1	0	1	4	4	4
Derby Co	3	2	0	0	3	0	0	0	1	0	3	4
Charlton A	3	1	0	0	2	0	1	0	1	1	4	4
Stoke C	3	1	0	1	5	2	0	1	0	2	2	3
Manchester U	3	1	0	0	4	0	0	0	1	1	3	3
Brentford	3	1	0	0	1	0	0	1	1	2	3	3
Chelsea	3	1	1	0	4	3	0	0	1	0	1	3
Grimsby T	3	1	1	0	2	0	0	0	1	0	4	3
Aston Villa	3	1	0	1	3	2	0	0	1	0	1	2
Sunderland	3	1	0	1	4	2	0	0	1	2	5	2
Wolves	3	0	1	0	2	2	0	1	1	1	2	2
Huddersfield T	3	0	0	1	0	1	1	0	1	2	2	2
Portsmouth	3	1	0	0	2	1	0	0	2	1	4	2
Preston NE	**3**	**0**	**2**	**0**	**0**	**0**	**0**	**0**	**1**	**0**	**2**	**2**
Blackburn R	3	0	1	0	2	2	0	0	2	1	3	1
Middlesbrough	3	0	1	0	2	2	0	0	2	1	6	1
Leeds U	3	0	0	2	0	2	0	1	0	0	0	1

1946-47 DIVISION 1

	P	W	D	L	F	A	W	D	L	F	A	Pts
Liverpool	42	13	3	5	42	24	12	4	5	42	28	57
Manchester U	42	17	3	1	61	19	5	9	7	34	35	56
Wolves	42	15	1	5	66	31	10	5	6	32	25	56
Stoke C	42	14	5	2	52	21	10	2	9	38	32	55
Blackpool	24	14	1	6	38	32	8	5	8	33	38	50
Sheffield U	42	12	4	5	51	32	9	3	9	38	43	49
Preston NE	**42**	**10**	**7**	**4**	**45**	**27**	**8**	**4**	**9**	**31**	**47**	**47**
Aston Villa	42	9	6	6	39	24	9	3	9	28	29	45
Sunderland	42	11	3	7	33	27	7	5	9	32	39	44
Everton	42	13	5	3	40	24	4	4	13	22	43	43
Middlesbrough	42	11	3	7	46	32	6	5	10	27	36	42
Portsmouth	42	11	3	7	42	27	5	6	10	24	33	41
Arsenal	42	9	5	7	43	33	7	4	10	29	37	41
Derby Co	42	13	2	6	44	28	5	3	13	29	51	41
Chelsea	42	9	3	9	33	39	7	4	10	36	45	39
Grimsby T	42	9	6	6	37	35	4	6	11	24	47	38
Blackburn R	42	6	5	10	23	27	8	3	10	22	26	36
Bolton W	42	8	5	8	30	28	5	3	13	27	41	34
Charlton A	42	6	6	9	34	32	5	6	10	23	39	34
Huddersfield T	42	11	4	6	34	24	2	3	16	19	55	33
Brentford	42	5	5	11	19	35	4	2	15	26	53	25
Leeds U	42	6	5	10	30	30	0	1	20	15	60	18

1947-48 DIVISION 1

	P	W	D	L	F	A	W	D	L	F	A	Pts
Arsenal	42	15	3	3	56	15	8	10	3	25	17	59
Manchester U	42	11	7	3	50	27	8	7	6	31	21	52
Burnley	42	12	5	4	31	12	8	7	6	25	31	52
Derby Co	42	11	6	4	38	24	8	6	7	39	33	50
Wolves	42	12	4	5	45	29	7	5	9	38	41	47
Aston Villa	42	13	5	3	42	22	6	4	11	23	35	47
Preston NE	**42**	**13**	**4**	**4**	**43**	**35**	**7**	**3**	**11**	**24**	**33**	**47**
Portsmouth	42	13	5	3	44	17	6	2	13	24	33	45
Blackpool	42	13	4	4	37	14	4	6	11	20	27	44
Manchester C	42	13	3	5	37	22	2	9	10	15	25	42
Liverpool	42	9	8	4	39	23	7	2	12	26	38	42
Sheffield U	42	13	4	4	44	24	3	6	12	21	46	42
Charlton A	42	8	4	9	33	29	9	2	10	24	37	40
Everton	42	10	2	9	30	26	7	4	10	22	40	40
Stoke C	42	9	5	7	29	23	5	5	11	12	32	38
Middlesbrough	42	8	7	6	37	27	6	2	13	34	46	37
Bolton WE	42	11	2	8	29	25	5	3	13	17	33	37
Chelsea	42	11	6	4	38	27	3	3	15	15	44	37
Huddersfield T	42	7	6	8	25	24	5	6	10	26	36	36
Sunderland	42	11	4	6	33	18	2	6	13	23	49	36
Blackburn R	42	8	5	8	35	30	3	5	13	19	42	32
Grimsby T	42	5	5	11	20	35	3	1	17	25	76	22

1948-49 DIVISION 1

	P	W	D	L	F	A	W	D	L	F	A	Pts
Portsmouth	42	18	3	0	52	12	7	5	9	32	30	58
Manchester U	42	11	7	3	40	20	10	4	7	37	24	53
Derby Co	42	17	2	2	48	22	5	7	9	26	33	53
Newcastle U	42	12	5	4	35	29	8	7	6	35	27	52
Arsenal	42	13	5	3	51	18	5	8	8	23	26	49
Wolves	42	13	5	3	48	19	4	7	10	31	47	46
Manchester C	42	10	8	3	28	21	5	7	9	19	30	45
Sunderland	42	8	10	3	27	19	5	7	9	22	39	43
Charlton A	42	10	5	6	38	31	5	7	9	25	36	42
Aston Villa	42	10	6	5	40	36	6	4	11	20	40	42
Stoke C	42	14	3	4	43	24	2	6	13	23	44	41
Liverpool	42	5	10	6	25	18	8	4	9	28	25	40
Chelsea	42	10	6	5	43	27	2	8	11	26	41	38
Bolton W	42	10	4	7	43	32	4	6	11	16	36	38
Burnley	42	10	6	5	27	19	2	8	11	16	31	38
Blackpool	42	8	8	5	24	25	3	8	10	30	42	38
Birmingham C	42	9	7	5	19	10	2	8	11	17	28	37
Everton	42	12	5	4	33	25	1	6	14	8	38	37
Middlesbrough	42	10	6	5	37	23	1	6	14	9	34	34
Huddersfield	42	6	7	8	19	24	6	3	12	21	45	34
Preston NE	**42**	**8**	**6**	**7**	**36**	**36**	**3**	**5**	**13**	**26**	**39**	**33**
Sheffield U	42	8	9	4	32	25	3	2	16	25	53	33

1949-50 DIVISION 3 NORTH

	P	W	D	L	F	A	W	D	L	F	A	Pts
Doncaster R	42	9	9	3	30	15	10	8	3	36	23	55
Gateshead	42	13	5	3	51	23	10	2	9	36	31	53
Rochdale	42	15	3	3	42	13	6	6	9	26	28	51
Lincoln C	42	14	5	2	35	9	7	4	10	25	30	51
Tranmere R	42	15	3	3	35	21	4	8	9	16	27	49
Rotherham U	42	10	6	5	46	28	9	4	8	34	31	48
Crewe A	42	10	6	5	38	27	7	8	6	30	28	48
Mansfield T	42	12	4	5	37	20	6	8	7	29	34	48
Carlisle U	**42**	**12**	**6**	**3**	**39**	**20**	**4**	**9**	**8**	**39**	**31**	**47**
Stockport Co	42	14	2	5	33	21	5	5	11	22	31	45
Oldham A	42	10	4	7	32	31	6	7	8	26	32	43
Chester	42	12	3	6	47	33	5	3	13	23	46	40
Accrington S	42	12	5	4	41	21	4	2	15	16	41	39
New Brighton	42	10	5	6	27	25	4	5	12	18	38	38
Barrow	42	9	6	6	27	20	5	3	13	20	33	37
Southport	42	7	10	4	29	26	5	3	13	22	45	37
Darlington	42	9	8	4	35	27	2	5	14	21	42	35
Hartlepools U	42	10	3	8	37	35	4	2	15	15	44	33
Bradford C	42	11	1	9	38	32	1	7	13	23	44	32
Wrexham	42	8	7	6	24	17	5	4	14	15	37	32
Halifax T	42	9	5	7	35	31	3	3	15	23	54	32
York C	42	6	7	8	29	33	3	6	12	23	37	31

1950-51 DIVISION 3 NORTH

	P	W	D	L	F	A	W	D	L	F	A	Pts
Rotherham U	46	16	3	4	55	16	15	6	2	48	25	71
Mansfield T	46	17	6	0	54	19	9	6	8	24	29	64
Carlisle U	**46**	**18**	**4**	**1**	**44**	**17**	**7**	**8**	**8**	**35**	**33**	**62**
Tranmere R	46	15	5	3	51	26	9	6	8	32	36	59
Lincoln C	46	18	1	4	62	23	7	7	9	27	35	58
Bradford	46	15	3	5	46	23	8	5	10	44	49	54
Bradford C	46	13	4	6	55	30	8	6	9	35	33	52
Gateshead	46	17	1	5	60	21	4	7	12	24	41	50
Crewe A	46	11	5	7	38	26	8	5	10	23	34	48
Stockport Co	46	15	3	5	45	26	5	5	13	18	37	48
Rochdale	46	11	6	6	38	18	6	5	12	31	44	45
Scunthorpe U	46	10	12	1	32	9	3	6	14	26	48	44
Chester	46	11	6	6	42	30	6	3	14	20	34	43
Wrexham	46	12	6	5	37	28	3	6	14	18	43	42
Oldham A	46	10	5	8	47	36	6	3	14	26	37	40
Hartlepools U	46	14	5	4	55	26	2	2	19	9	40	39
York C	46	7	12	4	37	24	5	3	15	29	53	39
Darlington	46	10	8	5	35	29	3	5	15	24	48	39
Barrow	46	12	3	8	38	27	4	3	16	13	49	38
Shrewsbury T	46	11	3	9	28	30	4	4	15	15	44	37
Southport	46	9	4	10	29	25	4	6	13	27	47	36
Halifax T	46	11	6	6	36	24	0	6	17	14	45	34
Accrington S	46	10	4	9	28	29	1	6	16	14	72	32
New Brighton	46	7	6	10	22	32	4	2	17	18	58	30

1951-52 DIVISION 3 NORTH

	P	W	D	L	F	A	W	D	L	F	A	Pts
Lincoln C	46	19	2	2	80	23	11	7	5	41	29	69
Grimsby T	**46**	**19**	**2**	**2**	**59**	**14**	**10**	**6**	**7**	**37**	**31**	**66**
Stockport Co	46	12	9	2	47	17	11	4	8	27	23	59
Oldham A	46	19	2	2	65	22	5	7	11	25	39	57
Gateshead	46	14	7	2	41	17	7	4	12	25	32	53
Mansfield T	46	17	3	3	50	23	5	5	13	23	37	52
Carlisle U	46	10	7	6	31	24	9	6	8	31	33	51
Bradford	46	13	6	4	51	28	6	6	11	23	36	50
Hartlepools U	46	17	3	3	47	19	4	5	14	24	46	50
York C	46	16	4	3	53	19	2	9	12	20	33	49
Tranmere R	46	17	2	4	59	29	4	4	15	17	42	48
Barrow	46	13	5	5	33	19	4	7	12	24	42	46
Chesterfield	46	15	7	1	47	16	2	4	17	18	50	45
Scunthorpe U	46	10	11	2	39	23	4	5	14	26	51	44
Bradford C	46	12	5	6	40	32	4	5	14	21	36	42
Crewe A	46	12	6	5	42	28	5	2	16	21	54	42
Southport	46	12	6	5	36	22	3	5	15	17	49	41
Wrexham	46	14	5	4	41	22	1	4	18	22	51	39
Chester	46	13	4	6	46	30	2	5	16	26	55	39
Halifax T	46	11	4	8	31	23	3	3	17	30	74	35
Rochdale	46	10	5	8	32	34	1	8	14	15	45	35
Accrington S	46	6	8	9	30	34	4	4	15	31	58	32
Darlington	46	10	5	8	39	34	1	4	18	25	69	31
Workington	46	8	4	11	33	34	3	3	17	17	57	29

1952-53 DIVISION 3 NORTH

	P	W	D	L	F	A	W	D	L	F	A	Pts
Oldham A	46	15	4	4	48	21	7	11	5	29	24	59
Port Vale	46	13	9	1	41	10	7	9	7	26	25	58
Wrexham	46	18	3	2	59	24	6	5	12	27	42	56
York C	46	14	5	4	35	16	6	8	9	25	29	53
Grimsby T	**46**	**15**	**5**	**3**	**47**	**19**	**6**	**5**	**12**	**28**	**40**	**52**
Southport	46	16	4	3	42	18	4	7	12	21	42	51
Bradford	46	10	8	5	37	23	9	4	10	38	38	50
Gateshead	46	13	6	4	51	24	4	9	10	25	36	49
Carlisle U	46	13	7	3	57	24	5	6	12	25	44	49
Crewe A	46	13	5	5	46	28	7	3	13	24	40	48
Stockport Co	46	13	8	2	61	26	4	5	14	21	43	47
Chesterfield	46	13	6	4	40	23	5	5	13	25	40	47
Tranmere R	46	16	4	3	45	16	5	1	17	20	47	47
Halifax T	46	13	5	5	47	31	3	10	10	31	37	47
Scunthorpe U	46	10	6	7	38	21	6	8	9	24	35	46
Bradford C	46	14	7	2	54	29	0	11	12	21	51	46
Hartlepools U	46	14	6	3	39	16	2	8	13	18	45	46
Mansfield T	46	11	9	3	34	25	5	5	13	21	37	46
Barrow	46	15	6	2	48	20	1	6	16	18	51	44
Chester	46	10	7	6	39	27	1	8	14	25	58	37
Darlington	46	13	4	6	33	27	1	2	20	25	69	34
Rochdale	46	12	5	6	41	27	2	0	21	21	56	33
Workington	46	9	5	9	40	33	2	5	16	15	58	32
Accrington S	46	7	9	7	25	29	1	2	20	14	60	27

1953-54 DIVISION 3 NORTH

	P	W	D	L	F	A	W	D	L	F	A	Pts
Port Vale	46	16	7	0	48	5	10	10	3	26	16	69
Barnsley	46	16	3	4	54	24	8	7	8	23	33	58
Scunthorpe U	46	14	7	2	49	24	7	8	8	28	32	57
Gateshead	46	15	4	4	49	22	6	9	8	25	33	55
Bradford C	46	15	6	2	40	14	7	3	13	20	41	53
Chesterfield	46	13	6	4	41	19	6	8	9	35	45	52
Mansfield T	46	15	5	3	59	22	5	6	12	29	45	51
Wrexham	46	16	4	3	59	19	5	5	13	22	49	51
Bradford	46	13	6	4	57	31	5	8	10	20	37	50
Stockport Co	46	14	6	3	57	20	4	5	14	20	47	47
Southport	46	12	5	6	41	26	5	7	11	22	34	46
Barrow	46	12	7	4	46	26	4	5	14	26	45	44
Carlisle U	46	10	8	5	53	27	4	7	12	30	44	43
Tranmere R	46	11	4	8	40	34	7	3	13	19	36	43
Accrington S	46	12	7	4	41	22	4	3	16	25	52	42
Crewe A	46	9	8	6	30	26	5	5	13	19	41	41
Grimsby T	**46**	**14**	**5**	**4**	**31**	**15**	**2**	**4**	**17**	**20**	**62**	**41**
Hartlepools U	46	10	8	5	40	21	3	6	14	19	44	40
Rochdale	46	12	5	6	40	20	3	5	15	19	57	40
Workington	**46**	**10**	**9**	**4**	**36**	**22**	**3**	**5**	**15**	**23**	**58**	**40**
Darlington	46	11	3	9	31	27	1	11	11	19	44	38
York C	46	8	7	8	39	32	4	6	13	25	54	37
Halifax T	46	9	6	8	26	21	3	4	16	18	52	34
Chester	46	10	7	6	39	22	1	3	19	9	45	32

1954-55 DIVISION 3 NORTH

	P	W	D	L	F	A	W	D	L	F	A	Pts
Barnsley	46	18	3	2	51	17	12	2	9	35	29	65
Accrington S	46	18	2	3	65	32	7	9	7	31	35	61
Scunthorpe U	46	14	6	3	45	18	9	6	8	36	35	58
York C	46	13	5	5	43	27	11	5	7	49	36	58
Hartlepools U	46	16	3	4	39	20	9	2	12	25	29	55
Chesterfield	46	17	1	5	54	33	7	5	11	27	37	54
Gateshead	46	11	7	5	38	26	9	5	9	27	43	52
Workington	**46**	**11**	**7**	**5**	**39**	**23**	**7**	**7**	**9**	**29**	**32**	**50**
Stockport Co	46	13	4	6	50	27	5	8	10	34	43	48
Oldham A	46	14	5	4	47	22	5	5	13	27	46	48
Southport	46	10	9	4	28	18	6	7	10	19	26	48
Rochdale	46	13	7	3	39	20	4	7	12	30	46	48
Mansfield T	46	14	4	5	40	28	4	5	14	25	43	45
Halifax T	46	9	9	5	41	27	6	4	13	22	40	43
Darlington	46	10	7	6	41	28	4	7	12	21	45	42
Bradford	46	11	7	5	29	21	4	4	15	278	49	41
Barrow	46	12	4	7	39	34	5	2	16	31	55	40
Wrexham	46	9	6	8	40	35	4	6	13	25	42	38
Tranmere R	46	9	6	8	37	30	4	5	14	18	40	37
Carlisle U	46	12	1	10	53	39	3	5	15	25	50	36
Bradford C	46	9	5	9	30	26	4	5	14	17	29	36
Crewe A	46	8	10	5	45	35	2	4	17	23	56	34
Grimsby T	46	10	4	9	28	32	3	4	16	19	46	34
Chester	46	10	3	10	23	25	2	6	15	21	52	33

DIVISION 3 NORTH

	P	W	D	L	F	A	W	D	L	F	A	Pts
Grimsby T	46	20	1	2	54	10	11	5	7	22	19	68
Derby Co	46	18	4	1	67	23	10	3	10	43	32	63
Accrington S	46	17	4	2	61	19	8	5	10	31	38	59
Hartlepools U	46	18	2	3	47	15	8	3	12	34	45	57
Southport	46	12	9	2	39	18	11	2	10	27	35	57
Chesterfield	46	18	1	4	61	21	7	3	13	33	45	54
Stockport Co	46	16	4	3	65	22	5	5	13	25	39	51
Bradford C	46	16	5	2	57	25	2	8	13	21	39	49
Scunthorpe U	46	12	4	7	40	26	8	4	11	35	37	48
Workington	**46**	**13**	**4**	**6**	**47**	**20**	**6**	**5**	**12**	**28**	**43**	**47**
York C	46	12	4	7	44	24	7	5	11	41	48	47
Rochdale	46	13	5	5	46	3	4	8	11	20	45	47
Gateshead	46	15	4	4	56	32	2	7	14	21	52	45
Wrexham	46	11	5	7	37	28	5	5	13	29	45	42
Darlington	46	11	6	6	41	28	5	3	15	19	45	41
Tranmere R	46	11	4	8	33	25	5	5	13	26	59	41
Chester	46	10	8	5	35	33	3	6	14	17	49	40
Mansfield T	46	13	6	4	59	21	1	5	17	25	60	39
Halifax T	46	10	6	7	40	27	4	5	14	26	49	39
Oldham A	46	7	12	4	48	36	3	6	14	28	50	38
Carlisle U	46	11	3	9	45	36	4	5	14	26	59	38
Barrow	46	11	6	6	44	25	1	3	19	17	58	33
Bradford	46	13	4	6	47	38	0	3	20	14	84	33
Crewe A	46	9	4	10	32	35	0	6	17	18	70	28

1955-56 DIVISION 1

	P	W	D	L	F	A	W	D	L	F	A	Pts
Manchester U	42	18	3	0	51	20	7	7	7	32	31	60
Blackpool	42	13	4	4	56	27	7	5	9	30	35	49
Wolves	42	15	2	4	51	27	5	7	9	38	38	49
Manchester C	42	11	5	5	40	27	7	5	9	42	42	46
Arsenal	42	13	4	4	38	22	5	6	10	22	39	46
Birmingham C	42	12	4	5	51	26	6	5	10	24	31	45
Burnley	42	11	3	7	37	20	7	5	9	27	34	44
Bolton W	42	13	3	5	50	24	5	4	12	21	34	43
Sunderland	42	10	8	3	44	36	7	1	13	36	59	43
Luton T	42	12	4	5	44	27	5	4	12	22	37	42
Newcastle U	42	12	4	5	49	24	5	4	13	36	46	41
Portsmouth	42	9	8	4	46	38	7	1	13	32	47	41
WBA	42	13	3	5	37	25	5	2	14	21	45	41
Charlton A	42	13	2	6	47	26	4	4	13	28	55	40
Everton	42	11	5	5	37	29	4	5	12	18	40	40
Chelsea	42	10	4	7	32	26	4	7	10	32	51	39
Cardiff C	42	11	4	6	36	32	4	5	12	19	37	39
Tottenham H	42	9	4	8	37	33	6	3	12	24	38	37
Preston NE	42	6	5	10	32	36	8	3	10	41	36	36
Aston Villa	42	9	6	6	32	29	2	7	12	20	40	35
Huddersfield T	**42**	**9**	**4**	**8**	**32**	**30**	**5**	**3**	**13**	**22**	**53**	**35**
Sheffield U	42	8	6	7	31	35	4	3	14	32	42	33

1956-57 DIVISION 2

	P	W	D	L	F	A	W	D	L	F	A	Pts
Leicester C	42	14	5	2	68	36	11	6	4	41	31	61
Nottingham F	42	13	4	4	50	29	9	6	6	44	26	54
Liverpool	42	16	1	4	53	26	5	10	6	29	28	53
Blackburn R	42	12	6	3	49	32	9	4	8	34	43	52
Stoke C	42	16	2	3	64	18	4	6	11	19	40	48
Middlesbrough	42	12	5	4	51	29	7	5	9	33	31	48
Sheffield U	42	11	6	4	45	28	8	2	11	42	48	46
West Ham U	42	12	4	5	31	24	7	4	10	28	39	46
Bristol R	42	12	5	4	47	19	6	4	11	34	48	45
Swansea T	42	12	34	6	53	34	7	4	10	37	56	45
Fulham	42	13	1	7	53	32	6	3	12	31	44	42
Huddersfield T	**42**	**10**	**3**	**8**	**33**	**27**	**8**	**3**	**10**	**35**	**47**	**42**
Bristol C	42	13	2	6	49	32	3	7	11	25	47	41
Doncaster R	42	12	5	4	51	21	3	5	13	26	56	40
Leyton O	42	7	8	6	34	38	8	2	11	32	46	40
Grimsby T	42	12	4	5	41	26	5	1	15	20	36	39
Rotherham U	42	9	7	5	37	26	4	4	13	37	49	37
Lincoln C	42	9	4	8	34	27	5	2	14	20	53	34
Barnsley	42	8	7	6	39	35	4	3	14	20	54	34
Notts Co	42	7	6	8	34	32	2	6	13	24	54	30
Bury	42	5	3	13	37	47	3	6	12	23	49	25
Port Vale	42	7	4	10	31	42	1	2	18	26	59	22

1957-58 DIVISION 2

	P	W	D	L	F	A	W	D	L	F	A	Pts
West Ham U	42	12	8	1	56	25	11	3	7	45	29	57
Blackburn R	42	13	7	1	50	18	9	5	7	43	39	56
Charlton A	42	15	3	3	65	33	9	4	8	42	36	55
Liverpool	42	17	3	1	50	13	5	7	9	29	41	54
Fulham	42	13	5	3	53	24	7	7	7	44	35	52
Sheffield U	42	12	5	4	38	22	9	5	7	37	28	52
Middlesbrough	42	13	3	5	52	29	6	4	11	31	45	45
Ipswich T	42	13	4	4	45	29	3	8	19	23	40	44
Huddersfield T	42	9	8	4	28	24	5	8	8	35	42	44
Bristol R	42	2	5	4	52	31	5	3	13	33	49	42
Stoke C	42	9	4	8	49	36	9	2	10	26	37	42
Leyton O	42	14	2	5	53	27	4	3	14	24	52	41
Grimsby T	42	13	4	4	54	30	4	2	15	32	53	40
Barnsley	42	10	6	5	40	25	4	6	11	30	49	40
Cardiff C	42	10	5	6	44	31	4	4	13	19	46	37
Derby Co	42	11	3	7	37	36	3	5	13	23	45	36
Bristol C	42	9	5	7	35	31	4	4	13	28	57	35
Rotherham U	42	8	3	10	38	44	6	2	13	27	57	33
Swansea T	42	8	3	10	48	45	3	6	12	24	54	31
Lincoln C	42	6	6	9	33	35	5	3	13	22	47	31
Notts Co	42	9	3	9	24	31	3	3	15	20	49	30
Doncaster R	42	7	5	9	34	40	1	6	14	22	48	27

1958-59 DIVISION 2

	P	W	D	L	F	A	W	D	L	F	A	Pts
Sheffield W	42	18	2	1	68	13	10	4	7	38	35	62
Fulham	42	18	1	2	65	28	9	5	7	31	35	60
Sheffield U	42	16	2	3	54	15	7	5	9	28	33	53
Liverpool	42	15	3	3	57	25	9	2	10	30	37	53
Stoke C	42	16	2	3	48	19	5	5	11	24	39	49
Bristol R	42	13	5	3	46	23	5	7	9	34	41	48
Derby Co	42	15	1	5	46	29	5	7	9	28	42	48
Charlton A	42	13	3	5	53	33	5	4	12	39	57	43
Cardiff C	42	12	2	7	37	26	6	5	10	28	39	43
Bristol C	42	11	3	7	43	27	6	4	11	31	43	41
Swansea T	42	12	5	4	52	30	4	4	13	27	51	41
Brighton & HA	42	10	9	2	46	29	5	2	14	28	61	41
Middlesbrough	42	9	7	5	51	26	6	3	12	36	45	40
Huddersfield T	42	12	3	6	39	20	4	5	12	23	35	40
Sunderland	42	13	4	4	42	23	3	4	14	22	52	40
Ipswich T	42	12	4	5	37	27	5	2	14	25	50	40
Leyton O	42	9	4	8	43	30	5	4	12	28	48	36
Scunthorpe U	42	7	6	8	32	37	5	3	13	23	47	33
Lincoln C	42	10	5	6	45	37	1	2	18	18	56	29
Rotherham U	42	9	5	7	32	28	1	4	16	10	54	29
Grimsby T	42	7	7	7	41	36	2	3	16	21	54	28
Barnsley	42	8	4	8	34	34	2	3	16	21	57	27

1959-60 DIVISION 2

	P	W	D	L	F	A	W	D	L	F	A	Pts
Aston Villa	42	17	3	1	62	19	8	6	7	27	24	59
Cardiff C	42	15	2	4	55	36	8	10	3	35	26	58
Liverpool	42	15	3	3	59	28	5	7	9	31	38	50
Sheffield U	42	12	5	4	43	22	7	7	7	25	29	50
Middlesbrough	42	14	5	2	56	21	5	5	11	34	43	48
Huddersfield T	42	13	3	5	44	20	6	6	9	29	32	47
Charlton A	42	12	7	2	55	28	5	6	10	35	59	47
Rotherham U	42	9	9	3	31	23	8	4	9	30	37	47
Bristol R	42	12	6	3	42	28	6	5	10	30	50	47
Leyton O	42	12	4	5	47	25	3	10	8	29	36	44
Ipswich T	42	12	5	4	48	24	7	1	13	30	44	44
Swansea T	42	12	6	3	54	32	3	4	14	28	52	40
Lincoln C	42	11	3	7	41	25	5	4	12	34	53	39
Brighton & HA	42	7	8	6	35	32	6	4	11	32	44	38
Scunthorpe U	42	9	7	5	38	26	4	3	14	19	45	36
Sunderland	42	8	6	7	35	29	4	6	11	17	36	36
Stoke C	42	8	3	10	40	38	6	4	11	26	45	35
Derby Co	42	9	4	8	31	28	5	3	13	30	49	35
Plymouth A	42	10	6	5	42	36	3	3	15	19	53	35
Portsmouth	42	6	6	9	36	36	4	6	11	23	41	32
Hull C	42	7	6	8	27	30	3	4	14	21	46	30
Bristol C	42	8	3	10	27	31	3	2	16	33	66	27

1960-61 DIVISION 2

	P	W	D	L	F	A	W	D	L	F	A	Pts
Ipswich T	42	15	3	3	55	24	11	4	6	45	31	59
Sheffield U	42	16	2	3	49	22	10	4	7	32	29	58
Liverpool	42	14	5	2	49	21	7	5	9	38	37	52
Norwich C	42	15	3	3	46	20	5	6	10	24	33	49
Middlesbrough	42	13	6	2	44	20	5	6	10	39	54	48
Sunderland	42	12	5	4	47	24	5	8	8	28	36	47
Swansea T	42	14	4	3	49	26	4	7	10	28	47	47
Southampton	42	12	4	5	57	35	6	4	11	27	46	44
Scunthorpe U	42	9	8	4	39	25	5	7	9	30	39	43
Charlton A	42	12	3	6	60	42	4	8	9	37	49	43
Plymouth A	42	13	4	4	52	32	4	4	13	29	50	42
Derby Co	42	9	6	6	46	35	6	4	11	34	45	40
Luton T	42	13	5	3	48	27	2	4	15	23	52	39
Leeds U	42	7	7	7	41	38	7	3	11	34	45	38
Rotherham U	42	9	7	5	37	24	3	6	12	28	40	37
Brighton & HA	42	9	6	6	33	26	5	3	13	28	49	37
Bristol R	42	13	4	4	52	35	2	3	16	21	57	37
Stoke C	42	9	6	6	39	26	3	6	12	12	33	36
Leyton O	42	10	5	6	31	29	4	3	14	24	49	36
Huddersfield T	42	7	5	9	33	33	6	4	11	29	38	35
Portsmouth	42	10	6	5	38	27	1	5	15	26	64	33
Lincoln C	42	5	4	12	30	43	3	4	14	18	52	24

1961-62 DIVISION 2

	P	W	D	L	F	A	W	D	L	F	A	Pts
Liverpool	42	18	3	0	68	19	9	5	7	31	24	62
Leyton O	42	11	5	5	34	17	11	5	5	35	23	54
Sunderland	42	17	3	1	60	16	5	6	10	25	34	53
Scunthorpe U	42	14	4	3	52	26	7	3	11	34	45	49
Plymouth A	42	12	4	5	45	30	7	4	10	30	45	46
Southampton	42	13	3	5	53	28	5	6	10	24	34	45
Huddersfield T	42	11	5	5	39	22	5	7	9	28	37	44
Stoke C	42	13	4	4	34	17	4	4	13	21	40	42
Rotherham U	42	9	6	6	36	30	7	3	11	34	46	41
Preston NE	42	11	4	6	34	23	4	6	11	21	34	40
Newcastle U	42	10	5	6	40	27	5	4	12	24	31	39
Middlesbrough	42	11	3	7	45	29	5	4	12	31	43	39
Luton T	42	12	1	8	44	37	5	4	12	25	34	39
Walsall	42	11	7	3	42	23	3	4	14	28	52	39
Charlton A	42	10	5	6	38	30	5	4	12	31	45	39
Derby Co	42	10	7	4	42	27	4	4	13	26	48	39
Norwich C	42	10	6	5	36	28	4	5	12	25	42	39
Bury	42	9	4	8	32	36	8	1	12	20	40	39
Leeds U	42	9	6	6	24	19	3	6	12	26	42	36
Swansea T	42	10	5	6	38	30	2	7	12	23	53	36
Bristol R	42	11	3	7	36	31	2	4	15	17	50	33
Brighton & HA	42	7	7	7	24	32	3	4	14	18	54	31

1963-64 DIVISION 1

	P	W	D	L	F	A	W	D	L	F	A	Pts
Liverpool	42	16	0	5	60	18	10	5	6	32	27	57
Manchester U	42	15	3	3	54	19	8	4	9	36	43	53
Everton	42	14	4	3	53	26	7	6	8	31	38	52
Tottenham H	42	13	3	5	54	31	9	4	8	43	50	51
Chelsea	42	12	3	6	36	24	8	7	6	36	32	50
Sheffield W	42	15	3	3	50	24	4	8	9	34	43	49
Blackburn R	42	10	4	7	44	28	8	6	7	45	37	46
Arsenal	42	10	7	4	56	37	7	4	10	34	45	45
Burnley	42	14	3	4	46	23	3	7	11	25	41	44
WBA	42	9	6	6	43	35	7	5	9	27	26	43
Leicester C	42	9	4	8	33	27	7	7	7	28	31	43
Sheffield U	42	10	6	5	35	22	6	5	10	26	42	43
Nottingham F	42	9	5	7	34	24	7	4	10	30	44	41
West Ham U	42	8	7	6	45	38	6	5	10	24	36	40
Fulham	42	11	8	2	45	23	2	5	14	13	42	39
Wolves	42	6	9	6	36	34	6	6	9	34	46	39
Stoke C	42	9	6	6	49	33	5	4	12	28	45	38
Blackpool	42	8	6	7	26	29	5	3	13	26	44	35
Aston Villa	42	8	6	7	35	29	3	6	12	27	42	34
Birmingham C	42	7	7	7	33	32	4	0	17	21	60	29
Bolton W	42	6	5	10	39	35	4	3	4	18	45	28
Ipswich T	42	9	3	9	38	45	0	4	17	18	76	25

1962-63 DIVISION 1

	P	W	D	L	F	A	W	D	L	F	A	Pts
Everton	42	14	7	0	48	17	11	4	6	36	25	61
Tottenham H	42	14	6	1	72	28	9	3	9	39	34	55
Burnley	42	14	4	3	41	17	8	6	7	37	40	54
Leicester C	42	14	6	1	53	23	6	6	9	26	30	52
Wolves	42	11	6	4	51	25	9	4	8	42	40	50
Sheffield W	42	10	5	6	38	26	9	5	7	39	37	48
Arsenal	42	11	4	6	44	33	7	6	8	42	44	46
Liverpool	42	13	3	5	45	2	4	7	10	26	37	44
Nottingham F	42	12	4	5	39	28	5	6	10	28	41	44
Sheffield U	42	11	7	3	33	20	5	5	11	25	40	44
Blackburn R	42	11	4	6	55	34	4	8	9	24	37	42
West Ham U	42	8	6	7	39	34	6	6	9	34	35	40
Blackpool	42	8	7	6	34	27	5	7	9	24	37	40
WBA	42	11	1	9	40	37	5	6	10	31	42	39
Aston Villa	42	12	2	7	38	23	3	6	12	24	45	38
Fulham	42	8	6	7	28	30-	6	4	11	22	41	38
Ipswich T	42	5	8	8	34	39	7	3	11	25	39	35
Bolton W	42	13	3	5	35	18	2	2	17	20	57	35
Manchester U	42	6	6	9	36	38	6	4	11	31	43	34
Birmingham C	42	6	8	7	40	40	4	5	12	23	50	33
Manchester C	42	7	5	9	30	45	3	6	12	28	57	31
Leyton O	42	4	5	12	22	37	2	4	15	15	44	21

1964-65 DIVISION 1

	P	W	D	L	F	A	W	D	L	F	A	Pts
Manchester U	42	16	4	1	52	13	10	5	6	37	26	61
Leeds U	42	16	3	2	53	23	10	6	5	30	29	61
Chelsea	42	15	2	4	48	19	9	6	6	41	35	56
Everton	42	9	10	2	37	22	8	5	8	32	38	49
Nottingham F	42	10	7	4	45	33	7	6	8	26	34	47
Tottenham H	42	18	3	0	65	20	1	4	16	22	51	45
Liverpool	42	12	5	4	42	33	5	5	11	25	40	44
Sheffield W	42	13	5	3	37	15	3	6	12	20	40	43
West Ham U	42	14	2	5	48	25	5	2	14	34	46	42
Blackburn R	42	12	2	7	46	33	4	8	9	37	46	42
Stoke C	42	11	4	6	40	27	5	6	10	27	39	42
Burnley	42	9	9	3	39	26	7	1	13	31	44	42
Arsenal	42	11	5	5	41	31	6	2	13	27	44	41
WBA	42	10	5	6	45	25	3	8	10	25	40	39
Sunderland	42	12	6	3	45	26	2	3	16	19	48	37
Aston Villa	42	14	1	6	36	24	2	4	15	21	58	37
Blackpool	42	9	7	5	41	28	3	4	14	26	50	35
Leicester C	42	9	6	6	43	36	2	7	12	26	49	35
Sheffield U	42	7	5	9	30	29	5	6	10	20	35	35
Fulham	42	10	5	6	44	32	1	7	13	16	46	34
Wolves	42	8	2	11	33	36	5	2	14	26	53	30
Birmingham C	42	6	8	7	36	40	2	3	16	28	56	27

1965-66 DIVISION 1

	P	W	D	L	F	A	W	D	L	F	A	Pts
Liverpool	42	17	2	2	52	15	9	7	5	27	19	61
Leeds U	42	14	4	3	49	15	9	5	7	30	23	55
Burnley	42	15	3	3	45	20	9	4	8	34	27	55
Manchester U	42	12	8	1	50	20	6	7	8	34	39	51
Chelsea	42	11	4	6	30	21	11	3	7	35	32	51
WBA	42	11	6	4	58	34	8	6	7	33	35	50
Leicester C	42	12	4	5	40	28	9	3	9	40	37	49
Tottenham H	42	11	6	4	55	37	5	6	10	20	29	44
Sheffield U	42	11	6	4	37	25	5	5	11	19	34	43
Stoke C	42	12	6	3	42	22	3	6	12	23	42	42
Everton	42	12	6	3	39	19	3	5	13	17	43	41
West Ham U	42	12	5	4	46	33	3	4	14	24	50	39
Blackpool	42	9	5	7	36	29	5	4	12	19	36	37
Arsenal	42	8	8	5	36	31	4	5	12	26	44	37
Newcastle U	42	10	5	6	26	20	4	4	13	24	43	37
Aston Villa	42	10	3	8	39	34	5	3	13	30	46	36
Sheffield W	42	11	6	4	35	18	3	2	16	21	48	36
Nottingham F	42	11	3	7	31	26	3	5	13	25	46	36
Sunderland	42	13	2	6	36	28	1	6	14	15	44	36
Fulham	42	9	4	8	34	37	5	3	13	33	48	35
Northampton T	42	8	6	7	31	32	2	7	12	24	60	33
Blackburn R	42	6	1	14	30	36	2	3	16	27	52	20

1966-67 DIVISION 1

	P	W	D	L	F	A	W	D	L	F	A	Pts
Manchester U	42	17	4	0	51	13	7	8	6	33	32	60
Nottingham F	42	16	4	1	41	13	7	6	8	23	28	56
Tottenham H	42	15	3	3	44	21	9	5	7	27	27	56
Leeds U	42	15	4	2	41	17	7	7	7	21	25	55
Liverpool	42	12	7	2	36	17	7	6	8	28	30	51
Everton	42	11	4	6	39	22	8	6	7	26	24	48
Arsenal	42	11	6	4	32	20	5	8	8	26	27	46
Leicester C	42	12	4	5	47	28	6	4	11	31	43	44
Chelsea	42	7	9	5	33	29	8	5	8	34	33	44
Sheffield U	42	11	5	5	34	22	5	5	11	18	37	42
Sheffield W	42	9	7	5	39	19	5	6	10	17	28	41
Stoke C	42	11	5	5	40	21	6	2	13	23	37	41
WBA	42	11	1	9	40	28	5	6	10	37	45	39
Burnley	42	11	4	6	43	28	4	5	12	23	48	39
Manchester C	42	8	9	4	27	25	4	6	11	16	27	39
West Ham U	42	8	6	7	40	31	6	2	13	40	53	36
Sunderland	42	12	3	6	39	26	2	5	14	19	46	36
Fulham	42	8	7	6	49	34	3	5	13	22	49	34
Southampton	42	10	3	8	49	41	4	3	14	25	51	34
Newcastle U	42	9	5	7	24	27	3	4	14	15	54	33
Aston Villa	42	7	5	9	30	33	4	2	15	24	52	29
Blackpool	42	1	5	15	18	36	5	4	12	23	40	21

1967-68 DIVISION 1

	P	W	D	L	F	A	W	D	L	F	A	Pts
Manchester C	42	17	2	2	52	16	9	4	8	34	27	58
Manchester U	42	15	2	4	49	21	9	6	6	40	34	56
Liverpool	42	17	2	2	51	17	5	9	7	20	23	55
Leeds U	42	17	3	1	49	14	5	6	10	22	27	53
Everton	42	18	1	2	43	13	5	5	11	24	27	52
Chelsea	42	11	7	3	34	25	7	5	9	28	43	48
Tottenham H	42	11	7	3	44	20	8	2	11	26	39	47
WBA	42	12	4	5	45	25	5	8	8	30	37	46
Arsenal	42	12	6	3	37	23	5	4	12	23	33	44
Newcastle U	42	12	7	2	38	20	1	8	12	16	47	41
Nottingham F	42	11	6	4	34	22	3	5	13	18	42	39
West Ham U	42	8	5	8	43	30	6	5	10	30	39	38
Leicester C	42	7	7	7	37	34	6	5	10	27	35	38
Burnley	42	12	7	2	38	16	2	3	16	26	55	38
Sunderland	42	8	7	6	28	25	5	4	12	23	33	37
Southampton	42	9	8	4	37	31	4	3	14	29	52	37
Wolves	42	10	4	7	45	36	4	4	13	21	39	36
Stoke C	42	10	3	8	30	29	4	4	13	20	44	35
Sheffield W	42	6	10	5	32	24	5	2	14	19	39	34
Coventry C	42	8	5	8	32	32	1	10	10	19	39	33
Sheffield U	42	7	4	10	25	31	4	6	11	24	39	32
Fulham	42	6	4	11	27	41	4	3	14	29	57	27

1968-69 DIVISION 1

	P	W	D	L	F	A	W	D	L	F	A	Pts
Leeds U	42	18	3	0	41	9	9	10	2	25	17	67
Liverpool	42	16	4	1	36	10	9	7	5	27	14	61
Everton	42	14	5	2	43	10	7	10	4	34	26	57
Arsenal	42	12	6	3	31	12	10	6	5	25	15	56
Chelsea	42	11	7	3	40	24	9	3	9	33	29	50
Tottenham H	42	10	8	3	39	22	4	9	8	22	29	45
Southampton	42	13	5	3	41	21	3	8	10	16	27	45
West Ham U	42	10	8	3	47	22	3	10	8	19	28	44
Newcastle U	42	12	7	2	40	20	3	7	11	21	35	44
WBA	42	11	7	3	43	26	5	4	12	21	41	43
Manchester U	42	13	5	3	38	18	2	7	12	19	35	42
Ipswich T	42	10	4	7	32	26	5	7	9	27	34	41
Manchester C	42	13	6	2	49	20	2	4	15	15	35	40
Burnley	42	11	6	4	36	25	4	3	14	19	57	39
Sheffield W	42	7	9	5	27	26	3	7	11	14	28	36
Wolves	42	7	10	4	26	22	3	5	13	15	36	35
Sunderland	42	10	6	5	28	18	1	6	14	15	49	34
Nottingham F	42	6	6	9	17	22	4	7	10	28	35	33
Stoke C	42	9	7	5	24	24	0	8	13	16	39	33
Coventry C	42	8	6	7	32	22	2	5	14	14	42	31
Leicester C	42	8	8	5	27	24	1	4	16	12	44	30
QPR	42	4	7109	20	33	0	3	18	19	62	18	

1969-70 DIVISION 1

	P	W	D	L	F	A	W	D	L	F	A	Pts
Everton	42	17	3	1	46	19	12	5	4	26	15	66
Leeds U	42	15	4	2	50	19	6	11	4	34	30	57
Chelsea	42	13	7	1	36	18	8	6	7	34	32	55
Derby Co	42	15	3	3	45	14	7	6	8	19	23	53
Liverpool	42	10	7	4	34	20	10	4	7	31	22	51
Coventry C	42	9	6	6	35	28	10	5	6	23	20	49
Newcastle U	42	14	2	5	42	16	3	11	7	15	19	47
Manchester U	42	8	9	4	37	27	6	8	7	29	34	45
Stoke C	42	10	7	4	31	23	5	8	8	25	29	45
Manchester C	42	8	6	7	25	22	8	5	8	30	26	43
Tottenham H	42	11	2	8	27	21	6	7	8	27	34	43
Arsenal	42	7	10	4	29	23	5	8	8	22	26	42
Wolves	42	8	8	5	30	23	4	8	9	25	34	40
Burnley	42	7	7	7	33	29	5	8	8	23	32	39
Nottingham F	42	8	9	4	28	28	2	9	10	22	43	38
WBA	42	10	6	5	39	25	4	3	14	19	41	37
West Ham U	42	8	8	5	28	21	4	4	13	23	39	36
Ipswich T	42	9	5	7	23	20	1	6	14	17	43	31
Southampton	42	3	12	6	24	27	3	5	13	22	40	29
Crystal P	42	5	6	10	20	36	1	9	11	14	32	27
Sunderland	42	4	11	6	17	24	2	3	16	13	44	26
Sheffield W	42	6	5	10	23	27	2	4	15	17	44	25

1971-72 DIVISION 1

	P	W	D	L	F	A	W	D	L	F	A	Pts
Derby Co	42	16	4	1	43	10	8	6	7	26	23	58
Leeds U	42	17	4	0	54	10	7	5	9	19	21	57
Liverpool	42	17	3	1	48	16	7	6	8	16	14	57
Manchester C	42	16	3	2	48	15	7	8	6	29	30	57
Arsenal	42	15	2	4	36	13	7	6	8	22	27	52
Tottenham H	42	16	3	2	45	13	3	10	8	18	29	51
Chelsea	42	12	7	2	41	20	6	5	10	17	29	48
Manchester U	42	13	2	6	39	26	6	8	7	30	35	48
Wolves	42	10	7	4	35	23	8	4	9	30	34	47
Sheffield U	42	10	8	3	39	26	7	4	10	22	34	46
Newcastle U	42	10	6	5	30	18	5	5	11	19	34	41
Leicester C	42	9	6	6	18	11	4	7	10	23	35	39
Ipswich T	42	7	8	6	19	19	4	8	9	20	34	38
West Ham U	42	10	6	5	31	19	2	6	13	16	32	36
Everton	42	8	9	4	28	17	1	8	11	9	31	36
WBA	42	6	7	8	22	23	6	4	11	20	31	35
Stoke C	42	6	10	5	26	25	4	5	12	13	31	35
Coventry C	42	7	10	4	27	23	2	5	14	17	44	33
Southampton	42	8	5	8	31	28	4	2	15	21	52	31
Crystal P	42	4	8	9	26	31	4	5	12	13	34	29
Nottingham F	42	6	4	11	25	29	2	5	14	22	52	25
Huddersfield T	42	4	7	10	12	22	2	6	13	15	37	25

1970-71 DIVISION 1

	P	W	D	L	F	A	W	D	L	F	A	Pts
Arsenal	42	18	3	0	41	6	11	4	6	30	23	65
Leeds U	42	16	2	3	40	12	11	8	2	32	18	64
Tottenham H	42	11	5	5	33	19	8	9	4	21	14	52
Wolves	42	13	3	5	33	22	9	5	7	31	32	52
Liverpool	42	11	10	0	30	10	6	7	8	12	14	51
Chelsea	42	12	6	3	34	21	6	9	6	18	21	51
Southampton	42	12	5	4	35	15	5	7	9	21	29	46
Manchester U	42	9	6	6	29	24	7	5	9	36	42	43
Derby Co	42	9	5	7	32	26	7	5	9	24	28	42
Coventry C	42	12	4	5	24	12	4	6	11	13	26	42
Manchester C	42	7	9	5	30	22	5	8	8	17	20	41
Newcastle U	42	9	9	3	27	16	5	4	12	17	30	41
Stoke C	42	10	7	4	28	11	2	6	13	16	37	37
Everton	42	10	7	4	32	16	2	6	13	22	44	37
Huddersfield T	42	7	8	6	19	16	4	6	11	21	33	36
Nottingham F	42	9	4	8	29	26	5	4	12	13	35	36
WBA	42	9	8	4	34	25	1	7	13	24	50	35
Crystal P	42	9	5	7	24	24	3	6	12	15	33	35
Ipswich T	42	9	4	8	28	22	3	6	12	14	26	34
West Ham U	42	6	8	7	28	30	4	6	11	19	30	34
Burnley	42	4	8	9	20	31	3	5	13	9	32	27
Blackpool	42	3	9	9	22	31	1	6	14	12	35	23

1972-73 DIVISION 1

	P	W	D	L	F	A	W	D	L	F	A	Pts
Liverpool	42	17	3	1	45	19	8	7	6	27	23	60
Arsenal	42	14	5	2	31	14	9	6	6	26	29	57
Leeds U	42	15	4	2	45	13	6	7	8	26	32	53
Ipswich T	42	10	7	4	34	20	7	7	7	21	25	48
Wolves	42	13	3	5	43	23	5	8	8	23	31	47
West Ham U	42	12	5	4	45	25	5	7	9	22	28	46
Derby Co	42	15	3	3	43	18	4	5	12	13	36	46
Tottenham H	42	10	5	6	33	23	6	8	7	25	25	45
Newcastle U	42	12	6	3	35	19	4	7	10	25	32	45
Birmingham C	42	11	7	3	39	22	4	5	12	14	32	42
Manchester C	42	12	4	5	36	20	3	7	11	21	40	41
Chelsea	42	9	6	6	30	22	4	8	9	19	29	40
Southampton	42	8	11	2	26	17	3	7	11	21	35	40
Sheffield U	42	11	4	6	28	18	4	6	11	23	41	40
Stoke C	42	11	8	2	38	17	3	2	16	23	39	38
Leicester C	42	7	9	5	23	18	3	8	10	17	28	37
Everton	42	9	5	7	27	21	4	6	11	14	28	37
Manchester U	42	9	7	5	24	19	3	6	12	20	41	37
Coventry C	42	9	5	7	27	24	4	4	13	13	31	35
Norwich C	42	7	9	5	22	19	4	1	16	14	44	32
Crystal P	42	7	7	7	25	21	2	5	14	16	37	30
WBA	42	8	7	6	25	24	1	3	17	13	38	28

1973-74 DIVISION 1

	P	W	D	L	F	A	W	D	L	F	A	Pts
Leeds U	42	12	8	1	38	18	12	6	3	28	13	62
Liverpool	**42**	**18**	**2**	**1**	**34**	**11**	**4**	**11**	**6**	**18**	**20**	**57**
Derby Co	42	13	7	1	40	16	4	7	10	12	26	48
Ipswich T	42	10	7	4	38	21	8	4	9	29	37	47
Stoke C	42	13	6	2	39	15	2	10	9	15	27	46
Burnley	42	10	9	2	29	16	6	5	10	27	37	46
Everton	42	12	6	2	29	14	4	5	12	21	34	44
QPR	42	8	10	3	30	17	5	7	9	26	35	43
Leicester C	42	10	7	4	35	17	3	9	9	16	24	42
Arsenal	42	9	7	5	23	16	5	7	9	26	35	42
Tottenham H	42	9	4	8	26	27	5	10	6	19	23	42
Wolves	42	11	6	4	30	18	2	9	10	19	31	41
Sheffield U	42	7	7	7	25	22	7	5	9	19	27	40
Manchester C	42	10	78	4	25	17	4	56	12	14	29	40
Newcastle U	42	9	6	6	28	21	4	6	11	21	27	38
Coventry C	42	10	5	6	25	18	4	5	12	18	36	38
Chelsea	42	9	4	8	36	29	3	9	9	20	31	37
West Ham U	42	7	7	7	36	32	4	8	9	19	28	37
Birmingham C	42	10	7	4	30	21	2	6	13	22	43	37
Southampton	42	8	10	3	30	20	3	4	14	17	48	36
Manchester U	42	7	7	7	23	20	3	5	13	15	28	32
Norwich C	42	6	9	6	25	27	1	6	14	12	35	29

The Last Words

IT is a far cry from the gentle calm of Glenbuck to the roar of the Reds at Wembley Stadium. When Mr and Mrs Shankly celebrated the birth of their son Willie, back in 1913, they could have had no idea that he would make the family name famous throughout the world. They must have been delighted when baby Willie took his first faltering steps, even though they had no idea then that those footsteps were leading to football fame and were also going to be followed by many others who would have their own stairway to stardom as soccer celebrities.

By his own admission, Shankly retired too early. He didn't actually say those words, but he once told Ian St John, "The man who invented retirement should be shot!" It was an indication of his frustration at not being involved in the day-to-day running of a football club. For his family it was rather like calling in a loan, they had him back at last. He still cleaned the cooker, and he made a brave attempt at gardening although, to Bill, anything that wasn't labelled, or instantly recognisable, was a weed – consequently, many of Nessie's acquisitions from the local gardening centre found themselves on a one-way ticket to the compost heap.

The conclusion is simply that Bill Shankly was a man born for football. It was in his blood. Other people have red and white corpuscles, Bill Shankly had liniment coursing through his veins. He needed football to keep him alive. The plants that he tried so hard to understand lived by photosynthesis – he lived by football-synthesis, the need to kick round things, feel adrenalin, emit passion, and be judged a winner.

When he moved out of mainstream soccer on his retirement from Liverpool, he bequeathed the Shankly Legacy to the nation – the cosmopolitan soccer nation. To anyone who was prepared to lift the lid, look inside and pick what they needed, it was available.

They could select his attitude, his positive approach, his total self-belief. They could grasp his instinctive flair for psychology. They could use his training techniques, his preparation plans, his masterpieces of match-winning tactics, his eye for talent and how to get the most from it. They could use his discipline, his guidance for young players.

Many have, as we have already seen. It is no accident that three of the most successful managers in English soccer graduated from the Shankly University – or that many others have gone on to be coaches and scouts – all former pupils at one of the greatest soccer schools ever known.

The Shankly Legacy is still there for all to use. If you are a manager in the Premiership, or just running a pub team, If you are a player at any level whatsoever, If you are a youth coach, a schoolteacher or a young lad with ambition and a love for football, then you will find something in the Shankly Legacy to both inspire and instruct.

"Bernard, what would the world be like without football?" He once said to me – and immediately answered the question himself. "Football has saved lives – soldiers have taken time off in wars, put down their guns, and played football. It has made Princes of paupers, it has given hope to the hopeless, and brought smiles to the faces of the depressed. It has given something to those who had nothing... That's football! It's a wonderful game Bernard, there's nothing like it."

What would he have thought of today's game – the soccer of the 1990s? Today, football is very different. The heavy boots over the ankles have given way to carpet-slippers with studs. The ball has the lightness of a shuttlecock. Newsagents' shelves have a kaleidoscope of all-colour football magazines. National newspapers give over pages and special supplements daily to this one aspect of sport. Prime-time television and radio feeds on football like an insatiable square-eyed monster.

Soccer stars earn tens of thousands of pounds each week for playing football, and tens of thousands more for wearing the right baseball cap when they are in front of the television camera. A generation from now will read this book and scoff at these figures as their stars of the future add another '0' to their income.

Football has usurped pop music in its fan appeal. Just as most Beatles fans never actually saw their heroes in the flesh, so the majority of Liverpool and Manchester United fans today never experience that unique occasion of seeing their team live. Most soccer stars accept their responsibility of maintaining a good, clean, athletic image. Some, of course, do not – and therefore must take a share of the guilt in the disrepute that occasionally sullies the game – a stigma that creates an obstacle to football being the family sport that it could and should be.

What would Shankly have thought of the four-letter choruses from the terraces? How would he have viewed those cigar-chewing barons, the 'agents', who manipulate so many player movements these days? Yes, football has much to enjoy about it – but still a great deal to put right. It was dubbed 'The Beautiful Game' by Pelé, but there is still a Mr Hyde to good natured Dr Jekyll.

We cannot know, of course, what Bill Shankly would have thought of today's soccer. He saw something good in just about everything so he would have gleaned some positives from all the negatives, and loved every little bit of the positives themselves. But we also know that he believed in discipline, self-respect and pride from hard-earned achievement. He did not like bad language, excessive drinking, immorality or bad manners, and therefore we can draw our own conclusions from the features of football today – the good, the bad and the ugly.

Mentioning Pelé, he once explained the difference between European and South American soccer, saying: "Our football comes from the heart, theirs comes from the mind."

Shankly's football came from the body and soul. Sir Walter Scott could have written the following just for him.

> Then strip lads and to it, though sharp be the weather
> And if, by mischance, you should happen to fall,
> There are worse things in life than a tumble in the heather,
> And life itself is but a game of football.

When Bill Shankly died, soccer celebrities were phoning the press to pay tribute. Usually it is the other way about, with pressmen desperately trying to contact suitable people for quotes. Ian St John echoed the words of Bob Paisley:

"The Shankly legend will live on long after we've all packed it in"

It's true! When this book first appears on the shelves it will be almost exactly 15 years since Bill passed away on 29 September 1981. Yet in the last year or so there have been three other books charting his life. The legend does indeed live on.

The Shankly Legacy also lives on, a wealth of wisdom, wit and winning ways. He would have been really proud to have still been there at the top of the game, at least in personification if not in person.

Let's allow Ian St John to have almost the last word.

"His influence through the Shankly Legacy will live on for ever. Shanks would like that. He just loved the game. It was his life."

But, of course, when Shankly was around, only one person really had the last word. In his personal autobiography, *Shankly by Bill Shankly*, he wrote his own epitaph, not long after his retirement.

'Above all, I would like to be remembered as a man who was selfless, who strove and worried so that others could share the glory, and who built up a family of people who could hold their heads up high and say, "We're Liverpool".'

Who could ever forget him? He still lives – through the Shankly Legacy.

INDEX